The Family in Contemporary Society

THE REPORT OF A GROUP
CONVENED AT THE BEHEST OF
THE ARCHBISHOP OF CANTERBURY
WITH APPENDED REPORTS FROM
THE U.S.A., CANADA, AND INDIA

LONDON

S · P · C · K

1958

First published in 1958
by S.P.C.K.
Holy Trinity Church
Marylebone Road
London N.W.1

Printed in Great Britain by
The Talbot Press (S.P.C.K.), Saffron Walden, Essex

Contents

NOTE

The Report has been prepared by a Group convened by the Church of England Moral Welfare Council at the behest of the Archbishop of Canterbury. The Group met for four whole days, and the theological members for two days more; there were other consultations between members, and an extensive exchange of papers.

The signed Report is unanimous.

The papers in Appendix 1 were prepared for the use of the Group, and although they are all accepted by the Group for attachment to the Report, individual signatories are not committed to all their details as they are to the Report itself.

Members of the Group are greatly indebted to Dr Gertrude Willoughby for Chapters 1 to 8 in Appendix 1, the drafting of which involved a great deal of work in a very short time.

Appendix 2 was prepared by the Department of Christian Social Relations of the Protestant Episcopal Church of the U.S.A., at the request of the Presiding Bishop, for submission to the Archbishop of Canterbury. The Department had the helpful advice and participation of Canon Howard Johnson, of the Cathedral of St John the Divine, and of the Reverend Wood B. Carper, Jr, D.D., of the General Theological Seminary. The first draft of the manuscript was prepared by members of the staff of the Department, and written by Mrs Muriel S. Webb, on the basis of consultations, a wide range of source materials, and their own knowledge and experience. The draft was seen by twenty-one associates of the Department, and their criticisms and suggestions were used in the preparation of the final draft. The Department kept in touch with the Church of England Moral Welfare Council throughout.

Appendix 3 was prepared by the Department of Christian Social Service of the Anglican Church of Canada.

Appendix 4 is a Report prepared by a Special Committee appointed by the Metropolitan of the Church of India, Burma, Pakistan, and Ceylon, as requested by the Episcopal Synod of that Church.

All the above material has been prepared for the use of the Lambeth Conference, 1958.

MEMBERS OF THE GROUP
CONVENED AT THE BEHEST OF THE
ARCHBISHOP OF CANTERBURY

The Reverend Canon M. A. C. WARREN, M.A., D.D., *Chairman*

The Very Reverend MERVYN ARMSTRONG, O.B.E., M.A. (Social and Industrial Council)

The Reverend D. SHERWIN BAILEY, PH.D. (Church of England Moral Welfare Council)

Miss E. M. BATTEN, O.B.E., B.SC. (Econ.), M.A., Principal, William Temple College

The Reverend Canon G. B. BENTLEY, M.A., Canon of St George's, Windsor

Mrs KATHLEEN BLISS, M.A., D.D.

Sir ALEXANDER CARR-SAUNDERS, K.B.E., F.B.A., LL.D., LITT.D., D. en DROIT, Formerly Director, London School of Economics

W. H. CHINN, Esq., C.M.G., Social Welfare Adviser to H.M. Secretary of State for the Colonies

Miss FREDA H. GWILLIAM, O.B.E., M.A., Woman Educational Adviser to H.M. Secretary of State for the Colonies

A. L. HUTCHINSON, Esq., M.A., County Education Officer, Isle of Wight (Church of England Youth Council)

Sir CHARLES JEFFRIES, K.C.M.G., O.B.E., Formerly Deputy Under-Secretary of State for the Colonies (Overseas Council)

The Reverend Canon R. H. PRESTON, M.A., B.SC., Lecturer in Christian Ethics, University of Manchester

The Reverend Canon I. T. RAMSEY, M.A., Nolloth Professor of the Philosophy of the Christian Religion, University of Oxford

Professor T. S. SIMEY, M.A., Professor of Social Science, University of Liverpool

Miss E. M. STEEL, B.A. (Church of England Moral Welfare Council)

J. K. THOMPSON, ESQ., B.A., A.K.C., Head of Social Services Department, Colonial Office.

Professor R. M. TITMUSS, Professor of Social Administration, University of London, at the London School of Economics

Miss GERTRUDE WILLOUGHBY, M.A., Doc. de l'Univ. Paris, *Research Assistant*

The Reverend G. R. DUNSTAN, M.A., F.S.A. (Church of England Moral Welfare Council), *Secretary*

The Report

To His Grace the Lord Archbishop of Canterbury
YOUR GRACE,

In our writing of this Report we have felt acutely a dilemma of authorship. We would gladly have furnished your Grace with such reading as, being set before your Grace's guests at Lambeth in July 1958, would have been to the satisfaction of them all. But if we had done so, we should have acted irresponsibly. The nature of our subject, and the responsibilities which our Christianity imposes upon us, oblige us to offer some things which the Bishops might understandably not have chosen for themselves, some from which their first inclination might have been to turn away; but things which, in our judgement, their Lordships may properly be asked to receive, and inwardly to digest, when they gather at your Grace's conference table. They will, perhaps, uphold our decision when they recall, as we do, the prayer of Archbishop William Laud :

> Most gracious Father, we humbly beseech thee for thy holy Catholic Church. Fill it with all truth; in all truth with all peace. Where it is corrupt, purge it; where it is in error, direct it; where anything is amiss, reform it; where it is right, strengthen and confirm it; where it is divided and rent asunder, make up the breaches of it, O thou Holy One of Israel.

1. INTRODUCTION

Our subject was given us with two sub-titles : "The Family in Contemporary Society : (*a*) Problems of Population; (*b*) Effects of Rapid Social Change on Family Life." It became clear to us in discussion that the sub-sections are not separable : the demographic factor—that is, the number and density of population and its distribution by age and sex—is one of the essential determinants of economic and social conditions; demographic change necessarily involves economic and social change, and economic and social changes are never unrelated to the population structure. The family is involved at every point, causally in creating (or arresting) the

1

population change, consequentially in the economic and social changes which follow.

Our study has therefore been of some intricacy. We have come to it as Christians, seeking to understand, first what the facts of our situation are, and secondly what our Christian duty is before them. It is not to be expected that our understanding of either should be unequivocal or complete—we have worked within severe limits of time as well as of human finitude; neither have we felt ourselves obliged or even able to dogmatize, to pronounce facts or changes to be in themselves good or bad, or to declare what "the Church" should do, forbid, or sanction in relation to them. But if, as we must believe, this complex situation is yet one in which God rules, in which it is his children, redeemed by his Son for eternal life with him, who act and suffer, then clearly it is one in which the Christian has to determine his duty to God and God's children—to decide what, in these circumstances, the command to love his neighbour demands of him. We account it an axiom that the Church—each local Church—has a duty, under the Holy Spirit, to study the local situation and so to order its teaching and pastoral ministry and organization that it can perceive and do the will of God in that situation. Our aim in compiling this Report and its Appendix[1] is simply to help the Church in the discharge of this duty in relation to some of the problems confronting the family and society in different parts of the world to-day.

These problems, we have said, are not separable, and the major difficulty is so to act that in satisfying one principle we do not violate another; in meeting one claim, we deny not another equally valid, equally demanding. There is a transcendental element in the family, a point at which it mirrors the Godhead "from whom every family in heaven and earth is named",[2] something therefore "given" of God and so absolute in itself. Yet the cultural patterns in which the family shows itself are many and various; and these patterns have a value in themselves, providing moral, emotional, and economic security in the bonds of kinship and the tacitly regulated interplay of personal life. This family and kindred are interwoven at many points with a wider society—the tribe, the community, or the nation —another entity enjoying the sanction of the God who is God of "all the nations upon earth". Between these two entities there may well be many conflicting legitimate demands. Family and society together, albeit imperceptibly, create a "population problem" : the specific and sacred family act of begetting and bearing puts out of balance local resources and the people who feed and live upon them.

[1] Appendix 1.
[2] Eph. 3. 15.

2

With the simultaneous advance of an ethic in which to preserve life is an imperative and of a natural science which makes that task more widely possible, a new conflict of absolutes is introduced : "to save life" is a command of God, even though in the long run obedience to it produces the threat of, or actual, starvation; to "feed the hungry" is another command of God, and one which drives us, in an age of vast technological and economic resources, into a seemingly endless labyrinth of natural and applied sciences and departments of human organization. And so, with the application of technology—with industrialization and the radical transformation of societies which goes with it—in our effort to "feed the hungry" we create a set of lawful claims apparently in conflict with the equally lawful claims of family pattern and personal life. So we come full circle : a problem which is social, demographic, economic, once it is recognized and understood, may confront a man and a woman with personal decisions over the specific act of their married life, that act by which another child may be begotten. It is within this network of conflicting valid claims that we have to work; and if, as we must, we discuss them one by one, their inherent interconnection must not be overlooked.

The papers in Appendix 1 furnish the facts, so far as we can ascertain them, and the arguments upon which this Report is based. We treat first of population, then of the place of the family and the Church in the wider community. Our treatment of population begins with a general discussion, which is then made more precise by reference to certain countries and regions where over-population is or threatens to become a major concern. Social and economic conditions in these regions are described because the remedy has to be found very much in social and economic adjustment : these are the conditions, this the inter-play of forces, in which the local Church has to find its obedience to God, and which distant Churches have to ponder if they are to act and pray as one Body in Christ. We follow with a section on Western society where there is now relative demographic stability, but still marked, and indeed revolutionary, social changes, which have resulted partly from the new demographic trends appearing in the last generation and the one before it, and partly from industrial, commercial, and technological developments. These are, of course, interconnected processes, and they are, again, bound up with the fundamental changes in the values and beliefs which ultimately determine the social behaviour of individual men and women.

These are complex problems. Our study is far from complete : first, because our purpose limited us to selected regions, and even within these it seemed wiser to select a few representative areas

3

than to attempt a shallower treatment of them all : secondly, because the evidence, especially on social change, is fragmentary and still in many instances hypothetical. We have tried to make it clear where we are arguing from evidence which we may fairly assume to be conclusive, and where from suggestions or hypotheses still open to challenge or contradiction. We would hope that the same self-discipline may be observed in any discussions which may ensue upon our work.

Local studies of the family have been undertaken by groups similar to our own in other provinces within the Anglican Communion—in the U.S.A.,[3] Canada,[4] Australia, New Zealand, South Wales, Scotland, and Northern Ireland, to name only those known to us.[5] Since this work has all been proceeding at the same time, and against time, it has not been possible to collate it all; nevertheless it is only by regional studies of this sort that an informed discussion can be assured when the Bishops assemble from these regions for the Lambeth Conference.

2. Population

Over-population is not a new problem. What is new is the scale of it, and this because of man's discovery and use of the powers entrusted to him by God. New power demands new responsibility. What is the Christian responsibility in this new situation? It is first to try to understand the problem. Chapters 1 to 7 in Appendix 1 are written as an aid to that understanding. Here we would condense the argument and underline the imperatives.

Malthus, on the evidence open to him in his day, concluded that, since human beings increase in geometric progression, that is by multiplication, while resources increase only in arithmetic progression, that is by simple addition, population must outstrip resources unless checked. To the "natural" checks of disease, war, misery, and want are added abortion and infanticide to keep the population within its means of subsistence; but population will always increase up to the level of those means, even allowing for the "moral restraint" of a postponement of the age of marriage accompanied by strict sexual continence. But already when Malthus wrote[6] two forces had begun to work which were destined to raise the problem to an entirely new scale. The first was industrialization,

[3] See Appendix 2.

[4] See Appendix 3.

[5] A Report on Family Planning, by a Special Committee appointed by the Metropolitan of India, Pakistan, Burma, and Ceylon, is printed as Appendix 4 to this volume.

[6] *Essay on Population*, 1st ed., 1798; 2nd to 6th editions, revised and enlarged, 1803-26.

4

which, with economic conditions in its native Britain and markets abroad alike wholly favourable to its rapid expansion, so increased resources in the West as to make the Malthusian conclusion appear unduly pessimistic. The second was the invasion made by science upon some at least of the "natural" checks at the behest of an ethic that to save every life that can be saved, to combat disease, to relieve misery and want, is an absolute obligation.

The assault on the mortality rate in Britain and the West did not assume significant proportions until after the increase of resources by industrialization was well under way—and after improved agriculture had made industrialization and urbanization possible; it was carried to its present pitch of effectiveness only by the advance of social and educational services and of nutritional standards which industrialization with its consequent wealth (in the widest sense) made possible. It is of cardinal importance to observe that this same assault on disease and death has been made in the East, and in the Caribbean, before industrialization has really got under way—in advance, therefore, of the means of providing the enlarged and multiplying population with food and the barest necessities of life, to say nothing of the spiritual, educational, and social betterment which make that life worth living. It is this fact which invalidates some of the optimistic analogies with the experience of the West. Education itself, a vital factor in the reduction of population, is hampered and retarded by poverty and the very social conditions which over-population creates. The problem of over-population to-day cannot be left to solve itself; the starvation of millions, the remaining "natural check" (excluding annihilation in an atomic war), is intolerable to the conscience of mankind.

A third force, which Malthus could not foresee, entered into the history of the West to replace, in large measure, the added checks of abortion and infanticide. This was the control of conception made possible by the application of scientific knowledge, giving rise to "family planning" and a reduction of the birth rate ultimately sufficient to match the reduction of the infant mortality rate, and so to stabilize the population, as in England and Wales. The motivation of family planning as the personal decision of each husband and wife involved is complex and requires deeper study;[7] as a social phenomenon, however, at least in the West, it appears to be a consequence of social and economic development,[8] characterized by the

[7] We would refer to a paper by Dr John B. Wyon, "Motivation for Family Planning, with Special Reference to Field Studies", presented at the Third All-India Conference on Family Planning, Calcutta, January 1957.

[8] Not immediately; the immediate effect may be to increase the birth rate, but later the birth rate begins to fall.

spread of education, the adoption of an urban way of life, and a potentially higher level of living; it then becomes itself a determinant, with important social and demographic consequences of its own. This third force is therefore too important to be ignored in relation to the over-populated countries. Once the means to control conception are established—and the tendency of research is to make those means far simpler and more generally acceptable than before—then their use becomes, not a matter of personal decision or social attitude only, but also a concern of government and a potential instrument of its social and political policy. The history of several European countries since 1919 demonstrates the effectiveness with which the modern state, of whatever political complexion, can invade, by direct and indirect means, the innermost recesses of family life in the interests of the population policy of the government of the time.

There are, therefore, these three factors in the population problem in relation to which we have to determine our Christian obedience—first, the attempt to increase resources in order to sustain the existing and coming population, by means of economic and social development, with all the consequences which that entails; secondly, the continued reduction of mortality, especially infant mortality, and the continued fight against disease, with the inevitable consequence that thereby the population will multiply still further; and thirdly, the attempt to control this multiplication by means of family planning, fostered in some countries as an instrument of government policy. It appears to us that the first and third of these activities have not had from the Church the enthusiastic approbation enjoyed by the second. It is right, therefore, that in this context we should consider them in turn.

3. Economic and Industrial Development

The struggle to deliver peoples from poverty is now world-wide. As an undertaking it is not contingent upon the goodwill of the Church : it is happening; governments are committed to it; vast monetary interests are vested in it; it is bound up with racial, political, nationalistic, and other ideologies which may be entirely irrelevant to it, often to its own hindrance; it is both pawn and king on the chessboard of diplomacy. Yet the Church must have a part in it; first, to declare it to be in principle God's work; secondly, because it is an inescapable fact in the lives of millions of God's people, fraught with enormous consequence for good or ill, an experience of life into which the Church must enter if it is to be true to its mission in the theology of the Incarnation.

In the supposedly Christian West the first era of industrialization left scars which have scarcely healed in time for the second era which is now upon us, because basic human needs were ignored or, where considered, misunderstood. The great social surveys did not begin until the crowded industrial areas had taken shape; people had been swept from a rural into an urban and industrial way of life without any study of what effect so radical a change might have upon them; and the Church, albeit late but with magnificent enterprise, hastily extended to the towns its ancient, essentially rural, parochial pattern to overtake them. But the Church has never yet caught up : social service, the healing of consequential ills, is one duty, in which the Church has expended loving care; it is no substitute for the other, for social study and social integration—the shaping of community according to human needs and human destiny in the Kingdom of God. It is this second duty which we conceive to be the vocation of the Church wherever there is social change to-day. Where the Church is incarnate in the life of man it has the opportunity of helping to shape the new societies from or near the beginning, of lessening the toll which rapid change otherwise will take in human suffering, in the distortion of family and community life, and in multiplying the occasions of sin. The other duty, the healing service, will continue with new effectiveness. But two conditions of both are participation in life, and study.

We have anticipated several steps in our argument in order to establish the concern which we feel, that the Church should nowhere regard economic development—the attempt to give people more food, more material things and the opportunity to enjoy them, with less toil, less sheer drudgery in keeping alive—either as evil and mischievous in itself, or as an inevitable "high level" enterprise in which the Church has no part but to grieve for the disruption of the familiar scene, and to labour among the remnant as before. The theologians among us have contributed a paper[9] outlining the dispositions with which Christians ought to welcome material development. Others, with specialist knowledge of the areas which we have considered, have convinced us of the dire poverty in which those areas stand, and of the place which economic development must take, in planned conjunction with other remedies, if the level of living is to be raised and sheer disaster, with all its possibilities of social and moral disintegration, is to be averted.

The papers in Appendix 1 give examples of this need, and of measures taken where possible to meet it, in economic terms. India,[10]

[9] Appendix 1, Chap. 8, Sect. 3: "The Christian Attitude to Material Development".
[10] Appendix 1, Chap. 2.

7

where the deaths of children under 5 equal or exceed the deaths at all ages from 5 to 54, where the expectation of life is even now only 39 years, where population is even so increasing at four and a half to five millions a year, adding yearly to the unemployed and under-employed, and to the numbers trying to live off holdings already too small—India has come to the end of one Five Year Plan, aimed at increasing by irrigation the land available for agriculture, and by raising the yield of land by better farming. It has embarked on a second, in which industrialization will play an increasing part. But the very shackles of the situation will keep the wheels slow : India must forego the economic advantages of large-scale, centralized manufacture in order to preserve the village industries and such employment and social satisfaction as they afford;[11] foreign currency, necessary for the import of capital goods, has to be diverted to the import of even more precious food. India's rulers are hobbled in their race with the tide of population growth; and they cannot go at even the pace they have planned without external aid.

The picture in the West Indies[12] is more sombre still; the problems are, if anything, more acute, the remedies more elusive. Here density is added to fecundity : the islands are small, with little room for their inhabitants to support life. There is but a limited demand for what little the territory can export, and therefore a limit to what it can earn to meet the cost of improving its agriculture, to capitalize industries, or to raise purchasing power. The islands have few attractions for industrialists from abroad—except as holiday resorts. Those who write with knowledge of the economic possibilities of the West Indies do so in tones of anxious searching, with an under-current of despair. We read the reports of an impressive procession of expert commissions and advisers, each disappointed in the hope that those before were wrong : there is no note of optimism that can be struck. In economic terms the problems of the Caribbean are insoluble from within; they are probably insoluble still with external aid, unless at the same time revolutionary changes occur in the out-look of the masses of the people.

Egypt[13] presents a wholly different challenge to the Christian conscience. It is not a member of the British Commonwealth, so it has no claim upon Commonwealth resources; its political policies

---

[11] Compare China : "So vast is the population . . . that the Chinese cannot afford to mechanize, for the simple reason that unemployment on an un-precedented scale would result. Mechanization must wait until the new industries can absorb the teeming peasantry. In every part of China today you see tens of thousands of labourers at work with no instrument more complicated than a couple of baskets dangling from a bamboo pole. They are building China with the methods used for building the pyramids." (*The Times*, 2 Oct. 1957).

[12] Appendix 1, Chap. 3.   [13] Appendix 1, Chap. 5.

excite no sympathy for it in the United States of America and the monetary sources so largely in American control. Yet it must grow or import more food to feed its multiplying population. It cannot irrigate extensively without external aid; it cannot trade without export goods. It remains a "test case", trying the prudence and the humanity of the West precisely because it has no title to Western aid; a case of conscience for Christian statesmanship.

The materially more advanced countries of the world have a duty to help the under-developed countries in their economic and social development—a duty all the more insistent where there are population pressures like those which we have described. "Under-developed" is a relative term, but it applies to many independent nations as well as to Colonial territories. For the latter there is a clear responsibility (confirmed in the United Nations Charter) falling upon their respective metropolitan countries, each of which has its own methods of operation. Much excellent work is already being done in this way, and we hope that as national resources permit (even at some sacrifice to progress in the already much higher standards of living at home) it will be expanded and accelerated.

Such territories, as well as the independent nations, can also draw upon the services of the various international agencies, the International Monetary Fund, the World Health Organization, and the rest, in their respective fields. These agencies themselves depend mainly on the wealthier nations for their finances and the expert services which money represents.

It is customary to think of assistance to under-developed countries in terms of finance for capital development or of expert assistance in development plans and projects—perhaps too much in terms of the second, when the more urgent need is for the first.[14] The wealthier nations with diversified economies could make a perhaps even more important contribution by adopting liberal trade and fiscal policies which permit the under-developed countries—whose economic potentialities are often restricted by nature to a small range of products—to develop those commodities which they are specially suited to produce, and to market them in other countries at sufficiently rewarding prices with the minimum of trade restrictions. Prosperity through trade is better for economic, social, and moral stability than artificial aid.

[14] Cf. Professor P. M. S. Blackett, f.r.s., in his presidential address to the British Association, 5 Sept. 1957: "Admirable as many of the schemes of technical aid have been, particularly those in education, medicine and agriculture, the sending of experts to poor countries without the capital to carry out their plans could be as irritating as to send a trained cook to a family unable to pay the baker. Unless followed up by massive financial aid, some of the West's present aid programme may yet merit the war-time wisecrack of 'offering all aid short of help'." (*The Listener*, 5 Sept. 1957, p. 332).

We would suggest also that when financial assistance is given, it should be directed towards promoting the wealth of the recipient country by economic development or scientific research, or by development work in the social services such as the building of schools, improved housing, or the eradication of disease. This is preferable to the external subsidizing of recurrent services, which, in our view, is not consistent with self-government in any real sense. In the long run, the heavy recurrent costs of an improved standard of administration and social services can only be financed from the taxable wealth of the country itself. It is in measures to increase that wealth that the materially advanced countries can make their most useful contribution.

If the duty which we have stated be a valid one, and if the policies sketched in the last four paragraphs be sound, then Christians who are also citizens of the materially advanced countries have a clear field in which to interpret the divine precept, to give to those in need. They ought, in our view, to use every influence to secure such sacrifices in their nation's relatively high standard of living as may make some contribution at least towards meeting the needs of the under-developed countries;[15] they ought themselves to remain sensitive to a distinction between the necessities of an already ample life, and the luxuries which are continually attaching to it, and to commend this distinction to their nation. They ought to resist the erection of prohibitive tariff and other barriers by which their own national economy is protected at the expense of the much more precarious economies of countries which must market their few commodities in order to live. They ought to exercise a liberalizing influence on public opinion, disposing it towards accepting a concern for other peoples in need, and against inverted national or sectional self-interest; inculcating sympathy with the sensitiveness of the communities which they seek to help, their self-respect and desire for autonomy, and their suspicion of gifts trailing political "strings".

Christians in the "new" nations of Asia, Africa, and the Levant have a similar task in the face of combative nationalisms of their own. Communities and nations which need assistance, and seek it, must endeavour to overcome the hostility and suspicion that are "natural" even in an individual to whom good is done. With persons who have been brought together in this way we have learned to deal through a better understanding of the relationship in which they

15 Cf. Blackett, *loc. cit.* Of the £1,000m. a year needed as a free gift or as long term loans "Britain would pay £150m. a year, and this would postpone by less than a year the expected rise of 50 per cent in British living standards over the next quarter of a century. . . . With nations, as with individuals, the ultimate hypocrisy of the rich is to preach the virtue of poverty to the poor." See also "An Essay in Crusoe Economics", Appendix 1, Chap. 9, below.

stand; deeper meanings of the word "charity" have been made apparent to us, and have influenced our conduct. Between communities or nations the problems of giving and receiving are much greater. The recipient must learn to overcome the brash self-assertiveness, associated with feelings of inferiority, which is greatly reinforced when consciousness of race or colour intervenes. Tensions between "advanced" and "backward" have also to be overcome within communities as well as between them. Difficulties arising in this way require much more understanding and spiritual insight than we possess at the moment if adequate solutions are to be found for them.

The opportunities open to the Church in lands where this economic development is taking place will be discussed below when we consider social change. Our purpose so far has been to examine the economic factor in the population problem. We are convinced that agricultural and industrial development must take place as rapidly as circumstances permit; that it must command the most generous aid from countries already materially advanced; and, on the best evidence that we could find, that even so there are countries, inhabited by many millions of people, in which no programme of development yet foreseeable can hope by itself to win the race with population multiplying at its present rate. Even allowing for the application of atomic energy to industrialization, to irrigation—even, for example, to the creation of artificial lakes for stocking with fish, a most prolific form of food—this pessimistic conclusion is the only one to which responsibly we can come. It is with this in mind that we turn to the remaining two factors in the population problem, the reduction of mortality and the reduction of fertility.

4. THE REDUCTION OF MORTALITY

The science and skill which have already in the West changed the death of an infant from a common to a rare occurrence, are now advancing all across the world, with results which the figures in our papers tell, exciting wonder and grateful admiration. So do the measures which combat epidemics and disease, which lessen sickness and suffering, enriching and prolonging life. That far more can yet be done is manifest : the infant mortality rate in Britain is 26.5 per thousand; in India it is about 200. But every child kept alive is a potential parent. So the dense populations are also young populations, with an expectation of life and prolific parenthood before them such as their fathers hardly dreamed of. The Church has from the first accepted the care and healing of the sick as its privilege; "medical missions" were the spearhead of the great expansion of the

11

if we may do so without presumption, this method of procedure : it is, in our view, typical of the way in which a Church ought, in full consultation with other workers and specialists involved, to study, and form its mind, and frame its action, upon problems of local importance. The Medical Consultative Committee of The Commission of the Churches on International Affairs emphasized recently the necessity for the Churches to "intervene" to give religious sanction to responsible family limitation in the face of this world problem.[21]

We have considered very carefully what we ought to say in the face of these facts, having within our view the very different conditions facing Christians in different regions of the world. We could hardly be expected to enunciate a formula which could be applied to them all. The theologians among us have prepared a paper, which we print in Appendix 1,[22] setting out three considerations of the use of contraceptives, by means of which much, though not all, family planning is achieved. We observe that, although the first of these exemplifies the argument from given premisses by which a negative judgement is commonly reached, the theologians conclude that :

> In spite of the manifest divergences between these three treatments of the question, there is a meeting point of practical importance in the judgement that a conscientious decision to use contraceptives would in certain circumstances be justified.[23]

At the same time we are bound to record the existence of thoughtful opinion, both clerical and lay, in the Church of England which would go much further than this properly cautious theological conclusion, in a positive acceptance of the use of contraceptives within Christian marriage and family life.

Those who hold this opinion affirm very positively the wholeness, the one-ness of marriage, the expression of married love in coition, and the integrity of the family with children growing up within it. They would deny equally strongly that the use of contraceptives is an attempt to extract selfish pleasure out of the man-woman relationship at the expense of the duty and obligations of parenthood. Within the married partnership of a responsible, freely consenting man and woman, coition is part of the marriage, enhancing its unity and its harmony; children, as the outcome of the marriage, themselves also in turn enhance the unity and the harmony; the marriage, the metaphysical unity, is the controlling

21 *Medical Bulletin No 1*, January 1957.
22 Chap. 8, Sect. 2.
23 Below, p. 131.

14

concept between the coition and the children, and as such we may liken it to a reservoir which is the centre of control between the inflowing mountain streams and the outflow of hydraulic or electric power. The use of contraceptives, on this view, enables the marriage to be enriched with consequent benefit to the family, and the demand of this interpretation is not less responsibility but more. It is in terms like these that Christian men and women, earnestly seeking to fulfil the will of God for them in relation to the circumstances of their life, justify, to those who ask, the use of contraceptives within Christian marriage. (They would perhaps add that between themselves this decision has passed beyond the need of conscious justification.) It may be said that their contention cannot be overthrown unless we are prepared to maintain that the nature of coition is "given" in every particular and for ever, in all its physical and metaphysical aspects, and so placed outside the realm of human decision.

The more we understand of our procreative powers, the more responsible we are for the way in which we use them. The price of this generation's knowledge is therefore a heavier burden of responsibility. Christian parents who participate in that knowledge, whether they accept contraception or not, cannot but feel obliged to "space" and "plan" their families according to their understanding of themselves, of the well-being of their children, and of the needs of the society of which they are part. To produce children without regard to consequences is to use procreative power irresponsibly, the more so when there is involved the imposition of one partner's will upon the other. If our conscience will not tolerate, when we know how to prevent it, a torrent of infant deaths, no more should we, with the knowledge we have, encourage an ungoverned spate of unwanted births. If fatalism has given place to upholding the sanctity of life for the living, should it not yield also to a responsibility for those whom we cause to be born?

So we may bring together our consideration of the three aspects of the population problem. If those whose duty it is to know declare that there are parts of the world where, even given all the economic development possible in the time, resources cannot keep pace with human need if population continues to multiply at its present rate, we can find no ground on which responsibly to contradict them. We find nothing Christian in the suggestion that the so-called "natural checks" should be left to exercise their own restraint upon population —that men and women and infants should be left to die, that pestilence should walk unchecked, or war or abortion take their toll. If, therefore, governments resolve that it is their duty to encourage (but not to enforce) the adoption of family planning in conjunction with their best endeavours to raise the level of living in other ways, we cannot say that Christians ought to withhold their support. How, indeed, *could* we say that? The catastrophe of which Malthus warned the West has been averted here by two factors—by industrialization, which is now apparently to take vast new strides, and by family limitation which is now largely accepted in all levels of society irrespective of religious profession. These two factors do not yet operate in the under-developed areas of the world—the remaining four-fifths of it; therefore the gap between the developed and the under-developed is widening rapidly.[24] To "him that hath" is being given, and from "him that hath not" is being taken away even that which he hath, because he is reproducing himself more rapidly than forces can be marshalled in his environment which will enable his progeny to be fed.

Before such an aggravation of the world situation the Christian Church cannot remain detached and unmoved. It would be presumptuous for the Church in the West, which cannot look with complacency on the way in which it has guided or failed to guide its people in these matters, to seek to inhibit by religious sanction one of the two means, economic expansion and family limitation, by which under-developed areas may be able to save themselves from disaster. The Churches in the regions where the issues are both urgent and new have the opportunity to show themselves wiser in their generation, and to lead their people, through a deeper understanding of sex, marriage, and the family, of the State and of society, to undertake new responsibilities in fuller dependence upon God.

6. SOCIAL CHANGE

We have reserved from our discussion of the population problem (p. 6 above) a fuller treatment of the vocation of the Church in lands where industrial and economic development are taking place, in order to consider it in a wider context of social change— for in many regions social change is taking place unconnected with industrialization. We have suggested (p. 7 above) that the Church in the West, despite its heroic record of money and pastoral

[24] "In addition to maintaining its existing wealth, the western world is saving and investing productively some 10 per cent. of its income of £300 a year a head: that is, some £30 a year is being invested in additional plant and machinery to create more wealth. The pre-industrial countries of Asia have only about £20 a year to live on, that is, for both consumption and production goods. The West is thus saving more than the East is spending on everything. No wonder that the gap in wealth between the West and Asia is steadily widening!" Blackett, *loc. cit.*

16

zeal outpoured, never overtook the first industrial revolution because it set out too late and because it had no means of understanding the complexity of the change in which it was involved. To-day, as a second industrial revolution gathers speed, the Church has another opportunity : it need not, if it will but run, be left behind; and it has at hand the means of study, if it will but run in harness with those whose profession is to observe objectively what is happening in society. In service, too, the Church has potential allies as never before in an age when governments and government-sponsored international agencies have an ethical as well as a political interest in social and educational betterment and are contributing money and trained men and women towards it.

Those who know most about Western society to-day tell us how little is really known about the effect of present working conditions on human behaviour, and on family life in particular. They can write with some assurance of the influences of the first industrialization—the effects of which can still be traced in our pattern of family life, and which still provide many of the casualties in the social worker's care. On the new situation, however, which developed with widespread electrification in the 1930s, and which is advancing now under the name of "automation", they insist that they can but state hypotheses; they observe and deduce, but they do not claim to know.[25] If truth be a condition of prophecy, a like modesty would well adorn the Church : its utterances would gain thereby in effectiveness what they may lose sometimes in effect. At all events, we are hardly in a position to offer countries coming new to this enterprise lessons and warnings from our older experience : we are only now beginning to formulate what those lessons are. Even if, as one of our number has written, we can communicate principles of action,

> even here our motives in desiring to fund and pass on the lessons of experience must have that quality of disinterested-attachment on which empires, either of a material or ideological kind, are assuredly not built.

The Church may reasonably be expected, however, to challenge society to examine its goals, and to determine what must at all costs be preserved and what may be put in jeopardy in the planning of social change : and where, on the best available evidence, the family is threatened with more than it can be expected to bear, the Church

[25] See Richard M. Titmuss, "Industrialization and the Family", a paper delivered in plenary session at the International Conference of Social Work, Munich, 1956. The quotation immediately following is drawn from this source.

has a duty to say so,[26] accepting that in so doing it commits itself also to the search for a remedy.

We do not envisage the problem as one of exclusive choice—social change *or* the family; the reality of the situation is social change *and* the family, where some changes, some conditions of working life, make Christian family life more difficult, temporarily or with a threat of permanence, and others strengthen it, at least for a time. How do we receive a mixed blessing? "Automation" and the highly developed industrial processes of the West leave work-people with more leisure and more reserves of physical energy—a potential good, inviting all sorts of creative uses for the time and energy set free; they may also require shift-working, even over week-ends, with the corollary that a Christian family may not always be free to worship or sit at table or meet together on Sunday—a potential ill, and one disturbing to the Christian conscience. Is the Church to oppose the development, renouncing the good because of the ill? Or is the Church, for the sake of the good, to strengthen its people for Christian living in new conditions with new demands for personal decision? It is to be remembered that many Christians, those by whom the world's work was done, had to wait for Constantine to give them Sunday as a holy day, free from work; and that modern society has for long required work from some on Sundays—shift-work from railwaymen and others in the public services, work on any or every Sunday from farmers, doctors, nurses, and many more, whose strength either of churchmanship or of family life has not been noticeably the less. At what point does extension of incidence change an ill from one to be borne to one to be opposed? It is in situations like these that we perceive the danger of assuming that one phase of Christian culture has an eternal validity.

Sociologists are interesting themselves more deeply in the interplay of work and home as influences upon people's lives. "Industrial man" is also a "family man" : neither he nor his welfare can be studied as

[26] Cf. the Bishop of Sheffield, in a House of Lords debate on the family : "Then, as we all know, there are industrial pressures, some due to the nature of the industry and some in the interests of efficient production, which bear hardly on the family. Full employment and good wages are, of course, an immense boon and blessing; but the price is high if it means a great increase in shift work and in the demand for mobility of labour. The rootlessness of urban industrial populations is a social evil, and incidentally it is somewhat inimical to the life of the Churches. Industry affects social life powerfully. Whilst someone has said that a family may be more corrupted by coddling than by difficulties, *we may ask industry in framing its economic policies to have thought for the consequence of those policies upon the life of the family and community, and to be prepared sometimes to sacrifice, for a short length of time, a little economic efficiency in order to maintain the stability of the family as a unit.*" (*Hansard* : Lords. vol. 182 (Apr. to June 1953), p. 662.)

though his working life were all his life. Professor R. M. Titmuss has pointed to

> differences in the norms of behaviour expected of the worker in the factory and of the same worker (though in other of his rôles as husband and father) in his home and in the community.[27]

In an industrial society, he suggests, the manual worker is given less and less room for self-determination : technology, the "rationalization of production", the increasing independence and omnicompetence of the machine, all tend to give him a sense of "irregularity and uncertainty in status and skill". The contemporary idea of "the good father", however, requires him to plan, provide, nurture his family to maturity in a stable home, and so on—all requiring of him the attributes denied him in his daily work. The loss of status attached to skill when the machine replaces skill in a given process appears to be important in several ways. Though both the total number of workers and the proportion of skilled workers employed in the factory concerned may be increased as a result, it may nevertheless leave a residue of manual or "process" workers who are in a sense left behind by the general advance of industrial technology, with even less of a way of promotion ahead of them comparable with that open to the craftsmen employed in the same shop. But whether these changes are likely to be typical of technological developments in the next decade is very much in doubt. The emphasis in the work of an operative controlling an automatic process will be on responsibility, for vigilance and speed and accuracy of response will be of the first importance. Feelings of subjection to the machine may thus give way to one of pride in mastery over it. The worker's increased responsibility may indeed lead him to become a more active citizen. But, on the other hand, if his status is lowered, and his future looks no different from, and no more rewarding to him, than the past, he may shirk responsibility both in the factory and in the world outside.

There is no final opinion that can be expressed in this matter. The effects of changes in productive techniques and industrial organization upon a man's position in his own home, among his own children, have indeed still to be understood : will the man without status at work feel that he has no status either at home or among his neighbours? Will he be submissive therefore at home, or authoritarian in compensation? We do not offer answers to these questions; but the fact that the sociologist asks them indicates to us what forces may be pulling a man this way and that in the interrelation of his work and his home in an industrial society. Where

27 Op. cit.

human relationships like these are in question the Church should be supremely concerned. Does the fellowship of the local Church enable this man "to become himself" in a way that he cannot at work? Has the Church in an industrial area a clergyman or social worker capable of understanding the social strains of this divided life, and so of helping the family to ride above them at a time of threatened breakdown? Has this life any significance for Church worship, the times and duration of service, the idiom of liturgy, sermon, and instruction, the content and practice of prayer, public and private? Does it demand a re-thinking of Christian education, the development of a special syllabus, for example, for boys and girls approaching the day of their first going to work? Are we preparing them adequately for the moral decisions which they may have to make as workers, so different from those of home and school?

Not only our work but also our living is now caught up in change. In the section on the family in Great Britain in Appendix 1 [28] we draw attention to the importance of a reconsideration of housing policy in relation to the deeper, less obvious family needs. If this is primarily the concern of housing authorities and sociologists, it is also a very real concern of the Church. Is the Church really abreast of the changes in where and how people are living to-day? There are areas at the centre of industrial and commercial cities apparently socially derelict, destitute of any social bond, where parochial clergymen spend themselves utterly, supported if at all by the familiar voluntary parochial team, but needing desperately the help which only trained social workers could give. There are, on the fringe of the cities, the new estates and satellite towns, artificially created, where families live often far from kindred and place of work, where the Church is striving to build a Christian community from the beginning—an attempt which is surely ripe by this time for a thorough, comparative survey of the highest academic competence. Further out are the villages and villas, to which those who can afford to do so repair daily when their work in the city is done, to which they "belong" in only a limited sense, and from which they could uproot themselves at will. Elsewhere, it is true, as in some of the textile towns and, as a recent survey shows, in some London boroughs, there is a stronger sense of neighbourhood and "belonging", based upon a network of kindred and acquaintance which has been many decades in growing. If, as we believe to be likely, the family is strengthened and supported in many ways by such a sense of community, then society—and the Church within it—must give much more serious attention to the factors contributing to community, and seek to arrest the present tendencies towards urban disintegration.

[28] Below, pp. 98 ff.

If we have begun with the industrial society of the West, it is only because it is the one in which we live, not because the problems of social change in Africa, India, Asia, the Caribbean, and South America are less crucial. There they are more obvious and pressing, because of the pace of social change and because of the wide territorial areas which may be involved. The papers in Appendix 1 touch upon some of those changes in relation to over-population and the need of rapid economic development to meet it. But we must emphasize that industrialization and economic development are not the only causes of social change. Christianity itself has been a potent disruptive force, undermining the authority of fear, breaking into established family and tribal structures, pronouncing new value judgements upon them—as, for instance, upon polygamy, which has social and economic aspects as well as the moral and theological— and imposing new structures, overlaying a new culture, upon the old. (How far the new remains as an insecure veneer upon the old, or how far it is yet rooted in place of the old, remains yet to be seen.) Education, whether "westernized" or not, is itself a disruptive force : by enlarging men's apprehension of what is elsewhere, and of what can be where they are, it leads to discontent and to a determined aspiration towards a "better life". The old charge against Christian missions, that they "make the natives discontented", was factually true though morally obtuse. If the Gospel be true, this we had to do : and if the Gospel be true, we are equally bound to the consequence. The education of women and girls, which, relatively speaking, has only just begun, is probably the most disruptive force of all in matters of family life : new attitudes towards marriage, towards motherhood, towards children, towards marital and family love— and a new understanding of a vocation for the unmarried—are all bound to emerge as women experience the liberation which we call knowledge.

That this is happening we know, among Moslems and Hindus as well as Christians; and standards which may be called vaguely "western" are sometimes being adopted without specific religious foundation, and without any religious power to meet the disruption which they cause. Where marriage has traditionally been an alliance of families more than a union of persons, there are strong family sanctions, social and economic, to hold the weak marriage together; this is true of those parts of Africa where the bride-price is paid, and of Hindu societies where marriages are "arranged" and a dowry paid. Substitute for this the marriage of choice, in which the family interest is diminished, over-ridden, or ignored, where the bride-price is either fictitious or paid out of the bridegroom's earnings, not from his family's cattle, and the marriage is left without these supporting

21

bonds. If there be no other bond—an inward bond of religious faith or of lasting love, or an outward social bond, girded about by a community which is a fellowship, which cares—then that marriage is unlikely to last; and many are the pitfalls, moral and social, which await the man and woman as they drift apart, perhaps in a friendless city or location far away from the tribal solidarity in which they were reared.[29]

That many are disturbed by the changes which they see is emphasized by the marked revulsion from change which erupts pictorially from time to time. The reversion abroad from European dress to native costume, the studied cultivation of regional languages, as Flemish, or Irish, or Welsh, against the cosmopolitan, the militancy of a regional culture, and the intense opposition advanced in its name to, for example, the flooding of a Welsh valley to provide water for Liverpool's industries—even the outbreak of the Mau Mau rebellion—these are different manifestations of the same resistance to a change which is, in the nature of things, irresistible, the movement towards one world of mutual awareness and dependence. The world will not run so headlong into change that it is careless of what is to be preserved.

Yet it must change : there are regions into which industry must come if their people are to survive; economic change, urban development and the consequent disruption of the village and tribal way of life must come. Education is both demanded and given by governments and international agencies as well as by the Christian Church. What duty does the Church owe to its people in such situations? How can it transform its deep pastoral concern into effective action in these new fields? Has it in itself the resources with which to integrate the new "dispersion", to create community where else there is but conglomeration? Can it create to-day in a technological age what its fathers built of old, a Christendom, a culture in which men and women can affirm their work and their family and social life to be their Christian life, and can offer its fruits in worship? Or must it retreat from this age, become a Church of the desert—of the solitary, or of the gathered, withdrawn, stockaded community—and deny that daily toil has any Christian relevance at all? For ourselves, we know but one answer : the Church of the Incarnate Lord must not withdraw; it must participate in life, all of

[29] The evidence for Africa is collected in *Survey of African Marriage and Family Life*, ed. Arthur Phillips, published for the International African Institute by Oxford University Press, 1953. cf. J. C. Carothers, *The Psychology of Mau Mau*, Nairobi, 1954, and J. V. Taylor, *Christianity and Politics in Africa*, Penguin, 1957. For Ceylon see T. L. Green, "Changes in the Family in Ceylon Consequent upon Education and Social Contacts", in *Familles dans le Monde*, Paris, Dec. 1956.

it, and be where men are. The lump must still be leavened, if it is to rise.

We have asked ourselves earnestly what this participation demands of the Church in these many different situations. The first demand, we believe, is one of conviction : the Church has to convince itself theologically of what its witness requires of it, what the will of God is for men and women in their families, in work, in society, in the nation and race. Without theological conviction, action would be half-hearted, or misdirected, or both. The Church, then, is called again to study : not, we suggest, to study in the abstract, but to study its theology in relation to the things that are— the "given" by revelation together with the "given" by situation.[30] In such study there is an essential element of exchange, of generative conversation between those with knowledge in different professions. We believe that a Church which hopes to make any impact in its local situation must set its theologians and its administrators to work with the men and women of integrity (be they Christians or not) engaged locally in academic study, field research, or administration or community service; in order, first to understand what the situation really is, and then to order Church life and activity within it accordingly. We regard such an exchange as essential, not only for this immediate, "practical" outcome, but also as the only way to lay the foundations of a contemporary Christian culture. Theology activates society, we believe, when it is embodied in cultural forms : medieval Christendom became what it was because theology found an expression, not only in the liturgical, but also in the social and economic, life of men; it broke when theology became circumscribed, partly by authority, partly by its own logic, and so unable any longer to admit other aspects of knowledge and truth. That danger is present to Christians in every age.[31] We would therefore recommend, as the means whereby in our own day a Christian culture may be developed, that the Church should encourage co-operative work on specific problems between those who are specialists working within the different disciplines of their diverse fields.[32] Cathedral foundations in particular (which in the past were the nurseries of schools and hence sometimes of universities) might well take the initiative in fostering such co-operation, and thus again offer a more ample and reasonable service to God and men.

An integration which begins thus at the centre—say in the Cathedral and University City, or in the diocesan office and

[30] Cf. A. R. Vidler, *Christian Belief and this World*, S.C.M. Press, 1956.
[31] See Appendix 1, Chap. 8, Sect. 4, "Religion as a Social Bond".
[32] Cf. a speech by the Bishop of Chichester (Dr Bell) in the Convocation of Canterbury, 2 October 1957.

23

government office—must grow also further afield. Those who know the under-developed countries, and those concerned with their advancement, assure us that to put capital into industrial and economic development without investing correspondingly in the social and educational services would not be simply to waste money; it would be to put it to dangerous use : for without tremendous social care, the social hurt of industrialization would be appalling. There is evidence enough already, at home and abroad, that this affirmation is true. Moreover, there is no reason to suppose that the economic and social plans which are being prepared in the less developed countries can be put into effect—or ever completed—unless great reserves of spiritual energy can be drawn on to provide the planning process with motive power. Without energy of this kind, the inhabitants of such countries may share with the adherents of the Cargo Cult of the South Seas an angry sense of deprivation when the commodities they lack are not made freely available to them by wealthier nations, coupled with a determination not to be "ordered around" any longer by "foreigners". It is for this reason that the foundations of economic planning must be laid in properly conceived social development schemes. Put bluntly, the urge to work is stillborn in a man who cannot expect that life has much to offer him in the future; if he cannot look ahead with confidence, he tends naturally to live in the present, if not in the past. The administrative problem may, indeed, be resolved in the last analysis into one of generating new energies and making new opportunities available. This is outwardly a social problem, but its core is spiritual, and it exists as a challenge to all Christian men and women.

Even the social and educational services as we know them, however, require people as well as money, the right men and women, with character, integrity, and vocation, and with the right training. We believe it to be a function of the Church to produce these men and women, and to set before them as a high vocation the study and service of society in this way, at home and abroad.

The Christians of the West have a solemn obligation to use their influence to ensure that men and women from the West shall go out to serve the world which they no longer rule. Service will no doubt call for judicious capital investment. But fundamentally it calls for something far deeper and more important—personal involvement by persons in the local situation, so that the experience of the "haves" can be mediated to the "have-nots" by processes which are organic to the local situation and not alien to it.[33]

[33] *C.M.S. Newsletter*, No. 193, April 1957, p. 7.

We believe that the Church must take more trained social scientists and social workers into its own service, as well as co-operating fully with those in the employ of government and local authorities and of voluntary organizations.

The acceptance of this proposition in principle will raise many questions of practical application. The Church of England would need to reconsider its whole policy in the training and use of lay people, especially of women, in church work. It would have to engage in close consultation with the university departments of social studies over the selection of students and their training. It would reassess the curriculum of its theological colleges, to see whether an introduction to "pastoralia" which did not convey some understanding of, so to speak, "the pastoral scene" could be considered adequate at all. (The continued use of the pastoral idiom may, indeed, blind us to the social realities of contemporary life.) If the Church came to accept the need of a social worker on the staff of the large industrial parish, or attached to a group of parishes, diocesan and parochial organization and finance would require adjustment accordingly. The fostering of vocations to this sort of ministry will call for more informed and imaginative preaching and teaching where Christian character is formed and ideals are seen, in the parish church, the youth fellowship, the school and college chapel, and the university student bodies. The task is formidable, but in our view the need is paramount and it must be met.

The pitch of vocation must be high. Overseas, we are told, until society understands the place of the unmarried woman within it, the Church and the social services need very much the help of unmarried women from abroad, especially for the education and advancement of women and girls. But the higher rate and lower age of marriage, in Britain at least, with its corollary that there will be steadily fewer unmarried women in our midst and a consequent strain upon our own social services, means that without a high pitch of Christian vocation Britain will not send out what the Church and society overseas most require. Our theology and our preaching, then, are confronted with this dual task—to proclaim a positive doctrine of marriage and the family, and, at the same time, a positive vocation to a service which may demand their renunciation; yet a renunciation which is also an affirmation of gender, a consecration of characteristic "manhood" or "womanhood" to the service of others and the glory of God.

The vocation to serve thus in the building up of a community and the integrating of family life within it is not to the individual only but also to the congregation. The disintegration of once-established cultures and communities is as real in some of the cities of England

25

as in regions, shall we say, of Africa; here, as there, are newly-populated areas which cannot be called "communities" because no power on earth seems capable of generating a recognizable community life in them for very long. Many who once had great faith in the "community centre" movement now speak sadly of the futility of trying to "bring people together" with no defined purpose or reason. The local Church is a potential nucleus of community : common prayer, a common participation in the sacraments, common aims, a common language and way of life—all this ought to produce a community, and does. But does it grow outwards? we cannot rest content if it stops with the faithful congregation. Theologically all human relationship and life in community are very much the Church's business. Therefore this way of "participation in life", the non-church life of the local people, must be the task of the Christian congregation. Reports from the few places where this is already realized show that a Church which genuinely sets out to permeate the local life by means of lay activity, geared to the real social needs of the place, does exert a cohesive force, laying the foundations of community. The prerequisite of such work is leadership—a ministering team, lay as well as clerical, appropriate to the locality.

The Church's first conquest of Europe was accomplished because the ecclesiastical organization developed step by step with the civilization—first the city diocese; then the staffed "mission" church at strategic points on routes or central for regions; then the parish, its shape economically determined (the parish was the area from which a Church took its tithe) and exactly suited to the manorial and municipal society of the day; then the supplementary ministries of friaries, guilds, and fraternities. Even the withdrawals from the general pattern, the monasteries of various sorts from the Celtic to the Cistercian, were cradles of a Christian community and culture, precisely because they were so exactly adapted to the social needs and systems of their several generations. The demand on the Church is no less to-day—to adapt the organization of its ministry closely to the local and contemporary patterns of society. Without this adaptation there can be no identification; without identification, no leavening, no healing for the broken sinews of society. We would therefore emphasize the need for active thinking about the organization of the Christian ministry.

As church responsibility overflows from the congregation to the neighbouring society, so it reaches out further through the wider society, the One Body which transcends distinctions of race and nation. We are aware of the deep concern felt in the Church about militant nationalism, racial tension, and colour conflicts—particularly in parts of Africa and North America, and in the

Middle East. The Church is concerned with these problems, not only because of the suffering they cause or because they are politically inflammable, but because at bottom they are matters of theological principle, concerning our fundamental beliefs about God and man. Further treatment of them is beyond our competence; we would only plead that should they become, as well they might, a matter for discussion at a future Lambeth Conference, years of study be given to them in preparation, perhaps by a permanent Commission of the Conference set up for the purpose. Even in our own limited sphere of interest—the effect of such problems upon population and the family—the subject is too intricate and important for hasty or ill-prepared comment.

On the level of Christian action, however, responsibility has already many channels into which to overflow. The presence in Britain of unaccustomed numbers of immigrants from the West Indies in recent years has challenged the Church here to show its concern for fellow-churchmen from overseas, often living here per-force in great discomfort and enduring all the publicity attached to what might have been magnified into a spectacular "social problem". At an "impersonal" level Christians here have acted responsibly, in the work of co-ordinating social services, in helping to keep down racial tension, and, often through the Press, in helping English people to accommodate these visitors to their midst. At the "personal" level, however, in the taking of West Indians into the heart of congregations and homes, the Church of England, for many reasons, has been less generous and successful than other Churches. A similar inhibition is discernible in the little regard we pay, as a Church, to the needs of students and others, from Africa, Asia and the West Indies, living in our larger cities for fairly long periods. The Methodist Church, with its International House organization, has been more generous in expressing its fellowship with members from overseas. It is, in our view, inadequate to dismiss the accommodation and happiness of overseas students as "a University problem"; these men and women, away from their own families for a considerable period of time, sometimes need that personal friend-ship which acceptance into English church and family life can give, if they are to be carried over a period of considerable social and emotional strain. There is room here for much closer co-operation between the parishes, the missionary societies, and such bodies as the East and West Friendship Council which work to integrate visitors into our society in a responsible way. We must envisage that more, not less, immigrants and students will be with us in future years; the responsibility of integrating them into the life of Church and society is correspondingly greater; so, of course, is the opportunity of cultural exchange and enrichment which that integration will bring.

7. Related Questions of Church Discipline

We conclude with a reference to problems facing particular Churches which, although thrown into relief by what is happening socially in their environment, are yet more particularly matters of church discipline and ultimately of theological understanding. There is, we believe, widespread conflict of opinion and practice among Christian communities in Africa over the recognition of marriages between Christians celebrated in accordance with native law and custom, and over the refusal of infant baptism to the children of such marriages. There appear to be divergences in some places between the local church law and the practice of the clergy. Instances are quoted in which it appears that acute injustice is done to some families, and that good people are sometimes driven to a moral despair, by the exercise of a discipline which concerns itself less with the true, internal nature of the marriage than with the place and form of its celebration—whether in church or according to native custom. If it be true that consent and consummation and an intention of lifelong union are the things which make a marriage, then the Church cannot, theologically, limit its recognition and acceptance to marriages which have been solemnized in church. If the argument be urged that customary marriages are potentially polygamous, then theologically it ought to be urged also against marriages in Britain and elsewhere which are potentially legally dissoluble with the right of remarriage. This group of problems, therefore, seems to call for an examination of two related questions : "What conditions are necessary for a marriage which can be recognized by the Church?" and, "What, in this context, are the conditions required for baptism?" These are theological questions, reaching into the very nature of the man-woman relationship; their study is a pre-requisite of any ecclesiastical regulation, and of any serious attempt to allay the moral unrest which is troubling many in Churches overseas and in Britain to-day.

We have knowledge of other issues, with serious social as well as theological implications, confronting Churches as far apart as Africa, Ceylon, the West Indies, and Polynesia, each in different ways. We read of traditional codes of family life having broken down—the authority of the tribe or kindred or family weakened, the pre-puberty instruction and initiation of boys and girls corrupted or outmoded, the bride-price or dowry become a formality or a burden but not a safeguard, the marriage ceremonies (both church and

28

customary) made prohibitively expensive, attended as they are by lavish entertainment and display. The old codes, while they lasted, may not have commended themselves easily to the European Christian mind : but at least they made for stability and cohesion, and their destruction leaves a void—social disintegration follows. Families from different tribes, for instance, thrown together in an urban location, finding that their respective tribal codes differ, cannot be blamed if they lose faith in them all; the consequent demoralization is no less painful. Local Churches are greatly exercised by these problems : a solution, capable of saving or replacing the cohesive forces and eliminating the disruptive, will come more easily as the churches develop more and more under native leadership and the European influence is lessened; and this will require the reconsideration of some ecclesiastical codes.

Polygamy, which has come intermittently before Lambeth Conferences since 1888, is another subject which will not be left alone. In many parts of Africa it is reported to be on its way out, and that for non-religious reasons. But it will be a long time a-dying, and while it lasts it is not sufficient to judge it through European eyes or simply in terms of the sexual need of the African man. It has to be seen also in terms of African society, involving the tilling of the fields, the relationships between kindred and clan, the affording of security to otherwise "unattached" women—for some the alternative has been a life of prostitution. Far be it from us to suggest that these conditions are immutable, or that they can dictate a final answer. But until they are changed, and that from within African society itself, it would be folly to ignore the social purpose which polygamy fulfils.

In order to express vividly the dilemma, therefore, facing the Church in parts of Africa to-day, we would quote the words of one of our number, written in another context but relevant also to ours.

The polygamous family, with its multiplication of kinship groups, plays a social, political and economic rôle in African society which must not be underestimated. We may well judge that it is inconsistent with the Western pattern of life which is being forced upon Africa. We may endorse the opinion that the "smaller" Western family of father, mother, and children, represents the ideal nucleus of the wider society of mankind. We may be right in believing that only that smaller family does justice to half the human race, and makes the fullest meaning of partnership possible for man and woman. We shall, as Christians, see all these judgements in the light of the New Testament value set upon personality. Polygamy cannot be

29

brought into any consistency with the values of man and woman as revealed by Jesus Christ our Lord. All that is legitimate Christian reasoning. Only, in reaching these conclusions, let us face the fact that in Africa we are dealing with a polygamous society in a state of violent transition.

The alternative to polygamy, with all its strict sanctions of taboo, in the framework of an ordered way of life is, for all too many, the sordid pursuit of promiscuous relationships with a mounting toll of illegitimacy and social delinquency. To those who look at Africa without blinkers the picture is a shattering one. Christ loves these African men and women, every one of them. He cares about the disintegrated patterns of their social life, the break-up of all their traditional loyalties. He suffers with them if what the New Testament says is true. A Church which is not a fellowship so strong that it can hold men and women, and their new family life, in its continually strengthening and forgiving embrace, and serve as a mutual benefit society in times of stress— as did the old polygamous family—such a Church is a very sad betrayal of its Lord. In the context of that betrayal, *wherever it occurs*, a legalistic insistence on monogamy *and* the penalty of ex-communication for any lapse, comes very near to the repudiation of a trust.

What is called for, let us face it frankly, is a real revival in the Church of the kind that affects family relationships and the sense of corporate responsibility. At the same time we need, I believe, a completely fresh appraisal of the traditional use of ex-communication as a means of discipline for the Church in Africa. This is a time of very rapid transition, and of widespread disintegration of the old patterns of society with their accepted sanctions. We cannot afford a moral theology which is so inflexible that it can make no provision for the needs of the bewildered mass of humanity such as is found in Africa today. Of course, there must be discipline. The visible Church is a society which lives within certain frontiers, else it would be invisible. The question we are entitled to ask is whether the means for safe-guarding these frontiers in Africa today are those best calculated to achieve their purpose, and at the same time to prepare for the day when the frontiers of the Church in Africa will coincide with that continent's coastline and with the depths of the human nature which lives within it.[34]

Further discussion of the topics raised in this final section of our Report would require much more study and experience than we can

[34] *C.M.S. Newsletter*, No. 196, July 1957, p. 5.

bring to them, and especially close consultation with the Churches concerned. They are matters upon which European judgement is necessarily less important than native judgement. We recommend that this group of subjects, like the racial and related problems, is of such importance that a standing commission of the Lambeth Conference be set up to study it, taking the best possible evidence from the field as well as from relevant theological, anthropological, and social studies.

Thus we conclude our Report. It would be presumptuous for us to describe it as a call to a new sense of social responsibility in the Church, for we know how concerned many Christians are about the world in which they live. Yet we know, from letters written to us[35] and from our own observation, that this Christian concern to-day is more often a bewildered than an informed concern; that it is often felt more for the world across the sea than for the world at the church door—English church opinion, for instance, has been far more vocal over race relations in South Africa than over the living conditions of West Indians in England; and that the expression of this concern in much contemporary writing and speaking suffers, not only from want of a norm by which to judge the changes seen, but from want of awareness that such a norm can be established. We return therefore to the test of truth. Christians would repudiate as dishonest the falsification of history in the interest of argument or moral exhortation : we would plead that contemporary society, which is history unfolding, be considered worthy of the same scrupulous regard.

4 October 1957

(*Signed*)	MAX WARREN (*Chairman*)	RONALD H. PRESTON
	MERVYN ARMSTRONG	IAN T. RAMSEY
	SHERWIN BAILEY	T. S. SIMEY
	E. M. BATTEN	ENA M. STEEL
	G. B. BENTLEY	J. KENNETH THOMPSON
	KATHLEEN BLISS	RICHARD M. TITMUSS
	A. M. CARR-SAUNDERS	
	W. H. CHINN	
	FREDA H. GWILLIAM	GERTRUDE WILLOUGHBY
	A. L. HUTCHINSON	(*Research Assistant*)
	CHARLES JEFFRIES	G. R. DUNSTAN (*Secretary*)

[35] Archbishops and Metropolitans were invited to advise the Group of particular problems in their provinces.

Appendix I

AN ASSESSMENT AND THEOLOGICAL
CONSIDERATION OF THE FACTS UPON
WHICH THE REPORT IS BASED

CONTENTS

1. INTRODUCTORY SURVEY

The Inter-relation of Population, Resources, and Urbanization

Population questions and the distribution of mankind over the face of the earth are to-day preoccupying all those who are concerned with the well-being of the human race. The rate of population growth in the world has never been so rapid as at the present time, and it is estimated that in one generation the world population might increase by 45 per cent;[1] in certain areas the rate of acceleration in population growth is probably without precedent in human history. The relationship between population trends and family life is so intimate and complex that the problems of the one cannot be separated from the other. Statistical material exists to indicate population trends; the effect of these changes on individual families may be conjectured, but, over a wide area, cannot be measured with any accuracy. Nevertheless, the pressure of population on raw materials, and on food supplies in particular, must have an effect on the standard of living in economically under-developed countries where the population is increasing rapidly.

The falling death rates in under-developed countries are a testimony to the effectiveness of modern disease control and programmes of medical care and health education. The people of these countries are living longer, but this does not mean that in other respects levels of living have risen to the same extent. The acceleration of population growth which results from this reduction of mortality requires that the production of goods and services be expanded at still more rapid rates if these countries are to progress towards a satisfactory level of living.

This very expansion is however hindered by increasing numbers. A larger part of the national income has to be devoted to the social services, particularly the services for the young, rather than to the capital investment which would ultimately raise the level of living.[2]

---

[1] *The Determinants and Consequences of Population Trends,* United Nations, 1953, p. 3.

[2] *Report on the World Social Situation* (U.N. Economic and Social Council), Part 1, 1957, p. 65.

In so far as a rapid increase in the population has in itself an effect on the development of resources, it may be useful at this point to illustrate the extent of the population problem by quoting some figures. The rate at which population is increasing in a given country will depend on natural growth, the number by which births exceed deaths, and the balance of migration. As will be seen when some study is made of the problems confronting a selected group of economically under-developed countries, emigration to-day has little effect, with the significant exception of in Ireland, in diminishing population pressure; internal migration from country to town is important particularly when consideration is given to its effects on the family.

Crude Annual Birth Rate per 1000 of Population [3]

	1947–49 average	1950–52 average	1953–55 average
Singapore	46.4	46.5	48.7
Jamaica	31.6	33.3	35.3
Puerto Rico	40.5	37.6	35.0
Japan	33.6	25.7	20.4
India		estimated	40.0
Mauritius	44.3	48.4	43.1
United Kingdom	18.6	15.9	15.6

It will be noted that in both Japan and Puerto Rico the birth rate has shown some decline : both countries are furthering a policy of family planning.

In the past, high birth rates were matched by high death rates and thus the population growth was restrained. To-day all countries are showing declining death rates, some more spectacular than others.

Average Crude Death Rates per 1000 of Population [4]

	1947–49	1950–52	1953–55
Singapore	12.5	11.7	9.8
Jamaica	13.2	11.8	10.4
Puerto Rico	11.6	9.7	7.6
Japan	12.7	9.9	8.3
India		estimated	28.0
Mauritius	20.1	14.5	15.0
United Kingdom	11.7	11.9	11.5

When comparing the death rates of different countries the relation of age-groups to the total population is important. The United

[3] Ibid., p. 22 for India; *Demographic Year Book, 1955* (United Nations) for others.

[4] See previous note.

Kingdom figure reflects the large proportion of her population falling into the over sixty-five group.

The decline in the infant mortality rate is particularly illuminating since this decline is in itself evidence of a rise in the levels of living. The control of the environment through sanitary measures and better medical services has a speedy influence on the mortality rate of children under one year : this rate is declining everywhere.

Annual Registered Infant Mortality Rate per 1000 Live Births [5]

	1947–49	1950–52	1953–55
Singapore	80	75.6	61.4
Jamaica	78.2	63.5	70.9
Puerto Rico	72.5	67	58.5
Japan	67.0	96.3	81.6
India		estimated	200
Mauritius	91.0	80.8	83.1
United Kingdom	37.9	30.2	26.5*

A comparison with 1935-39 shows that many of these rates have been halved in some 20 years.

These figures emphasize in a dramatic manner the differences in levels of living between countries. In the United Kingdom to-day it is rare for a baby to die from environmental causes; an infant mortality rate in India of 200 per 1000 live births is a tragic indication of the low environmental and nutritional standards at which the majority of families must be living. In India and Pakistan 50 per cent of total deaths are attributed to children under ten; in the United Kingdom the figure is six per cent.

The natural increase of a country's population is measured by relating birth to death rates. With the exception of Japan and the United Kingdom it will be noted that all the countries listed above have an annual average increase of population of nearly two per cent, some of nearly three. Where population is increasing at two per cent per annum the population would increase by 50 per cent in 20 years. Where the increase is at the rate of three per cent per annum a population would increase by 50 per cent in less than 15 years and would double itself in 25 years.

This rate of increase, unknown in the world before the present day, presents some countries with the problem of balancing population and resources which can only be solved by external aid, and possibly by taking measures to encourage a reduction in the birth rate. The solution is made more difficult by the predominance of the young age groups, as the following table indicates.

[5] *Report of the United Nations Economic and Social Council Population Commission* (1957), Table 22.

* In 1957 the death rate of children under one year in England and Wales was 23 per thousand, the lowest on record. (Registrar General)

Age Composition of the Population [6]

	Census Year	Under 15 years	15–59 years	60 years and over
India	1951	37.4	56.9	5.7
Japan	1950	35.4	56.9	7.7
Jamaica	1943	36.6	56.9	6.5
Puerto Rico	1950	43.2	50.7	6.1
United Kingdom	1951	22.6	61.7	15.7

Of importance to community and to family alike is the expectation of life at birth. How many families, for example, by the premature death of the husband, lose the bread-winner? To what extent can the community count on the survival of men within the working group on whom depends the provision, not only of day-to-day needs, but also of capital for investment?

Expectation of Life at Birth (both sexes) [7]

		According to estimates 1950–1955
Singapore	around	63
Jamaica	,,	50
Puerto Rico		
Japan	,,	66
India	,,	35
Mauritius		36
United Kingdom	,,	71

The significance of these figures becomes clearer if they are seen in terms of the family and community. Any consideration of population problems has to take into account the vast differences which exist between countries in culture, in resources, and in the administrative framework. But a few general deductions may be drawn from these figures before a more detailed study of a few countries is attempted.

High birth rates and high death rates must bring desolation and unnecessary suffering within the family circle. It is noticeable that the Indian Government's plan for family limitation lays particular stress on the need to reduce maternal mortality and the ill health which supervenes as a result of too frequent pregnancies, in itself a cause of high infant mortality rates. High infant mortality rates and high mortality rates for children under ten can frequently be traced to the same causes. This wastage of child life, immeasurable as it is in terms of human suffering, is to be assessed also as an economic loss to both family and nation. Here is wasted capital—a vital

[6] Ibid., Table 29.

[7] Ibid., Table 27.

38

consideration for families living at or near subsistence level—for the family has kept the child and now cannot benefit from any future contribution to the family economy; and in so far as the State has provided social services, the State too has lost. This same reasoning may be applied when the expectation of life is low; families lose their bread-winner and the nation loses the work of those best able to add to the national product.

The continuance of high birth rates combined with mortality rates which, in some countries, are approaching the low European rate, result in population increases which are out of balance with present resources. The present relatively high population increase in North America, Canada, Australia, and New Zealand serves to raise the level of living; the capital equipment, the resources, are there, and the additional power makes their more efficient exploitation possible. In the under-developed countries, however, unprecedented changes will have to take place in both agriculture and industry if the present levels of living are to be maintained, leave alone increased. But in these countries where the majority of families are living at a low level the mere increase in numbers militates against change. Families cannot save or improve the techniques of agriculture or of village industry, because of the need to provide for the larger families : the nation finds it difficult to finance capital investment by savings or by higher taxation. The introduction of innovations in agriculture is delayed because of the increasing division of peasant holdings, or because of the growing numbers who have to find work on and draw sustenance from the same holding, already too small. There is growing unemployment and under-employment in the country, and this results in migration to the towns.

This movement to towns, partly the result of rural distress and of better transport and the desire to improve one's lot, but in part the effect of better education, is bringing about an increase in urbanization greater than the increase in industrialization : rural poverty becomes urban poverty. It is noticeable that even the ambitious Indian Second Five Year Plan is based on the assumption that the rapid industrialization envisaged will only give work to the number of workers added each year by natural increase to the population : the reservoir of unemployed and under-employed remains untouched.

The Report of the Economic and Social Council Population Commission notes that urban housing in the cities of the under-developed countries has certainly deteriorated during the past few years, particularly because of the rapid influx into the larger cities. The country people, if they remain in the cities, generally continue

39

to have large families; slum areas then develop on the periphery of the towns and cities. Family life inevitably deteriorates.

With urbanization in economically under-developed countries, there is usually a transfer of poverty and under-employment from the country to the city, and social evils that have been laid to industrialization or to city life are often but an over-flow of rural distress. Urbanization also brings, however, in varying degrees, new problems arising from conflicts of culture, disruption of old customs and patterns of life, difficulties of personal adjustment, disorganization and re-organization of social structures. The family in particular, undergoes changes in its size, its functions— losing some functions and strengthening others—and in the status and rôles of its different members. The position of children, who are caught between the new culture and the old, is apt to become especially uncertain and precarious. The increase of juvenile delinquency, with urbanization, is a matter of widespread concern.[8]

The growth of population shows marked differences between countries : a global figure gives little indication of the problems involved. Three groups of countries are distinguished by the U.N. Population Commission, although it must be borne in mind that all these countries show wide differences amongst themselves in their demographic situation :

Group One. North-west, Central, and Southern Europe, Northern America, and Oceania, comprising 20 per cent of the world's population. Here fertility[9] and mortality have declined to low levels.

Group Two. Eastern Europe (including Asiatic U.S.S.R.), Latin America, and Japan, comprising 22 per cent of the world's population. In all of these death rates have fallen to moderate levels, whilst birth rates vary widely. Compared with countries in Group One both birth rates and death rates are substantially higher.

Group Three. The Middle East, the remainder of Asia, and Africa. Reliable vital statistics for these countries are in many instances lacking, but it seems clear that there has been progress in bringing down the death rate whilst fertility has remained high. This gives a large increase in absolute numbers, and these countries contain over half the population of the world. It is in these countries that the problem of population is seen in its most acute form, for here the economic situation is much less favourable than in the second group.

8 Op. cit., p. 16.
9 The level of fertility is the crude birth rate, the number of births per 1,000 of the total population.

The standard of living is highest in the first group of countries because of the development of industry and trade. In these countries the birth rate has been declining for many years, though recently there has been a tendency towards stability and, in some countries, a slight increase.

In all these countries, in varying degrees, the decline in family size has been preceded by a shift of population to the towns. It would appear, therefore, that the development of industry, with its corollary the growth of the urban population, influences the motivation of parents, and the small family unit is the result. It is now generally conceded that the reason for the fall in the average number of children per family must be sought not in a physical diminution of the powers of procreation but in changes of social attitudes and behaviour which result in family limitation. In a situation where the movement from country to town seems to have set in motion a desire on the part of parents to limit their families, though often with a considerable time lag, it may be asked what changes in the total situation directly or indirectly influence the decisions taken.

Generalizations in a matter so complex as this tend to obscure important differences between the countries falling into *Group One* and differences in the reactions of different social groups. It is, however, generally conceded that some or all of the following factors influence the attitudes of parents.

Life in a town allows of social mobility, the possibility of raising one's own social status and of aiding one's children to do likewise. In the country, status tends to be taken for granted. In the town, there is a greater merging of social classes, people have more leisure, economic and educational facilities are more readily available, and the prospect of raising one's standard of living appears realizable on condition that one limits one's liabilities. This leads to a limitation of the family.

The change in the status of women, and the education and occupational opportunities which have been opened to them, have changed the attitude of both men and women towards their rôle in the home; this subject will be developed later when discussing the English family. Clearly, however, this change in status and the desire for independence has had an influence in limiting the number of children which a woman is prepared to bear. Moreover, if she engages in gainful employment outside her home the standard of living of the family may rest on the additional income which she contributes to the family budget. Before industrialization she made this contribution by her work in the fields or in cottage industry,

3

work to which child-bearing brought little disruption. Work outside the home often presents her with the necessity of choice.

As a country becomes more industrialized and the national income increases this increase will ultimately be reflected in a rising level of living throughout the community. As standards rise the cost of child dependency does become heavier. Part of this extra cost may be assumed by the community through the provision of free education, free health services, family allowances, and so forth. Parents, however, will still be called upon to meet the rising standards in housing, in the provision of clothes, in food, holidays, extended education, and leisure time activities. Moreover, every State regulation which raises the school leaving age or the age of entry into paid employment, increases the financial burden resting on parents. Indirectly, if not directly, these considerations may weigh with parents when thinking about the size of their families.

The fall in mortality rates for children, especially the fall in the infant mortality rate, may well result in family planning. High birth rates and high death rates were common in England during the earlier part of the nineteenth century, as they are in the under-developed countries to-day. To ensure that at least two or more children survived, five had to be brought into the world.[10] When better environmental conditions and medical care ensure a high probability that five would survive, this factor might consciously or unconsciously influence parental attitudes and play some part in accounting for the fall in family size in England and in Europe generally towards the end of the nineteenth century.

These four factors can be stated and given due weight in striving to assess the effect of urbanization on the attitudes of parents. It is clear that many imponderable factors, some requiring psychological understanding, influence the behaviour of parents in this complex situation. It has been argued, for example, that the declining influence of the Churches on the behaviour of individuals has affected their attitudes towards family planning: ecclesiastical pronouncements in a matter so personal, intimate, and complex are questioned and sometimes rejected. The Report of the Royal Commission on Population gave some consideration to this matter when assessing the various factors which had influenced population trends:

There is some evidence—though the statistical information on the subject is scanty—that the trend of family size has differed

[10] In 1856 Archbishop Tait, while Dean of Carlisle, lost five daughters within one month through scarlet fever; he was left with Crauford, aged 6, and Lucy, aged two months. (R. T. Davidson and W. Benham, *Life of Archibald Campbell Tait,* (1891), vol. I, pp. 189f.)

between people of different religious affiliation. The decline has been slower among Roman Catholics than among Protestants. But the extent of the difference can easily be overstated : there is little doubt that average family size has declined greatly even among Roman Catholics. Moreover, Roman Catholics of different occupational groups seem to differ in average family size in very much the same way as the non-Catholics.[11]

This same conclusion is reached in the United Nations Report already referred to. After stating that family size has declined greatly in Europe and in the United States the Report continues :

> Fertility differences between religious groups taken as wholes appear to be closely related to the economic and occupational differences discussed above. It has often been found, for example, that a greater proportion of Catholics than of Protestants is in occupations whose members have a high fertility. This is by no means the whole explanation, for among members of the same occupation and income group, Catholics are on an average more fertile than Protestants, but the differences in fertility between persons of the same religion but of different occupation, income, education, etc., are very great.[12]

The Government of the Irish Republic Commission on Emigration and other Population Problems, 1948-54, reports similar conclusions :

> The fertility material available from the 1946 Census has also been examined with reference to religions. It shows, first, that the fertility of Catholics is substantially higher than that of other religious denominations, and secondly, that this feature is found in each of the social groups. . . . In one respect, however, there is a distinct similarity between Catholics and other religious denominations; for both, the largest families occur in the farming group and among general and agricultural workers, while the smallest families occur in the higher professional group and among employers and managers.[13]

The West German Ministry for Family Affairs reports, in August 1957, the same occupational determinant upon Roman Catholics and Protestants, but with the lower fertility rate in the working class:

[11] *Report of the Royal Commission on Population,* 1949 (Cmd. 7695), para. 72.

[12] *The Determinants and Consequences of Population Trends,* p. 90.

[13] *Report of the Commission on Emigration and Other Population Problems, 1948-1954* (pr. 2541), para. 204.

The Report points out that there is now practically no difference between the birth rates of Roman Catholics and Protestants, but the difference between the workers and the "white collar" class has been reversed—officials, clerks, and self-employed people now have more children than workers.[14]

The determining influence of social and economic factors on family life has been exemplified by this brief study of the family attitudes in countries brought together under *Group One*. Where social and economic factors are very different the family also takes on a different pattern. Although a distinction must be drawn between certain of the countries falling into *Groups Two* and *Three*, in general both death rates and birth rates are higher than in the countries in *Group One*. In some countries falling into *Group Two* where industrialization has already made an impact on people's lives and attitudes, there is a realization of the consequences which follow on a high birth rate accompanied by a falling death rate : there is already a tendency for birth rates to fall, and Japan, and recently China, have adopted policies aided financially by the government to encourage family planning.

The *Third Group* of countries, and some of the Latin American countries, are usually referred to as under-developed countries, in most of which rapid social change is now taking place. These areas are characterized by high birth rates and comparatively high death rates, though the death rates in some countries have shown a spectacular fall. Even a slight fall in the death rate, however, accompanied by no corresponding fall in the birth rate, will result in an increase in population. The effect of this on the standard of living of the majority of families will be determined by the relationship between economic, social and demographic factors.

These relationships are among the matters which must be understood if the fundamental reasons for mass poverty, for the wastage of human and physical resources, and for the economic and cultural retardation of many of the world's peoples are to be known.[15]

Before examining in some detail the effects of demographic and economic changes on certain selected countries, it would be useful to consider some general factors which influence or may influence change in the economically under-developed countries.

The present demographic situation in the under-developed countries, with relatively constant fertility and rapidly decreasing

[14] *The Times*, 24 August 1957.
[15] *The Determinants and Consequences of Population Trends*, p. 3.

44

mortality, is leading to rates of population increase such as have never before been experienced in the history of the human race. Increases of 3 per cent per annum are not exceptional at present among the under-developed countries. Population growth at such a rate cannot fail to have important economic and social consequences, and their importance does not seem to have been recognised clearly by most of the governments.[16]

The Alleged Analogy with Western Europe

It is sometimes argued that there is a parallel with the increase of population in Europe during the nineteenth century, and the deduction has been drawn that as the birth rate fell in Europe so, for the same causes, the birth rate will ultimately fall in the developing countries. The circumstances are so different that the deduction may not be valid, or it may be valid only after a considerable lapse of time.

England was the first country to undergo an industrial revolution, with the consequent shift of population from country to town; other European countries followed the same course, though the rate of change was slower. Industrialization in many of the economically under-developed countries is taking place to-day at a far more rapid rate than in the England of the latter part of the eighteenth and the first half of the nineteenth centuries, and in a totally different setting. The English were a homogeneous people, speaking a common language and bound by a common culture; by 1835 the foundations of sound democratic government, central and local, had been laid. In Asia, on the other hand, industrialization is overtaking peoples where these bonds either do not exist at all or are not present in the same combination.

In England the fall in the death rate during the first half of the nineteenth century was unaccompanied by a fall in the birth rate, so that during the first half of that century the population doubled. The average annual rate of increase each year was 1.5 per cent, a much lower rate than that of many of the under-developed countries to-day; it was not until the latter part of the century that there was a marked fall in the birth rate.

A rise in the *per capita* level of living presupposes a rise in the national income. This in turn demands capital investment. England's wealth derived from her own resources : investment capital was available because she had a large national income in relation to her population, and this income was unequally distributed. A fact of paramount importance is that whilst her population was increasing

[16] *Background Facts on World Population and Population Trends*, 1957, United Nations Economic and Social Council, p. 1.

during the first half of the nineteenth century so also was capital investment : the national income increased at a higher rate than the rate of population growth. Thus there was on average a rising standard of living in spite of much poverty. More efficient agriculture was producing food more cheaply, food and raw materials were imported on favourable terms against manufactured goods, and manufactured goods were falling in price on the home market. The increased wealth of the country meant that resources could be devoted to improving the physical environment of the population; and after 1760 the more efficient health services, especially for the mother in child-birth and for the baby, resulted in a falling death rate.[17] All these factors are inter-related and help to explain the doubling of the population during the first half of the nineteenth century. It was not until towards the end of the century that the cumulative effect of all these changes brought about also a marked fall in the birth rate.

The salient points of resemblance and difference between the economic and social development of England and the changes now taking place in the under-developed countries will become clearer as individual countries are studied. But at this point certain comparisons may be drawn. In the under-developed countries the standard of living of masses of the people is considerably lower than that of England during the period of industrial change; local resources available for investment are in some countries almost negligible and in all insufficient for the changes which will have to occur in order greatly to raise the standard of living of the mass of the people. Some international funds will no doubt continue to be made available for capital investment, and the World Health Organization will continue its beneficent work. But more people are being kept alive to share the scanty resources of those who exist : the crux of the matter lies in the relationship of population and resources. How swiftly can the improvement in agriculture and the development of industrial resources provide the rise in the standard of living which might influence the desire of parents to limit their families? It is not inopportune to note the time which elapsed in England before the rising standard of living influenced family size and ultimately slowed down the growth of population.

A brief examination of the conditions existing in the under-developed countries to-day emphasizes further fundamental differences between them and the Europe of the nineteenth century. They have a different standard of living from that of the England of the industrial revolution; but, whereas in England the fall in the death rate had to wait on changes in economic and environmental

[17] G. M. Trevelyan, *History of England* (1926), p. 602.

conditions, medical knowledge to-day can be utilized through the World Health Organization and other international resources and forms of technical co-operation, and spectacular reductions can be wrought in the death rate in advance of such changes. British Honduras, British Guiana, Ceylon, and India, to single out only a few countries, have had their death rate halved or almost halved in the space of about twelve years. The decline in the death of children under one year has been spectacular. Birth rates have remained at their previous high level or have possibly increased, and the better health of mothers has meant that more babies live during the critical first months of life. Population is increasing at a rate hitherto unknown in the world's history.

Some of the countries where this is taking place are already densely populated, with a population living little, if at all, above subsistence level. The problem is twofold. The standard of living must be raised for the older generation, and the children must be provided for. Agriculture must be improved and industrialization must be accelerated. But the mere fact of increasing numbers makes these two desirable ends more difficult to attain. The sub-division of agricultural land continues in order to provide for the new families, thereby making more difficult the introduction of machinery. Moreover, since in many of the under-developed countries there is redundant labour until industry can be developed and thereby increase the possibility of other than agricultural employment, the standard of living of the agricultural population may well be still further depressed. The extension of industrial enterprise demands capital investment, and savings for investment become available as the national income increases. Industrial development also demands markets : Britain enjoyed the advantage of possessing overseas territories in which to market her goods; the developing countries have to find markets for their goods as they produce them.

This brief analysis brings out certain points. Industrial development raises the *per capita* level of living; but if population is growing at the same time, this growth necessarily offsets that advantage by distributing the benefit more widely. Europe, and England in particular, had capital resources which allowed the development of industry to take place more quickly than the rise in population, even when population was increasing rapidly. The effect was cumulative. It is common ground among the demographers that the rising standard of living towards the end of the nineteenth century is also related to the fall in family size. In the under-developed countries time is of the essence of the matter, for unless the changes in agriculture and industry can proceed more quickly than the rate of population growth, there would appear to be no reason to expect these countries to follow the same line of development as that of Britain and the older industrialized countries. The basis on which the whole structure is founded is lacking. In countries where population is outstripping resources, a decline in standards of living appears to be inevitable. Therefore, if the argument advanced above is valid, the determinants which in the West have limited family size will not apply.

The families in all three groups of countries alike are being faced with problems of adaptation to new situations. In *Group One,* of which England will be taken as an example, full employment, the fall in family size, and the social services have brought about the abolition of dire need for the vast majority of the population. In *Groups Two* and *Three,* some 80 per cent of the population are dependent upon agriculture, and life is lived, especially for the families in *Group Three,* largely by producing all that they need for themselves, which, in many cases, is barely adequate to sustain life. It would appear that the only way to raise the standard of living of these countries is to change age-long systems of agriculture, to develop industry, and to further the movement to towns. These changes may well involve a disruption of one culture without replacing it by another, unless raising the standard of living is taken to include educational and social values. A study of some of the countries where rapid social change is taking place relates these points to concrete situations.

2. INDIA

Population and Resources

The Indian Government has, in recent years, given much attention to population problems, and to furthering measures necessary to increase agricultural production and industrial investment so as to meet the needs of a rapidly growing population. The need to check the rate of population growth, if possible, is recognized, and financial aid is provided to facilitate the dissemination of the knowledge of family planning methods. The Government is thus proceeding by two lines of approach to raise the standard of living of the people : first by increasing resources and secondly by striving to correct the present imbalance between population and resources by reducing the rate of growth of the population through limiting what the 1951 Census terms "improvident births".

The compilers of the 1951 Census estimate that a fair standard of statistical accuracy has been attained for three quarters of the country, and that the statistics available may, without too great a margin of error, be extended to the country as a whole. Tables in the Census Reports give details of the vital statistics and of agricultural production; the two sets of statistics are then brought together to serve as a basis for the estimated increases necessary to maintain the population, even at its present low standard of living.

> Prior to 1921 the growth of population and cultivation were nearly in balance. Population increase was fitful and slow, and increase in cultivation managed to keep pace with it. After 1921, however, population growth has been rapid and uninterrupted, while increase in cultivation, even where it has occurred, has been small and proportionately much less than the increase in population.[1]

The Report then proceeds to the analysis of the birth and death rates in order to substantiate the earlier part of this quotation : migration is disregarded as having little effect on the final figures. The increase in population is due to natural growth, the diminution of the death rate, and the continuance of a high birth rate. The

[1] *Census of India, 1951.* Vol. 1, Part IB, Appendices to the Census Report, 1951, p. 1.

3*

average birth rate during 1941-1950 was 40 per 1,000. The average
death rate during the same period was 27 per 1,000. The percentage
population growth for ten yearly periods is shown as follows :[2]

India — Population Growth — Average per Decade

1921–1930	10.4	per cent
1931–1940	12.7	,, ,,
1941–1950	13.2	,, ,,

These figures may be compared with those for the United Kingdom :

U.K. — Population Growth — Average per Decade

| 1881–1930 | 1.9 | per cent |
| 1931–1950 | 2.2 | ,, ,, |

The increase of the population between 1941 and 1950 has been
larger than during previous decades. Figures are given in the Census
Report to show that whilst what may be termed "normal" deaths
have diminished slightly, there has been a steep fall in "abnormal"
deaths, those due to severe famines and to bubonic plague. Malaria
control and the work of the public health departments have reduced
both epidemic and endemic diseases; therefore the natural checks on
population growth, which resulted in the earlier period in a rate of
growth of only 1.7 per cent per annum, no longer take the same
yearly toll of lives. Nevertheless, the "normal" death rate is still very
high in India, and is likely to fall very considerably; therefore the
Census Report estimates that there will be an increase in the rate of
population growth up to 1961 and thereafter, if no steps are taken
to discourage still further "improvident maternity".

So far as maternity is concerned, our assessment of the past does
not indicate a trend which would justify us in assuming any very
materially different future unless something happens which leads
to the wide-spread adoption of contraception—a contingency
which we shall reserve for later discussion. The position is
different about mortality. Our assessment of the past would justify
us in assuming that a further decline of mortality might take
place in the next thirty years. It is perfectly obvious that a large
proportion of deaths which occur at present are preventable.
There is, therefore, quite considerable scope for reduction of
mortality, especially among infants and very young children.[3]

The possibility of a considerable increase in population through
the reduction of the infant mortality rate, and of an increase in the
expectation of life, is clear when the Indian figures are compared
with those of other countries. The deaths of children under 5 equal

[2] Ibid., p. 134.
[3] Ibid., p. 190.

50

or exceed the deaths at ages between 5 and 54, and exceed the deaths of people of 55 and over. The health programme adopted by the Indian government lays great stress on infant and maternal health, so that a fall in the mortality rates of children under 5 is likely to continue, with a consequent increase of population. Moreover, a lengthening of adult life would have the same effect, and in India there is the possibility of greatly extending the expectation of life.

The expectation of life at age 10 is 59 to 60 in England and Wales, Australia and New Zealand. It is 56 in the U.S.A., about 50 in Japan and 47 in Egypt. It is *now* 39 in India. We continue to retain the unpleasant distinction of having the lowest expectation of life among all the peoples for whom figures are available.[4]

Taking the possibility of a reduction of mortality rates into consideration the writer of the Report then arrives at what he suggests is a low estimate for population growth up to 1981.

India : Census and Estimated Population [5]

Census population	1951	360 million
Estimated population	1961	410 million
,, ,,	1971	460 million
,, ,,	1981	520 million

On these assumptions, population in India will increase more rapidly during the period 1951-80 than during the period 1921-50 unless the birth rate falls through the adoption of family planning. The writer of the Report regards this possibility as remote, and he proceeds to examine how far agricultural and industrial resources may be expected to increase at a rate which will balance the increase in population. He comes to the conclusion that agricultural production will have to increase by 21 per cent before 1961, by 37 per cent before 1971, and by 54 per cent by 1981.

The First Five Year Plan

Since 1891 there appears to have been a steady drop in the amount of land available per head of the population; productivity in many areas has fallen because of the steady division of land to meet the requirement of new families. How far can productivity be increased by the measures laid down in the First Five Year Plan? This Plan concentrated on the improvement of agricultural production; 45 per cent of planned expenditure was set aside for the development of irrigation and power as the most efficient method of increasing production. The agricultural classes account for 69.8 per

4 Ibid., p. 194.
5 Ibid., p. 187.

51

cent of the total population and most of the land in cultivation is held by peasants in small holdings.

In India 706 persons out of 1000 are engaged in producing their own food and a small surplus which just falls short of being sufficient for the other 294.[6]

The results of the first Five Year Plan have definitely increased the home-grown food supplies though not to the extent anticipated. Large irrigation schemes have enabled more land to be brought into cultivation and yields have increased through double cropping. But the possibility of far-reaching changes is limited by the steady growth of population in the rural areas and by the increasing numbers dependent on ever smaller holdings. The Census notes the increasing unemployment and under-employment in rural areas. That shortages of home-grown food still exist is shown by the Government's continued control of the marketing of food products and the increase of imported food stuffs. Clearly the need is to develop industry, providing thereby among other advantages an alternative to farming as a way of living. The argument so far, as seen by the Indian Government, may be summarized in the words of its Planning Commission :

The recent increase in the population of India and the pressures exercised on the limited resources of the country have brought to the forefront the urgency of the problem of family planning and population control. The application of medical knowledge and social care has lowered the death rate, while the birth rate remains fairly constant. This has led to the rapid increase in the growth of the population. While a lowering of the birth rate may occur as a result of improvements in the standard of living, such improvements are not likely to materialize if there is a concurrent increase of population. It is, therefore, apparent that population control can be achieved only by the reduction of the birth rate to the extent necessary to stabilize the population at a level consistent with the requirements of national economy. This can be secured only by the realization of the need for family limitation on a wide scale by the people. The main appeal for family planning is based on considerations of the health and welfare of the family. Family limitation or spacing of the children is necessary and desirable in order to secure better health for the mother and better care and upbringing of children. Measures directed to this end should, therefore, form part of the public health program.[7]

6 Ibid., p. 120.
7 Quoted, ibid., p. 213.

The Plan sets out a "Program for family limitation" :

(a) To obtain an accurate picture of the factors contributing to the rapid population increase in India;

(b) to discover suitable techniques of family planning and to devise methods by which knowledge of these techniques can be widely disseminated; and

(c) to make advice on family planning an integral part of the service of Government hospitals and public health agencies.[8]

Details of how these plans are to be carried out are laid down and a sum of money has been allotted to cover the training of medical staff and social workers and the installation of clinics; the Rockefeller Foundation has given funds to assist the project.

The Progress Report on the Plan states that the money allotted for the family planning project has not all been spent owing to the lack of trained workers; it proceeds to give some details of what has been accomplished.

The Central Government has, at present, three experimental centres for pilot studies in family planning methods. A family planning section has been established in the Ministry of Health. . . . In view of the vital importance of family planning and the pioneering work which has already been done, it is of the highest importance that the Central Government should provide effective and vigorous leadership in this field and should guide the States as well as voluntary organizations on the basis of a definite and carefully co-ordinated program of work.[9]

The Second Five Year Plan

The Second Five Year Plan begins by recounting the progress already made in bringing more land into cultivation and in increasing the yield from crops by the extension or irrigation projects, and the distribution of better seeds and of chemical manures.

These gains notwithstanding, the fact remains that living standards in India are amongst the lowest in the world. The average intake of food in India is below accepted nutritional standards; the consumption of cloth in 1955-56, at about 16 yards per capita, is still around the pre-war level; housing is very deficient; and only a half of the children in age group 6-11 and

8 *Government of India Planning Commission. First Five Year Plan,* Vol. 2, Chap. 33, p. 106.

9 *Government of India Planning Commission. Progress Report,* pp. 52-3.

less than one-fifth of the children in the age group 11-14 attend school.[10]

The Second Five Year Plan has to take account of these facts, of a population increase of from 4.5 to 5 million a year, of a large and increasing volume of unemployment, and of the hopes and aspirations of a population looking to the government to provide the means by which a substantial rise in the standard of living may be achieved.

The experience of the West has shown that it is by the knowledge of industrial techniques and by capital investment that the national income can be increased and a rise in the standard of living thereby made possible. The Second Five Year Plan lays down the route by which India sets out to travel so as to arrive at the same end.

The Indian government plans neither to follow the way of the West nor the way of communist countries in bringing about the economic changes which alone can raise the standard of living of the population. What is desired is the creation of "a socialist pattern of society".

A rising standard of life, or material welfare as it is sometimes called, is of course not an end in itself. Essentially, it is a means to a better intellectual and cultural life. A society which has to devote the bulk of its working force or its working hours to the production of the bare wherewithals of life is to that extent limited in its pursuit of higher ends. Economic development is intended to expand the community's productive power and to provide the environment in which there is scope for the expression and application of diverse faculties and urges. It follows that the pattern of development and the lines along which economic activity is to be directed must from the start be related to the basic objectives which society has in view. The task before an under-developed country is not merely to get better results within the existing framework of economic and social institutions, but to mould and refashion these so that they contribute effectively to the realisation of wider and deeper social values.[11]

India plans for a vast development, over the next five years, in transport, in irrigation and the building of dams, in the increasing of power resources of steel plants and of engineering works. These developments, which are basic to the increase in the productive power of the country, must be undertaken by the State. Economic change would certainly have been accelerated had the production of consumer goods also been taken over by large industrial units

[10] *Government of India Planning Commission. Second Five Year Plan,* 1956, p. 23.
[11] Ibid., p. 22.

54

supplied with capital for the investment in machinery. India is prepared deliberately to slow down industrialization by preserving the livelihood and traditional way of life of those millions of families wholly or partially dependent on small scale and village industries. The basic policy of the plan in this matter is set forth as follows :

(a) To avoid as far as possible, during the period of the second plan, further technological unemployment such as occurs especially in the traditional village industries;

(b) to provide for as large a measure of increased employment as possible during the plan period through different village and small industries; and

(c) to provide the basis for the structure of an essentially decentralized society and also for progressive economic development at a fairly rapid rate.[12]

Thus hand-loom weaving is not to be ousted by the power-driven mill, but weavers are to be assisted in every way by the allocation of funds to improve the loom itself and by the establishment of co-operatives. A part of the market in cloth is reserved for the hand-loom weaver. The hand pounding of rice is to be encouraged by a subsidy and by an exemption from the sales tax. Power-driven rice mills must be licensed and no more may be set up except in very special circumstances. Again, the making of leather footwear in the cottages is encouraged by loans for better equipment and for aid in setting up co-operatives; large-scale industry is discouraged. These examples of the desire to encourage village industries could be multiplied many times. It is expected that as the development of basic industry takes place the demand for all these village products will increase, thus ensuring a rise in the standard of living of the village families without disorientating their traditional way of life.

The basis of village life is, however, to be found in agriculture; village industries often form a part-time occupation. It is essential to the success of the plan that more home-grown food is produced in order to meet the needs of the increasing urban population, to feed the four or five million added yearly to the population, and to raise the standard of living by increasing the food intake of the people as a whole. The importing of food requires foreign currency, of which India is short, and such foreign currency as she possesses is needed for the import of capital goods. The problem of increasing agricultural production, particularly the increase of cash crops, is a formidable one. The majority of the villages have under 1,000

12 Ibid., p. 432.

3. THE WEST INDIES AND MAURITIUS

The Caribbean Federation is now coming into being, though it does not cover the whole area of the West Indies : British Honduras, British Guiana, and the Virgin Islands, at least for the present, remain outside. Within the federation, whilst each island has problems peculiar to itself, there are certain conditions of living which basically determine the pattern of society for them all. All the islands are separated by miles of ocean, all have limited resources, and all have a more or less acute population problem due to a falling death rate unmatched by a proportionate falling birth rate. In all the islands the social institutions and particularly the family patterns are influenced by the legacy of slavery. It is proposed, therefore, to treat in some detail the situation in Jamaica : the problems of Barbados and Trinidad are in essence the same as those of Jamaica as some statistics will make clear.

JAMAICA

Population

As the island completes its third century of British rule it stands poised, apparently, for population growth on a scale greater than anything it has experienced in the past.[1]

The Jamaican Census of 1943 shows that between 1921 and 1943 the population increased by 44.16 per cent. The population has continued to increase by some 2 per cent per annum, a rate which yields a population increase of about 50 per cent in twenty years. The immediate increase is due, in part, to the almost complete cessation of emigration to the United States as a result of the Immigration and Nationality Act, 1952. From 1943 to 1954 the total of emigrants to the United States, including contract workers, and to this country, amounted to some 30,000 people; during this same period the natural increase of population amounted to 330,000. Since 1950 there has been a marked increase in emigration to Britain; the exact number is not known, but it is estimated that 24,000 immigrants arrived from the West Indies in 1955, and 26,000 in 1956 when a smaller proportion came from Jamaica. At this rate,

[1] G. W. Roberts, *The Population of Jamaica,* 1957, p. 307.

therefore, emigration provides no permanent solution to the population problem of Jamaica.

But over a longer period the population increase has been influenced far more by the decline in mortality rates in conjunction with a fairly stable birth rate. The crude death rate per 1,000 of the population has been reduced from 23.51, the average for the years 1921 to 1925, to 15, the average for the years 1950 to 1955.[2] This rate may be compared with the United Kingdom average of 11.7 for the same period. In twenty-five years mortality rates in Jamaica have been reduced to a greater degree than in England during the seventy years from 1841 to 1911.[3] The Jamaican death rate now approaches the European level, and because of the age structure of the population and the progress which is being made in combating such diseases as yaws and venereal disease, it may well decline to the European rate within the next few years. The average birth rate, however, shows a wide difference. The Jamaican average rate for the years 1950 to 1955 is rather under 40 per 1,000 of the population : the United Kingdom rate for the same period is 15.8.

Population growth is influenced, in particular, by the infant mortality rate and by the survival rate of women of child-bearing age. The infant mortality rate in Jamaica has shown a spectacular decline from 1921. The average rate from 1921 to 1925 was 176.1 per 1,000 live births; the average for 1950 to 1954 is 72.8, and the *Demographic Year Book* gives a rate of 60.3 per 1,000 births for 1955. The average for the United Kingdom from 1953 to 1955 is 26.5. It is clear, therefore, that the Jamaican rate could be reduced very much further, and the present extension of maternal and child welfare care may well bring this about. Moreover, if the level of living rises this also will affect the infant mortality rate, for this rate is particularly sensitive to environmental conditions. The average rate conceals a sharp difference between a death rate of 59.2 per 1,000 live births of those born within legally recognized marriage, and one of 27 per 1,000 of those born outside.[4] Since the "illegitimate" rate in 1953 was 70.9 of total births, a diminution in the mortality rate of these babies would raise considerably the total infant survival rate.

There has been a steady decline since 1936 in the mortality rates of the age group fifteen to thirty-four. Taken together, this increase in the number of babies kept alive plus the greater number of potential parents who now survive cannot fail to have an influence

[2] *United Nations Economic and Social Council: Population Commission,* 1954, Table 29.

[3] Roberts, op. cit., p. 204.

[4] See below, p. 60-1.

on population growth both now and in the future. Further, the expectation of life at birth is still only about 50 while in the United Kingdom it is to-day about 71.[5]

Jamaica has been under British control since 1655, and the present-day population is descended almost wholly from the slaves who were imported from Africa from the beginning of the eighteenth century to work in the sugar plantations; the slave trade was declared illegal in 1807. At that time the slave population numbered 346,150. In 1834 the slaves were declared free and their owners were indemnified against loss. The Census of 1943 gives the racial composition of the island as follows :

Jamaica — Racial Composition, 1943. [6]

Black	78.1
Coloured	17.5
White	1.1
Chinese	1.0
East Indian	2.1
Others	0.2

Total Population, 1943 : 1,237,063

Both the Negro and Coloured people in the population have increased about threefold since 1844 and it is, therefore, to these two groups that the increase in numbers is due.

The Jamaican Family

The Jamaican family, as the Royal Commission of 1938 stated, "has been moulded almost entirely by social and economic forces operating during and since the days of slavery". The result is a complicated family pattern which should not be regarded as a deviant from the accepted pattern of western society but as the special form of family life which evolved during slavery. The slaves were not allowed to marry and promiscuity was encouraged under the mistaken belief that the birth rate was thereby increased. The diversity of family forms in Jamaica to-day dates back to the period of slavery; that this diversity continues suggests that it fits into the general pattern of living in that society.

According to the 1943 census about 30 per cent of families are based on Christian marriage; about 29 per cent on faithful concubinage described as "common-law marriage", though this phrase does not imply that there is any legal sanction; 35.6 per cent of the mothers fall into two groups in which the family pattern is based on limited or general promiscuity; 1.9 per cent of women are returned as widows and 0.2 per cent as divorced.

[5] Figures from Department of Statistics, British West Indies, 1956, Section 1, and *Health in the U.K. Dependencies*, H.M.S.O., 1956, Table III.

[6] *Jamaica Census, 1943*, Table 46.

Henriques distinguishes four types of family groups : Christian Family, Faithful Concubinage, Maternal or Grandmother Family, and Keeper Family.[7] Professor Simey has named the last two groups the Companionate Family and the Disintegrate Family.

The Christian Family, rather over 30 per cent of all families, is the only one which enjoys legal recognition. The upper-class and certain of the middle-class households are based on marriage. It is not uncommon for the husband and wife to have lived together for years before moving from faithful concubinage to marriage. As Henriques, himself a West Indian, says,

> There is no moral sanction against concubinage. Church congregations addressed by a priest on their sexual immorality will appear ashamed, but it is a momentary feeling and their behaviour will continue as before. . . . To the average black man the fact that he lives contentedly with his woman without the benefit of Church or Law cannot conceivably be immoral. He may be an assiduous churchgoer and he sees nothing contradictory in the two types of behaviour.[8]

Concubinage continues in the island, therefore, as a recognized form on which a household may be based. The relationship may endure for many years, and though the wife may wish for the greater security of marriage her attitude is ambivalent : legal sanction makes her more dependent, takes away her freedom of choice, and may lead to undue domination by the man. Men, on the whole, are reluctant to contract marriage until after some years of experimentation, if then.[9] The average peasant and town dweller has a very low level of living; there is much unemployment; living conditions are lamentable; concubinage fits in to these material conditions.

The Grandmother type of household, as the name suggests, has no man at its head.

> The Grandmother or Maternal Family is so-called because the grandmother or some female relative, perhaps a sister, usurps the function of the father and at times of the mother. Such a family can originate through the girl becoming pregnant while still living at home. The Household may consist of her mother, her mother's sister, and the girl's siblings. The girl may remain at

7 F. M. Henriques, *Family and Colour in Jamaica,* 1953, p. 105.

8 Ibid., p. 87.

9 This description may not apply in the same way to British Guiana. For attitudes to legal marriage there see Raymond T. Smith, *The Negro Family in British Guiana,* 1956, pp. 180 ff.

home and look after her child, but in many cases she leaves and the child is brought up by its grandmother.[10]

The household founded on a Keeper union, the least stable form of household, has much less permanence, for the man and woman live together in a temporary union; it is a casual relationship; the household may consist of children of different fathers. There may be a man contributing to the household, but frequently the woman and the older children provide for the family needs. On occasions a household which begins as a Keeper union may pass into Faithful Concubinage; especially is this true when the woman is under twenty.

This diversity of family structure cannot fail to affect the security of the children. The low level of living is in part the result of the frequent absence of a male head; the sustenance of the family has to be provided through the work of the mother and the older children. Thus, whilst the children are expected to treat the father as the head of the family, it is the mother to whom they look for both material and emotional security. Therefore, as Madeleine Kerr has pointed out,

> The boy . . . will have no consistent pattern of male behaviour on which to model himself. His father may never come near the home, may come and go, his mother may have taken another man, or there may be no residential male at all. He will therefore be tied both emotionally and financially to the female head of the house. This will result in a fixation on the mother combined with a belief that the world in general should look after him with maternal care.[11]

There is thus a cultural pattern in which the man tends not to accept his responsibilities either as citizen or as father, with unfortunate results both to the community and to the family. On the other hand, the girl grows up accepting the idea that the major responsibility for maintaining the family will devolve upon her. Professor Simey has pointed out the sense of insecurity which is inherent in this pattern of family life, an insecurity which affects adult attitudes and which is enhanced by the conflict of living in a community with two disparate culture patterns.[12] Moreover, the support which the extended family provides in most peasant communities is lacking for a large proportion of the poor families, and these are the families

[10] Henriques, op. cit., p. 110.
[11] *Personality and Conflict in Jamaica,* 1952, p. 167.
[12] T. S. Simey, *Welfare and Planning in the West Indies,* 1946, pp. 160 ff.

which most need the material and moral support which kinship gives.

A factor which militates against a more stable family life is inadequate housing.

> The most striking fact about West Indian people, as exemplified in their houses, is their poverty.[13]

The 1943 Jamaican Census gave figures to show that 10,177 persons lived in houses with a superficial area of less than 100 square feet at a density of more than six persons to each house. In 1952 the International Bank for Reconstruction and Development sent a mission to Jamaica. The Report of the mission states that

> Housing authorities in Jamaica have estimated that about 100,000 of the 325,000 units of housing in the Island are so poor as to require urgent replacement. In addition, 5,000 new dwellings or more should be built every year simply to take care of the increase in population. The existing housing programmes offer no prospect that these requirements will be met.[14]

In the country districts there is frequently no incentive to improve the houses because of insecurity of tenure; in the towns, in particular Kingston and its suburb St Andrew, the rate of movement into the town far exceeds the provision of houses; the result is a rapid growth of exceedingly bad slum property. As will be seen later, two factors are making for an excess of population on the land : one is the growth in the numbers, the second is the more efficient cultivation of sugar, which has reduced the amount of labour required. The rate of industrialization in the towns has not been sufficient to absorb all the newcomers into productive work, with the result that there is a growing body of men, women, and children who live by anti-social methods on the fringe of the law.

Social and Economic Prospects

In all the economically under-developed countries the people are demanding a higher standard of living; there is more contact with people from more favoured areas; urbanization itself is responsible for the spreading of new ideas back to the countryside. Education, however, inadequate, is opening up new horizons and creating dissatisfaction with present low levels of living and all that this material condition implies. The new ideals gathering around the United Nations and the change of status of many of these countries have

13 Ibid., p. 12.

14 *Report by a Mission of the International Bank for Reconstruction and Development*, O.U.P., 1952, p. 125.

raised expectations. In Jamaica the growth of self-government has encouraged high hopes among the population. How far do the facts warrant the assumption that the level of living may be substantially raised in the next few years?

The importance of agriculture in the island's economy has been steadily declining, but it still engages rather over half of the population : for this reason the prospect of land available for establishing the growing number of households as peasant proprietors must be considered as well as the prospects of employment for the agriculture worker.

Since 1911 there has been little land available for further land settlement. The island is only 4,410 square miles in extent, and much of this is mountainous. One important result of population growth has therefore been a rising density.

> At the first census (1844) the density was 86 per square mile, and this has risen steadily during the ensuing century, amounting to 280 by 1943. According to the population [figure] of 1951 (1,443,700) the density was 327 persons per square mile.[15]

Since 1882 there has been a large increase in the number of holdings of under five acres; holdings of this size constitute by far the largest number, suggesting that the demand for land has, in part, been met by the sub-division of holdings.

> The reason for the existence of so many small holdings seems to be that Jamaicans, for historical reasons, value land beyond anything else. It is the symbol of security, though in most cases it does not provide security to its owners, not only because of the size of holdings but also because of a cultural factor. Land transmitted to the eldest son according to the law tends to be regarded as family land, which is inalienable. The consequence is that the whole family has a claim on the produce. . . . Thus the factor which may contribute to family cohesion leads to a very serious wastage of land, which is under-used, save for the fruit trees planted by ancestors.[16]

Land is transmitted and held in a variety of ways; women have a right to transmit land equally with men; but the Census return makes clear that the unit of land held by the majority of families is too small for efficient production. Moreover, the peasant is unwilling to devote the whole of his land to a single crop for fear of fluctuation in demand, and this diversity of product again reduces the yield.

[15] Roberts, op. cit., p. 55.
[16] Robert Marier, *Social Welfare in Jamaica*, U.N.E.S.C.O., 1953, p. 43.

The rural population is largely dependent on wages, for the majority of peasant holdings are too small to keep a family. The farmer therefore has to rent additional land and work on the plantation or big farm. Jamaican crops are destined for the export market; bananas, sugar, and coffee are subject to fluctuation in world prices, though the United Kingdom has an agreement which maintains the selling price of sugar and provides price support for bananas and citrus fruit. The cultivation of sugar demands a high labour force for about six months of the year only. The demand for workers has diminished in recent years and is likely to diminish still further owing to the mechanization of the industry. Mechanization is nevertheless beneficial, for more efficient production makes possible the payment of higher wages and a rise in the level of living of the workers employed. But since the countryside affords no alternative employment the redundant workers remain unemployed or swell the numbers of those seeking work in the towns.

Professor Arthur Lewis has argued that since no family can live off the two or three acres which constitute many holdings, the number of holdings should be drastically reduced so as to permit the families remaining on the land to raise their level of living by acquiring more land, and thereby make possible more efficient agriculture. In his view the numbers engaged in agriculture should be reduced by 20 per cent during the next ten years. If this were done work would have to be found for some 74,000 extra workers outside agriculture.[17] This would require that industry be developed at a sufficient rate to employ the increasing number of potential workers who are added each year to the labour force, as well as to provide work for those diverted from the land.

The government of Jamaica has worked out a ten-years development plan and has invited various bodies to advise on the serious economic situation in which the island finds itself. The result of urbanization has been an increase in the numbers employed in the professions, in commerce, and in the service industries, but Jamaica remains a predominantly agricultural country with its economy based on the export of sugar and sugar products, bananas, fruit, and fruit products. Recently bauxite has been found in the island and is being exploited. The Jamaican plan rightly, according to the experts, lays the main stress on the development of agriculture, and the larger proportion of the development funds so far invested has been in improving agriculture. There have been irrigation projects, improvements in transport and roads, efforts to encourage the use of fertilizers, and measures to stop soil erosion. There is a good deal of malnutrition in the island which would be mitigated by an increase

[17] A. L. Lewis, *The Caribbean Economic Review*, Vol. 2, 1950, p. 1.

in the cultivation of fruit and vegetables for the home market, and experts from U.N.I.C.E.F. and F.A.O. are giving technical advice on the matter. But since the island depends so greatly on its export crops the expansion of these crops would seem to be essential to economic progress.

In 1955 Professor J. R. Hicks, invited with his wife by the Jamaican Government to review the island's economy, made a Report on Finance and Taxation. He concluded that there was little possibility of an increase in world demand either for sugar or for bananas, which together account for 60 per cent of Jamaica's exports; and that the development of secondary industries for the home market, except on a small scale, was also limited by the low purchasing power of the mass of the population. Three companies, two American and one Canadian, are exploiting the bauxite resources, and while the island is benefiting from the increased revenue which taxation brings, the industry employs relatively little labour. Capital equipment reduces the numbers actually employed on the mining operations, and the island cannot provide the power necessary for the production of aluminium from the ore. The tourist industry, encouraged by tax remission, is employing an increasing number of people—Jamaica has been called "The American Riviera"—and this industry could be expanded still further.

Need of Capital

Is a country with limited resources better served by investment in its human resources or by investment in capital equipment which may lead to increased employment and a rise in the level of living? Better education, better housing, better health, are obviously not only blessings in themselves, but also they increase the efficiency and endurance of the worker, and so, in turn, aid industrial development. Every economically under-developed country with little investment capital is thus faced with a dilemma in the use of limited funds. Jamaica with its rapidly growing population has been obliged to spend relatively large sums on social services to the detriment of its investment programme. Professor Hicks, commenting on this, remarks :

Under social development we classify schools, hospitals, housing estates and similar works. There is a crying need for such services in every under-developed country, but it has to be realized that their provision does nothing to raise the national income or taxable capacity of the country, save in the very long run. If they are provided by borrowing, they contribute nothing towards the service of the debt which arises. . . They are of the best fruits of economic development but they do not easily produce such economic development by themselves.[18]

Economic development has been reviewed also by a Mission of the International Bank for Reconstruction and Development and by a group of British industrialists who visited the island and reported in 1953. The Mission from the Industrial Bank reviewed every aspect of the Jamaican economy and produced two development plans.

Despite a not inconsiderable economic potential and rising production, Jamaica suffers from chronic unemployment and widespread poverty. Wasteful and poor utilization of land, a growing population and lack of sufficient capital have all been responsible for this situation. Preoccupation with the increasing population pressure has in particular tended to produce rather pessimistic evaluations of the island's future. The future does indeed pose serious questions. Jamaica, which does not adequately support its present population, must provide for an additional 18 per cent by the end of the next decade. Although unemployment is already between 15 per cent and 20 per cent of the available labour force, 130,000 more people will be seeking work in the next ten years. There is therefore urgent need for a stock-taking on Jamaican economic capabilities and for the adoption of a development programme which will meet the twin requirements of more jobs and higher living standards.[19]

Further industrialization was considered essential by the Mission but the difficulties inherent in the situation were stressed. The Mission emphasized the lack of technical skill and saw little hope of finding an outlet on the foreign market for manufactured goods. What is required, according to the Mission, is capital investment in small industries; the difficulty is to find the capital.

The vicious circle must be broken; this can only be done by an investment programme financed to a considerable extent by private capital imports and public borrowing abroad.[20]

Jamaica would gain considerably if British firms would establish enterprises in Jamaica as American firms have done in Puerto Rico. The British industrialists who visited Jamaica studied the prospects of industrialization generally and considered whether British firms

18 J. R. and U. K. Hicks, *Report on Finance and Taxation in Jamaica*, 1955, p. 42.

19 Op. cit., p. 4.

20 *International Bank Report*, p. 6.

might find it to their advantage to put capital into establishing branches in Jamaica. On the first point the Mission reported,

> In general we cannot hold out any hope that industrial expansion by itself will solve the population problem in the crowded territories. It can, however, be a valuable contribution to it. For instance, we estimate that the doubling of industrial production over the next ten years will be accompanied by an increase in the direct labour force engaged in manufacture of approximately 25 per cent in excess of those employed today, and that there will be a similar amount of additional employment in service industries such as public utilities, roads, transport, retail distribution and the like. This is admittedly a disappointingly small contribution to the population problem in, say, Jamaica, where the additional employment to be expected from industrial development over the next ten years will barely be equal to the increase in population in one year.[21]

The Mission came to the conclusion that labour costs in Jamaica would not be appreciably lower than in this country and that there would, therefore, be little encouragement for the British industrialist to invest capital in enterprise in the island.

The Unsolved Problem: Population Pressure

Is there any justification for claiming that the birth rate in Jamaica is likely to fall in the near future and that the rate of population growth will ultimately slow down? The rate of growth at the present time is rather over 2 per cent per annum. There is every reason to expect that the mortality rates for all age groups in the island will continue to decline, thereby increasing the total population and increasing the number of women of child-bearing age who will ultimately be added to the population. There was a slight decline in the birth rate before 1950, but since then the figures, as given in *The Demographic Year Book*, 1956, show a steady rise. It may be that the movement from agriculture into other occupations and the rising numbers living in towns may serve to stabilize the birth rate, if not to reduce it; but the possibilities of industrial development considered above do not appear likely to accelerate the growth of towns or appreciably to raise the level of living to such an extent as to bring about a reduction of the birth rate as in other countries. Emigration, while it is unlikely to take place at a rate which will effectively diminish population pressure, has, moreover,

[21] *Industrial Development in Jamaica, Trinidad, Barbados and British Guiana.* Report of Mission of U.K. Industrialists 1953. Colonial No. 294, p. 44.

the serious disadvantage of taking away from the island a high proportion of the skilled men on whom any future development of industry depends.

It has been suggested that, should the economic situation improve, this would lead to more stable unions and a reduction in the birth rate : but the 1943 census shows that though the majority of children are by Western standards illegitimate, in fact more children are born to couples who are married than to couples who are not. A movement, therefore, in favour of households based on legal marriage would probably increase the birth rate. Mr Roberts shows in his book that there is a relation between family size and literacy; since 1921 there has been a marked fall in the birth rate amongst the better educated in the urban areas. The long-term influence of a more literate population and an increase in the numbers living in towns may therefore affect the birth rate. But when all these factors are weighed, it would seem unduly optimistic to suggest that population pressure in Jamaica is likely to be reduced in the near future. The immediate problem remains of maintaining a level of living, inadequate though it is, and of providing work for a community with limited resources which is increasing in numbers by about 2 per cent per annum.

Jamaica today is at a crucial stage of its political and economic development. In the near future important steps in the direction of complete self-government will be taken. The success of this venture may well be jeopardized unless economic progress can also be assured. Jamaica can support its population under conditions of political and economic stability only if an imaginative, far sighted development programme is vigorously prosecuted. In this task the people of Jamaica face a great challenge.[22]

BARBADOS

The population problem which confronts Barbados is, if anything, more acute than that of Jamaica. There are 1,540 persons per square mile, one of the highest population densities in the world.

Population Growth since 1921

Year	1921	1930	1940	1950	1955
Total population	156,774	159,000	179,000	209,000	229,000

Birth rate per 1,000 of population

Year	1947	1950	1951	1952	1953	1954	1955
Birth rate	32.7	30.7	32	33.7	33.1	33.7	33.2

[22] *Report by a Mission of the International Bank,* p. 149.

	Death rate per 1,000 of population						
Year	1947	1950	1951	1952	1953	1954	1955
Death rate	16.3	12.8	14.2	14.7	13.6	11.3	12.6

	Infant Mortality rate per 1,000 of live births						
Year	1947	1950	1951	1952	1953	1954	1955
I.M.R.	166.3	125.2	136.5	145.5	138.6	109.4	134.6

It may be noted that the average infant mortality rate for 1935 to 1939 was 209.6. In 1954 the "illegitimate" birth rate amounted to 54.4 of the total live births. In 35 years the population has increased by 73,000, about 2 per cent per annum.[23]

In view of this rapid increase in population, a committee was appointed by the government of Barbados to examine the situation. The report states :

> The population of Barbados, according to the Census taken on 9th April, 1946, was 192,841. The population at 31st December, 1952, as calculated by the Registrar, was 223,000. From this it can be seen that in seven and a half years the increase amounts to approximately 30,000.
>
> It is interesting to note that the total number of people employed on the sugar estates and sugar factories amounts to 25,350; thus the increase in the population in the past seven and a half years far exceeds the entire labour force required for the growing and manufacture of sugar.
>
> The population at the end of 1961 has been estimated by Mr G. W. Roberts, Vital Statistics Officer attached to the Development and Welfare Organisation, as 255,600, or 1,540 per square mile, one of the densest in the world. The actual rate of increase has so far worked out in excess of Mr Roberts' estimate.

Barbados is almost entirely dependent on the sugar industry, which accounts for some 98 per cent of its exports.

Lord Simon of Wythenshawe made a study of the population problem of Barbados in relation to the island's resources in 1954. He noted the high rate of unemployment and under-employment which existed, calculated the possibility of a further expansion of the sugar industry, and came to the conclusion that although the industry had enjoyed boom conditions for the past five years with a consequent rise in the level of living,

> The prospect for the future is, unfortunately, very different. The population is increasing at nearly 2 per cent per annum and the rate of increase is steadily growing. It is almost certain that the national income will increase at less than $\frac{1}{2}$ per cent per annum. If

[23] Figures from U.N. Demographic Year Book, 1956.

these conditions continue, there will inevitably be a gradual decline in the standard of living and in the national financial situation, which might become alarming if there were one or two bad sugar crops in the next few years.[24]

This pessimistic view of the possibility of increasing production to absorb the growing population is endorsed by the government committee already referred to.

Small industries have sprung up in recent years and will continue to do so, and while they serve a useful purpose the number of people involved is small. Industry in this Island is faced with many disadvantages, such as lack of an adequate electricity supply, lack of raw materials, lack of expert knowledge and markets. In addition the cost of new industries . . . rules out any big undertakings. The Steele Report on Industrial Development recently published does not hold out any great hope for industry in Barbados.[25]

The social effects of population increase at this rate are clear. The government finds it difficult, if not impossible, to keep pace with the provision of social services, education, housing, health services, and the provision of an adequate income maintenance for those in need. The inadequacies of the present provision in Barbados were emphasized by the report made by Professor J. H. Richardson in 1954.[26]

The problems that confront the family are made especially acute in Barbados by the growing unemployment; this is especially severe for adolescents. In spite of a rise in the level of living in recent years the level is extremely low by European standards. It would appear that since there seems to be no possibility of emigration on a scale which would substantially reduce population pressure; the only possibility of raising the level of living is by limiting population growth by some other means.

TRINIDAD AND TOBAGO

The following figures illustrate the population growth of Trinidad and Tobago.

[24] Lord Simon of Wythenshawe, *Population and Resources in Barbados*, 1954, p. 112.

[25] *Report of the Joint Committee Appointed by the Two Houses of the Legislature to examine the question of Over-Population in Barbados and to make Recommendations for Dealing with this Problem*, p. 3.

[26] J. H. Richardson, *Report of Inquiry into Social Security in Barbados*, 1954.

Total population

Year	1921	1930	1940	1950	1955
Population	365,913	405,000	476,000	623,000	721,000

Birth rate per 1,000 of population

Year	1947	1950	1951	1952	1953	1954	1955
Birth rate	38.3	37.5	36.7	34.6	37.7	41.4	41.9

Death rate per 1,000 of population

Year	1947	1950	1951	1952	1953	1954	1955
Death rate	16.3	12.8	14.2	14.7	13.6	11.3	12.6

Infant Mortality rate per 1,000 of live births

Year	1947	1950	1951	1952	1953	1954	1955
I.M.R.	81.5	80.3	78.2	89.1	69.9	61.3	67.9

The average rate for 1935-9 was 103.6.

The "illegitimate" rate is 58.6 of total births, but it should be noted that the Indians who marry according to their own rite are not, officially, counted as married.

The increase of population between 1931 and 1946, the dates at which a census was taken, is the highest ever recorded; in these 15 years the population has increased by 37.00 per cent, an average increase of 2.13 per cent per annum.[27]

The birth rate in Trinidad is higher than that of Barbados and Jamaica and there is no evidence that the rate is likely to decline. Trinidad, unlike Jamaica and Barbados, has a large proportion of Indians in the population, the descendants of workers brought in as indentured labour; it is this section of the population which is increasing at phenomenal rates. In 1954, in a total population of 697,550 the Indians numbered 253,900—an increase of 58,153, or over 23 per cent, since the 1946 census. Mauritius and British Guiana have a similar problem.

Trinidad suffers from the social and economic difficulties which confront Jamaica and Barbados as a result of mounting population pressure. Population density has increased from 185 persons per square mile in 1921 to 282 in 1946; 37.5 of families live in one-room dwellings. Trinidad moreover has to meet the further complication of the changing relationship between ethnic groups due to the difference in the relative birth rates.[28]

MAURITIUS

It will be convenient to conclude this chapter with a study of another island, with similar problems, though far away in the Indian Ocean. The population problems of Mauritius have been studied in

[27] Figures from the *U.N. Demographic Year Book* and the 1946 Census of the West Indies.

[28] Figures from the 1946 Census, West Indies.

detail by a Population Committee set up by the Governor in 1953 with the following terms of reference :

To consider the problem presented by the present trend of increase of population of the Colony in relation to its economic resources and potential productivity; and to investigate and report on the practicability of any methods of resolving the problem.[29]

The present rate of population increase in Mauritius is one of the highest in the world and the concern of those responsible for the well-being of the population would appear to be justified when the following figures are studied.

Year		Percentage increase in population
1933–1937	average	7.6
1950		35.8
1951		32.6
1952		33.2
1953		30.2

In the short period 1947 to 1953 the resident population has increased by nearly 22 per cent : already in 1951 there was a density of 687 people per square mile, more than twice that of Jamaica. During five recent years the birth rate has been three times higher than the death rate.

Since 1948, in particular, the increase has been at a phenomenal rate; the Report of the Committee on Population ascribes the recent rapid growth of population to the following causes. First, the increase in marriages which was encouraged by the giving of family allowances to married service men : the percentage of married women to the total population rose from 41.7 in 1931 to 58.5 in 1944, and by 1944 a marked increase in the number of births was discernible. Secondly, the relative prosperity of the island in the post-war years has encouraged a high birth rate; the productivity of both agriculture and industry has greatly increased. Industrial production has increased by some 60 per cent above the pre-war level, there is full employment and wages have risen, especially those of the lower paid workers. The Report notes :

While, no doubt, as experience shows, a high standard of living entails, as a very long range consequence and because of the change in mental outlook, a lowering of the reproduction rate, a sudden improvement in the conditions of life of masses which are still backward has just the opposite effect. The prosperity which

[29] Mauritius Legislative Council, *Report of the Committee on Population, 1953-1954*. Unless otherwise stated the figures quoted are drawn from this Report. See also pp. 36-7, above, for comparative figures.

4

followed the First World War (1920-1925) has already demonstrated this.

Thirdly, there is the decline in the infant mortality rate and its influence on population increase.

Average infant mortality rates per 1,000 live births

1935–1939	151.2
1950–1954	83.1

Thus in fifteen years the infant mortality rate has been almost halved, and since the rate is still relatively high there is every reason to expect that it will be reduced still further in the years to come. The government is spending considerable sums on the Maternity and Child Welfare services and on Social Welfare Organization; illegitimate children are being cared for and subsistence grants are being given to destitute mothers.

Health conditions have greatly improved for the whole population, resulting in a fall in the crude death rate. The malaria eradication campaign of 1948 was eminently successful, and malaria has ceased to be a concern of the public health authorities. In 1948 there were 1,580 deaths from malaria; in 1954, 27. This control of malaria is again a factor in the increase of the live birth rate, since it reduces not only the death rate but also morbidity.

A consequence of importance to the composition of the island's population is the difference in the rate at which the three main ethnic groups are increasing.

Constitution of the Population : Percentages

Census Year	General	Indian	Chinese	Total
1846	64.5	35.5	—	100
1952	29.6	66.9	3.5	100

The 1954 percentage rate of increase is as follows :

Great Britain		Mauritius	
	General	Indian	Chinese
1.59	2.3	3.0	5.4

Fertility in the Chinese group surpasses any figure of which we have record.

Women marry early in all three ethnic groups and the marriage rate is high. The majority of families are dependent on agriculture, and since the children start to work in the fields at an early age no economic motive incites parents to limit their families. A low level of living, illiteracy, and a fatalistic attitude towards life, together with obedience to the local religious[30] influences in favour of large

[30] Most Christians in Mauritius are Roman Catholics; for Hindus a family is not complete until it contains a son.

74

families, have, in the past as in the present, influenced the family pattern on the island. But in the past the death rate has slowed down the population growth; the figures already given show how greatly the diminution in the death rate has changed the situation.

Given the unlikelihood in the near future of a reduction in the birth rate which would have any effect on population increase for some years to come, the Committee turned its attention to "Prospects of Expansion of the Island Productivity in regard to the Growing Population." Every aspect of the island's economy was brought under review and it was shown that, whilst between 1938 and 1953 the population had increased by 27 per cent, the output of agriculture and industry had increased by 26 per cent; an increase of 60 per cent in the output of sugar during the same period together with the increase in capital resources had resulted in a rise in the average level of living of between 30 and 35 per cent.

Nevertheless, looking to the immediate future, the Committee concluded that even if all the capital expansion which had been planned was in fact undertaken, the maximum which could find subsistence on the island at the present standard of living would have been reached, in all probability, by 1952; and that the employment of increasing numbers would present a grave problem.

Hence, when the full impact of the present births brings to bear, there will be 15,000 people who will annually be unable to contribute to the productivity of the island—in other words a growing group of 15,000 persons per annum appears to be the measure of future increasing unemployment in the island.[31]

Mauritius is faced now with the immense problem of providing for the rapidly increasing numbers at both ends of the life span. In 1945 the total of children in primary and secondary schools numbered 41,500; in 1953 the number was nearly 75,000, an increase of 81 per cent, and it is estimated that in the near future a further 19,700 children will grow to school age. Mortality rates have also declined for the older generation, and the Report notes that the chances of survival to the age of 60 have increased in the following proportions.

	Year 1944	Year 1952
Males surviving to 60	15.9% of number born.	44.8% of number born.
Females surviving to 60	22.5% „ „ „	52.3% „ „ „

The problem of old age pension and assistance grants obviously becomes acute when changes of this magnitude occur in such a limited space of time.

[31] *Report of the Population Committee*, p. 26.

Finally, the Committee directed its attention to the housing needs of the island. The Housing Adviser to the Colonial Office had recently made a report on housing, so that reliable estimates were available. It was estimated that to secure a noticeable improvement 10,000 houses would have to be provided each year, 4,000 to provide for the households added each year to the total number. The Committee noted that 2,000 to 2,500 residences of all types had been constructed annually in recent years, insufficient even to meet the needs of the new households. The result must be a steady deterioration of conditions already lamentable. It was considered quite impossible to provide the funds necessary for the government to undertake the provision of the necessary houses, and even if capital had been available the land was not : it was agreed that no agricultural land should be used for large-scale housing projects.

The Committee, faced with what appears to be an insoluble problem, turned its attention to methods of reducing the population. Emigration was first considered, but here little hope for the immediate future could be drawn from recent figures.

Increase and decrease of population
through migration

1931–1940	−2,331
1941–1950	−2,632
1951–1953	+ 830

Nevertheless, the Committee thought that serious attention might be given to the emigration of families to Madagascar if an agreement could be reached beween the two countries. In the near future there seemed little hope of resuming emigration on a scale which would affect population growth.

After this careful survey of population and resources and the possibility of easing the population pressure through emigration the Committee came to the conclusion that the furthering of a planned parenthood policy would have to be explored. India, China, Hong Kong, Japan, Malaya, Singapore, and Barbados were all approached for information on the course which these countries were following. The Committee agreed that the Government of Mauritius should be recommended to establish family planning clinics so that the facilities available to the better-off families for limiting their families should be made available also to the poorer classes.

4. AFRICA

The development of a new culture, which will be both African and modern, is without question one of the most challenging and complex problems of the contemporary world.[1]

Some of the problems which face Africans are indicated in the following chapter. Population pressure is not, as in the West Indies and in India, the main concern, though the influence of the medical services and the spread of education may well create a population problem in certain areas in the not far distant future. Africa's main problem is the transition from a traditional way of communal life in the tribe to the world of individual responsibility in a competitive society. The transition has to be made, for only so can the level of living be raised. The rise in the level of living can only come about through fundamental changes in the pattern of agriculture, for as an increasing number of Africans will be drawn into the wage-earning group, those who remain on the land (who will be the great number) will have to increase output to meet the needs of those living in towns as well as their own. Thus whilst the African in the towns faces the harder adaptation to changing circumstances, the countryman also has to adapt to changing economic and social conditions.

Population

The population of Africa is estimated at some 223 million, 8 per cent of the world total. For many territories vital statistics are almost completely lacking; in others only limited statistics exist. *The Demographic Year Book, 1956,* gives the following estimated averages.

	Population	Death rate	Birth rate
		(per 1,000 of population)	
North Africa	78 million	25	45

(Population increase 1.5 million, i.e., about 2 per cent per annum.)

	Population	Death rate	Birth rate
Tropical and Southern Africa	145 million	25	45

(Population increase 2.8 million, i.e., about 2 per cent per annum.)

These averages conceal wide variations in rates. The death rate for the Bantu population of South Africa was 179 in 1935, 125 in 1951.

[1] United Nations Economic and Social Council, Social Commission, *Report on the World Social Situation,* E/CN 5/324, 1957, p. 169.

The infant mortality rates for the non-white population are estimated as lying between 90 and 250 per 1,000 live births, with the higher rate being the more general.[2]

The various findings suggest that the populations in the extreme north and the extreme south of the African continent are at present increasing very rapidly, but that in the remainder of Africa there are wide variations—from stationary or even declining populations in some areas to fairly rapidly increasing populations in other areas. Whether European influence has resulted in an acceleration or retardation of population growth has depended both on the nature and intensity of the contact with the West, and on the degree to which native society could adjust itself to these new influences. In South Africa, where European penetration and the presence of a large local European population have had the most profound effect, population has been increasing rapidly in recent times.[3]

Among the non-white peoples of Africa population growth has been due primarily to declining mortality rates unmatched by declining birth rates. The health services have first set out to control epidemic diseases; the environment has been improved in some regions by the provision of safe water and by disposal systems. The control of malaria, as has been noted elsewhere in this report, has had a swift effect in reducing the death rate. The beginning of social welfare services, the development of educational systems and the chances of better nutrition have all conduced to the same end. But the death rate is still high; especially high among the non-European population is the infant mortality rate; and this is in part the effect of inadequate food.

General malnutrition is still no doubt one of the greatest factors influencing the mortality rates. The diet of the African is known to be insufficient and ill balanced. The reason is not only lack of education and food habits which tradition has fixed, but also the general poverty and the lack of means of transportation and storage.[4]

It is estimated that the population of Africa is increasing at a little over 2 per cent per annum, but there is clearly the possibility

[2] Figures from U.N. *Demographic Year Book*, 1956, Table A, p. 2, and *World Population Conference, Rome 1954*, Vol. 3, p. 159.

[3] U.N. *The Determinants and Consequences of Population Trends*, New York, 1953, p. 19.

[4] U.N. *Proceedings of the World Population Conference, Rome 1954*, Vol. 1, p. 358.

of a higher rate of increase in the near future. Health services may well reduce further mortality rates which are high by European standards. Efforts are being made to improve nutrition; a rise in the level of living would certainly reduce the infant mortality rate. But Africa is in a state of transition, and further industrialization and the accompanying movement to towns may affect the birth rate; there is some evidence that the African birth rate is lower in the towns.

Work and Wages : Migrant Labour

Africa south of the Sahara is predominantly rural; only 6 per cent of the population live in towns of over 20,000 and this 6 per cent is very unevenly distributed. Thirty per cent of the town dwellers are to be found in the Union of South Africa and 40 per cent in Western Nigeria, where there has been a long tradition of town dwelling : in Liberia and British East Africa no more than 1 to 3 per cent of the population live in towns. Nevertheless the influence of the town is much greater than these figures would suggest. As will be shown later, an acute problem is created by the extreme mobility of the African worker; he moves back and forth from town to country, usually leaving his wife behind, so that over a period of time about a half of the men may have had the experience of living and working in towns.

During the past 60 to 70 years many of the territories in Africa south of the Sahara have been undergoing a social and economic revolution, the speed of which has greatly quickened during recent years; the traditional subsistence economy has been steadily giving place to a market economy. The cultivation on a large scale of crops for export, ground-nuts, palm-products, coffee, cocoa, and cotton, the development of mining and industry, the accompanying growth of towns, have provided the opportunity for wage-earning which the African has seized upon.

Africans move into wage-earning employment for one or more of the following reasons.

(*a*) The necessity of a money income for the payment of taxes.

(*b*) The desire to possess certain highly valued consumer goods or implements.

(*c*) The need for money to meet the traditional payment of the bride price.

(*d*) The pressure of population on the land. This may be due not so much to an actual shortage of land as to the exhaustion of the soil or to crop failures.

(e) A growing desire in some of the younger men to break away from the monotony and controls of tribal life : migration is greater among the more educated men.

(f) The attraction of the town and the real or imagined opportunities for personal advancement and independence.

(g) To join members of the family already in the town. The social prestige which, in some tribes, is accorded to the man who has lived in the town.

(h) The pressure of labour recruiting agents; this was more important in the past, but still has some importance.[5]

For whatever reason the African forsakes his traditional way of life for a longer or shorter spell of work in city or in mine, on plantation or on the railway, economic and social consequences follow which profoundly affect the life of the whole community.

The mobility of the African worker has already been noted. If he moves into wage-earning employment with the object of amassing a given sum to pay for a specific object, he will return to his tribe when this end is achieved. But the demand for a higher level of living in the tribal areas, or a worsening of the food situation due to the pressure of increasing population density or to misuse of land, may result in a high percentage of the men having to absent themselves from the tribe at recurrent intervals. Dr Lucy Mair, in discussing the factors which influence married life in Africa under modern conditions, states :

> Throughout married life, until there are sons old enough to earn, the husband must make frequent journeys abroad to places of employment, and . . . the length of the period of absence is increasing. This inevitably reacts in many directions on family life. In the economic sphere, as Kgatla life is at present organised, the husband's man-power is indispensable in two contradictory directions at the same time. He must earn wages to supply the household with those of its necessities that are bought with cash, and he must plough the ground for the family to grow its food supply. Formerly many men organised their periods of employment so as to be home for the ploughing season. Now fewer and fewer do this. A man's relatives in the past would have done the work for him after they had ploughed their own fields and therefore sometimes too late to profit by the early rains. But as more and more men go away, fewer are left to undertake this extra work and it has to be done by women and children; this is one of

[5] Causes listed in U.N. Economic and Social Council, *Report on the World Social Situation*, 1957, p. 145.

the reasons why children cannot be kept at school for long enough to profit by their schooling.[6]

The members of the East African Royal Commission came to much the same conclusion.

> In the existing situation the migrant labour system appears to be the only one through which a considerable section of the African population can meet its needs, because the economic opportunities for more effective specialisation have either been absent or have been seriously circumscribed by legal and customary restrictions. For many Africans it is not possible to attain a higher income level for the support of their families without working both on the land and in urban employment. This means that, given the present productivity of Africans over large parts of the rural and urban sectors of the economy, the migrant labour system appears as the most economic choice which the African can make, however socially deleterious or otherwise undesirable it may be. . . . The replacement of the migrant labour system cannot be effectively accomplished merely by the introduction of special devices in the urban areas, but only as the result of a successful long term policy which includes both agricultural and non-agricultural employment.[7]

The African industrial worker, therefore, is frequently suffering from a sense of acute insecurity, and, moreover, he lacks the incentives which provide a motive for work in the older industrial regions of the world, and does not respond readily to them when they are introduced. A writer in the journal *Africa* sums up the situation thus :

> The average urban African is unhealthy, badly housed, un-educated, and he lacks any security in town even if he happens to have been born there. These are his greatest and his constant worries. . . . Neither money nor the work that he performs can release him from any of his real troubles. He cannot obtain better health, a better education for himself or for his children, or a better or more permanent home in the urban areas however much he may earn or save.[8]

6 *Survey of African Marriage and Family Life,* published for the International African Institute by Oxford University Press, 1953, pp. 23 f.

7 *East African Royal Commission, 1953-1955,* Cmd. 9475, H.M.S.O., 1945, p. 154, para. 20.

8 *Africa,* Vol. XXIII, 1953, p. 141.

4*

Social Consequences of Mobility

The effect of two world wars, of the spread of education, of greater transport facilities, the impact of new ideas from many sources, have, for some years, been loosening rigid tribal traditions— a process accelerated by economic and social change and by urbanization.

The absence of the men has meant that in some areas, Rhodesia, for example, an inadequate diet has been still further reduced, and because of the low wages which the African earns, he cannot, in general, send back to his family sufficient money to increase the level of living. Capital investment and technical aid are required to increase the productivity of the land; measures to increase the productivity of the African worker are also imperative.

The wages of the African worker are low because his productivity is low. The factors which influence African efficiency are summed up in an article in the *International Labour Review*.

A worker's productivity, after all, is no more than a particular manifestation of human behaviour and should be studied in the context of the whole man. The African has had a very violent shock and has suffered considerably as a result. In a closed society where all precautions have been taken to safeguard the individual against all the hazards of life, a revolution has suddenly exposed him to a variety of hazards for which he is wholly unprepared. He cannot be expected to behave as if nothing had happened. The African of today has no assured future ahead of him and finds it impossible to pin his faith either in the values of the Western world, to which in any event he has hardly any access, or in the values of his former world, whose foundations have been shaken.[9]

The African strives to keep a foot in both worlds and hence his extreme mobility; he remains in the unskilled or the semi-skilled class because few employers are prepared to train a man whose length of service is so precarious. On the other hand, some measure of security for old age is possible only by retaining his ties with his own people; and however inadequate the return from the land may be, some provision for wife and children who are left behind is thereby provided and his stake in the land maintained.

An inquiry carried out among African workers in the Dunlop works, Durban, showed that only 6 per cent of the men had their wives living with them. Seventy-six per cent of the men viewed with "anger and contempt" the idea that they might make a permanent

9 *International Labour Review*, Vol. LXXII, 1955, p. 137.

home in the city with their wives and children.[10] Most African workers leave their wives and families in the country; and they are led to do so for the reasons already given, reasons which are certainly enhanced by the lamentable housing conditions in which the majority of African workers live. The towns have been expanding rapidly but provision for the growing number of Africans seeking work in the towns has not been made.

In the whole of Africa, what has been called the growth of new towns . . . is first and foremost the conglomeration of uprooted human masses, who are camping in the expectation of remunerated labour; but who maintain ties, sometimes at very long distance, with the native bush, and for whom a true adaptation to urban life is not facilitated since it can be guaranteed only by adequate wages, lodging and security provisions.[11]

The economic consequences of this transitional period in the life of the African population may to some extent be measured. What is more difficult to appraise is the effect on his social institutions and particularly on his marriage customs.

Marriage in the traditional African society is not only an agreement between two individuals but also the agreement between two kinship groups. It is a basis of the system whereby co-operation in tilling the fields or herding the cattle is provided by people bound by the obligation of kinship and not by the relationship of wage earner to employer.[12]

The traditional part played by marriage in the tribal setting is rudely shaken by the changes which have been described. The coming of a money economy has had an influence on custom; men who have been working for wages in the town are not always willing to return to customary awards for labour. The spread of education and the knowledge of a freer society has bred in some men rebellion against the power of the elders to plan their lives; the absence of so many men from the tribe affects the whole agricultural routine. To what extent the foundations of traditional life are shaken will depend on the force of the extraneous influences and the power of adaptation within the group.

Much has been written on the life of the African worker living in the towns. Cut off as he is from the traditional restraints of his own

[10] *The African Factory Worker. A Sample Study of the Life and Labour of the Urban African Worker,* by The Department of Economics, University of Natal, Oxford University Press, 1950, p. 11.

[11] Quoted in *U.N. Economic and Social Council, Social Commission, 1957,* p. 147.

[12] U.N. *Report on the World Social Situation,* p. 166.

people and living in lamentable conditions, it is not surprising that there has been an increase in promiscuity and divorce. Insufficient wages, inadequate housing, and the traditional and steadily increasing expenses connected with marriage mean that many young men are unable to marry. There is, moreover, a serious imbalance between the sexes. In the urban centres of South Africa there are less than 50 women to 100 men; similar proportions are to be found in the towns of other territories. The result has been a notable increase in prostitution. It is also contended that some women refuse to marry under the traditional marriage custom because of the lack of freedom and the low status accorded to the wife.

Few married men have their wives and families with them for the reasons already given. There is, however, a growing number of men who now live permanently in the towns and whose families live with them. The African is encouraged to make his home in the town when housing adequate to his family needs is provided. When this is done, a growing number of Africans make their permanent homes in the towns. A problem is created by the low wages earned by the men, which makes it necessary for the wives and even the young children to work. Work for the women is not always available, and whereas in the country women are an asset, in the town they may well be a liability.

The effect of town life on the children, and in particular the weakness of the family bond, has led to a steadily increasing juvenile delinquency. In the tribal areas the training and the discipline of the members of the group was the concern of the extended family and not of the parents alone. Some parents, aware of the moral dangers which their children run, send them back to the tribe at about the age of ten. The United Nations report already cited states:

> The high rate of illegitimacy, parental neglect of their children, and the necessity for most children, legitimate or illegitimate, to learn to fend for themselves at an early age, are factors in turn contributing to the spread of juvenile delinquency in many cities.[13]

There is no going back for the African: discontent with the present level of living, the influences of education, of new ideas from whatever source, are going to precipitate change at an ever increasing rate. Nevertheless the price to be paid is a high one.

> The gulf between the traditional culture [and the life] of modern cities remains wider and deeper than the rural-urban gulf in any other major region of the world. The problem of transition, as a

13 *U.N. Economic and Social Council, Social Commission, 1957*, p. 168.

social and psychological problem, is thus encountered in Africa in an extreme form. In other economically under-developed regions, the process of transition is usually helped by the existence of certain cultural or religious elements that are common to both rural and urban life and thus serve as stabilising factors providing some sense of continuity and identity in a changing situation . . . Urbanisation for the African may imply, for example, a radical change in forms of political organisations, as well as in material and economic aspects of culture. The contradictions and conflicts he faces are often aggravated by different problems of race relations, which may be present to some extent also in the rural areas but are exacerbated in the cities.[14]

Racial Complications

Town life is further complicated by the heterogeneity of the population. Much has been written of the effect on the African of the dominant position of the white people. The African who has attained to professional status, the doctor or the lawyer, does not, in general, find himself accepted socially by his professional colleagues. The skilled or semi-skilled African worker has to meet hostility to his advancement from the white workers within the trade union movement itself. There is an increasing body of non-African small traders who, because of their greater commercial acumen, bar the advance of the African in trade and small commercial ventures.

To the heterongeneity normally existing in all modern cities, the African cities add the problems created by a multi-racial society, sometimes composed of Asian and Arab elements (the latter being especially numerous in East Africa) besides Europeans and Africans. In most of the coastal cities of West Africa traders of Arab (usually Syrian or Lebanese) origin, while constituting numerically small minorities, have traditionally exercised an important influence on commercial developments as intermediaries between the African producer and the large European firms. In many towns, each group is widely separated from the others not only by racial, linguistic and religious differences, but also (and often even more so) by wide variations in economic and social status and education and cultural advancement.[15]

These facts present local Churches with a complex of problems—political, social, economic, cultural, religious—which demand searching study and thought, action according to an informed conscience, and, sometimes, suffering as the price.

[14] Ibid., p. 147.
[15] U.N. *Report on the World Social Situation*, 1957, p. 146.

85

Prospect of a New Urban Society

What promise is there of a new and stable African society arising in the towns? Whilst the movement backwards and forwards to the tribal areas continues, the hope of evolving a new society rests on those who remain in the town. Where a number of men from the same tribe are found in one town they frequently group themselves and provide shelter and some security for the newcomer. On occasions an association is formed admitting men from various tribes as members. These associations maintain the links with the tribal areas and in some instances provide such services as aid for burial, expenses of sending back a widow and her children to her own tribe; their purpose, in fact, is comparable with that of the early Friendly Societies in this country. How far these associations retard or accelerate the adaptation of the African to a new way of life is disputed; certainly they keep alive the tribal association and the loyalty and the obligations due to the tribal group.

The size and diversity of towns has given rise to many other associations which cut across the tribal loyalties—organized association among occupational groups, trade unions, groups for the furtherance of some political idea, cultural and recreational associations, all with a valuable part to play in providing common purposes for men and women whose lives in the past have been given direction through tribal organization.

The spread of education and the emergence of an educated *élite* are essential to the economic and social progress of Africans; in other words, the rise of an educated middle class. One of the difficulties here is the slowness of income differentiation, the inability of the educated man to earn enough to take his place as a leader in his own society. Further, his own advancement is checked by the accepted liability to share his income with his less fortunate relations. Nevertheless, an African *élite* already exists, though the number who may be so designated is small; but here a fresh problem arises. How far will members of the *élite* identify themselves with the problems and aspirations of their fellow Africans, and how far will they strive to identify themselves with the educated members of the white population? At the moment members of the African *élite* are to be found in both camps.[16]

Community Development

Although the provision for the formal education of the African is still largely based on Western concepts, and is consequently inclined to draw the child away from his environment, there have been many

[16] See *Africa*, Vol. XXIII, 1953, p. 277; and Thomas Hodgkin, *Nationalism in Colonial Africa*.

deliberate attempts during the last thirty years to devise systems of both formal and informal education which would help the mass of the people to understand the problems of their own environment and give them both the desire and the means to improve their standards of life. Since 1948 a movement has been fostered in most African territories which is usually known by the term "community delopment". It brings together both the African tradition of communal effort to meet communal needs and the time-honoured function of the district officer in helping the people to realize and to meet their own needs. What is new in the movement is the conscious stimulation of popular initiative. Emphasis is placed on the building of a sense of community by means of working together, with rudimentary but adequate technical advice, to harness natural resources, including human resources, in a limited locality. An important part of the movement is the training given to women as well as men; in large areas of Kenya, for example, there is now a women's progress movement with some 70,000 members.

Through the community development movement, the African is enabled to improve his standards of life in association with his neighbours. But the results of the movement are not primarily measured in economic terms. It brings a sense of achievement and consequently a feeling of hope to communities which, because of sparse technical services over large rural areas, cannot otherwise participate fully in the improved facilities for health, education, and agriculture which contact with the outside world is bringing.

Marriage and the Family

The basis of African life is to be found in marriage and the family. The great majority of marriages take place in accordance with native law and custom, though this varies greatly between tribes. *The Survey of African Marriage and Family Life* had wide terms of reference relating exclusively to the marriage and family life of the Africans. The Report deals with various forms of marriage and judges on the evidence that

> It seems legitimate to conclude that African customary marriage has sufficient in common with marriage in other parts of the world (including "European" Marriage) to warrant the usage of describing it, in a context such as the present one, by the same generic term "marriage".[17]

From the point of view of the Christian Churches two aspects of African marriage present problems; one is the admission of polygamy and the other the payment of the bride price. The Report states :

17 Op. cit., p. xiii.

5. EGYPT AND THE MIDDLE EAST

The vital statistics for most of the countries in this area are either lacking completely or, where they exist—as in Palestine—are deficient or not typical. The estimates for birth rates lie between 40 and 50 per thousand of population; death rates are high, possibly between 25 and 30 per thousand of population. It is generally agreed that death rates are slowly falling throughout the area, and that, since the high birth rates are being maintained, population is increasing fairly rapidly. The statistics for Egypt are fairly reliable, and chief consideration will, therefore, be given to this country.

The demographic situation in Egypt is comparable with that of India and the West Indies : the following figures, taken from *The Demographic Year Book, 1956*, show a slow decline in the crude death rate but no decline in the birth rate. There is therefore a steady increase of population.

Egypt

Total population (in millions)

Year	1947	1948	1949	1950	1951	1952	1953
	19,068	19.494	19,888	20,393	20,872	21,473	21,987

(In 1897 the total population of Egypt was 9.71 millions; in the half century to 1947, therefore, it had almost doubled itself.)

Birth Rate per 1,000 of population

Year	1947	1948	1949	1950	1951	1952	1953
	43.6	42.7	41.8	44.4	44.8	45.1	40 (45?)[1]

Death Rate per 1,000 of population

Year	1947	1948	1949	1950	1951	1952	1953
	21.3	20.4	20.6	19.1	19.3	17.7	18.4

(probably under-estimated)

Infant mortality rate per 1,000 live births

Year	1947	1948	1949	1950	1951	1952	1953
	126.8	138.6	135.5	129.6	128.6	127.1	148.5

One result of high birth rates and low death rates, as in India and the West Indies, is a distribution of age groups within the population which differs greatly from that of countries where the population has been relatively stabilized. Some 40 per cent of the people of Egypt are under 15 years of age; only 6 per cent are over 60. The economic and social effects of such an age distribution have already been discussed; there is an ever-increasing demand for social services—health, education, housing—if the existing standard is to be

---

[1] Another U.N. source gives the 1953 rate as 45.

maintained, leave alone improved. This demand on government revenue has to be, or should be, met at a time when capital investment for industrial development is already claiming a higher proportion of government expenditure.

Egypt is predominantly an agricultural country; the rural population is 76 per cent of the whole. The population density has steadily increased until now there are over 500 persons to the square kilometre in the Nile valley, one of the most densely populated areas in the world.[2] The implications of the doubling of the population in the last fifty years were summed up in a paper contributed to the World Conference on Population, held in Rome in 1954 :

> There is every indication that it (the population) will at least double itself again in the next fifty years since the death rates are sharply declining while the birth rates are maintaining their high levels. In other words, if nothing very serious happens, the population of Egypt may reach about 40 million by the end of this century, even if the result of the latest census is rather exaggerated as some believe. Since the area of cultivated land has increased very little, the area of land per head has decreased in this period by over 30 per cent.[3]

The same speaker pointed out that, though during the period 1915 to 1950 crop production went up by 30 per cent, the population increased by 64 per cent. Hence, in spite of the growing volume of imported food, there is a serious problem of under-nourishment.

> The decrease in both agricultural and animal returns per head of the population has naturally led to a noticeable shortage of foodstuffs. The combination of imported foodstuffs with home produce has not been sufficient to provide for the minimum standard of necessary nutrition.[4]

Egypt's present rulers are committed to raising the low level of living, and, to that end, to furthering schemes to increase the amount of land available and to develop industry. Powers were taken to distribute among the peasants a certain amount of land held in large estates, and by 1955 some 200,000 families had benefited from these measures. A Land Reform Law in 1952 gave the government power to deal with extortionate rents.

The government of Egypt has, for many years, been adding to the land brought into cultivation by means of extensive irrigation

[2] U.N., *The Determinants and Consequences of Population Trends*, 1953, p. 268.

[3] *The World Conference on Population, Rome 1954*, Vol. V, p. 336.

[4] Ibid., p. 338.

schemes, of which the Aswan High Dam is an example; the plans for this, if realized, would not only bring more land into cultivation but would also provide much needed power. However, political considerations apart, the amount of water available sets limits to irrigation projects.

Since 1953 the government has given direct encouragement to industrial development by tax policy, by capital investment in mining and transport, and by the provision of motive power. The manufacturing industries are still on a small scale, engaging only 8.4 per cent of the gainfully employed in 1947, and very small workshops prevail. Lack of capital and the nature of the product favour the small unit of production, and so does government policy; in 1947, 3 per cent only of establishments employed over ten workers. This is as true of Israel and Turkey as of Egypt :

> Measures for supporting small-scale industry have been taken in all three countries. In Egypt . . . it has been government policy to encourage the development of industry—including handicrafts and small manufacturing shops—in rural areas to provide at least part-time employment and additional income for rural dwellers. Since 1948 the Ministry of Social Affairs has been encouraging handicrafts and village industries in congested areas. In 1955 it established a department for "village" industries, and allocated funds in its budget for the purpose of extending loans, grants and technical aid to light industries for which raw materials are available in rural areas.[5]

In Egypt there has been a rapid increase in the urban population, especially in Alexandria and Cairo; but this growth is not due to greater industrialization and the provision of more employment, but to rising population pressure on the land. The Report already quoted, commenting on this growth of urban population, states :

> . . . this resulted less from an increase in occupations related to commerce and other services than from the growth of the group defined as persons with "unspecified and unproductive occupations", a group which consists mostly of people without stable jobs, persons living on private means, and students.[6]

The government's policy of protecting and encouraging the spread of industries in rural areas will go some way towards discouraging the development of industries in the towns, but it will also lessen the uprooting of families or their disintegration through the departure

[5] U.N. Economic and Social Council: *World Economic Situation; Industrialization in Egypt, Israel and Turkey*, 1957, p. 30.
[6] Ibid., p. 16.

of the bread-winner to find work in the towns. In this Egyptian policy may be compared with Indian.

Despite Egypt's limited resources and rapidly increasing population, economic and social factors tend to perpetuate the large family. The country is primarily agricultural, and children are employed on the land from an early age; there is thus no obvious incentive to limit their number. Wage-earning and salaried workers benefit from an allowance to meet the high cost of living, and this, together with the government tax policy, favours the large family. Both Muslim and Christian opinion accord high prestige to the parents of large families. To some extent the giving birth to a large number of children affords a measure of protection to the mother, since, in the event of divorce, alimony has to be paid for each child; further encouragement to the large family is given by the Muslim law of inheritance.

Culture and tradition have up to now discouraged the partici-pation of women in economic and social activities, except in so far as married women share in the work of farm and workshop. Replies to a recent inquiry,[7] however, emphasize the changing attitudes of the middle and educated classes. More women are qualifying for entry into the professions; the educated Egyptian is seeking to marry an educated wife rather than one selected for him by his family. For the great majority of women status remains low; but that the number of educated women is increasing is significant, and this may ultimately affect the family pattern.

[7] World Council of Churches, Questionnaire, 1957 (unpublished).

6. EUROPE AND GREAT BRITAIN

Although the world's population is increasing at an ever accelerating rate, there is a marked difference in the rate of growth as between areas. Thus while the annual percentage rate of increase from 1951 to 1955 is estimated at 2.2 for Africa and 1.7 for Asia, the rate for Europe is 0.7;[1] within Europe this overall rate masks a considerable difference between countries. Three groups may be distinguished; the birth rates of three countries within each group illustrate the wide difference which existed before the second world war; since the war it will be noted that the difference in birth rates still persists but that there has been a tendency for rates to rise in the low birth rate countries and to fall in countries where previously the rate was high.

Annual Crude Birth Rates (per 1,000 of Population)[2]

	1930-34	1935-39	1947-49	1950-52	1953-55
Group 1 (low pre-war fertility)					
France	17.3	15.1	22.0	19.9	18.8
Sweden	14.4	14.5	18.2	15.8	14.9
United Kingdom	15.8	15.3	18.6	15.9	15.6
Group 2 (intermediate pre-war fertility)					
Denmark	17.9	17.9	20.4	18.1	17.5
Ireland [3]	19.5	19.4	22.3	21.5	21.2
Netherlands	21.7	20.3	25.6	22.5	21.6
Group 3 (high pre-war fertility)					
Portugal	29.3	27.1	25.6	24.5	23.3
Spain	27.6	22.0	22.2	20.4	20.4
Italy	24.5	23.2	21.5	18.6	18.0

It is interesting to note the high birth rates which marked the immediate post war period in countries in Group 1, even in neutral Sweden.

The crude death rate of the European population has decreased slightly from 1947 : most of the countries to-day show a rate lying between 10 and 12 per 1,000 of the population; Norway and Sweden have a rate of 9.6 and 8.5 respectively. The infant mortality rates

[1] U. N. Economic and Social Council, *Population Commission 1957*, p. 4.

[2] U.N. *Report on the World Social Situation*, 1957, Table 12, p. 11.

[3] Thirty-two counties; i.e. the Irish Republic and Northern Ireland together.

show a wider divergence : France has a rate of 40.4, Sweden has 18.2—the lowest in Europe—and the United Kingdom, 26.5.[4]*

THE FAMILY IN GREAT BRITAIN

Population

The demographic situation in Britain to-day closely resembles that of many European countries in which birth rates have fallen substantially over the past one hundred years : mortality rates, especially infant mortality rates,* have been steadily reduced and a situation created in which the population is more or less stabilized. The social and economic consequences of this conjuncture influence directly the life of family and nation.

The Royal Commission on Population, 1949, impressed by the falling birth rate during the 1930s, took a cautious view of this country's population prospects;[5] recent forecasts, as the following table shows, display more optimism.

United Kingdom
How the Population is Expected to Change[6]
(millions)

Year	Ages			Total Population
	0-14	15-64	65 and over	
1955	11.7	33.8	5.8	51.3
1965	11.0	34.7	6.5	52.2
1975	10.8	34.4	7.8	53.0
1985	10.8	34.2	8.3	53.3
1995	10.4	34.1	8.3	52.8

This forecast is based on the assumption that births, deaths, and migration, the determinants of population trends, follow much the same course as to-day. A change in the size of families, or in the balance between those leaving the country and those entering it, could affect the calculations; but, all in all, the figures suggest that the total population of this country is unlikely to change very much up to the end of this century.

The 1951 Census, however, revealed that certain changes are taking place which are important for this study. The previous census had been taken in 1931. The increasing proportion of older people in the country and the growing number of pensioners is important both to the community and to individual families. Families in all sections of the community had been diminishing in size for many years, though the latest figure indicated a slight check in the tendency.

4 U.N. Economic and Social Council, *Population Commission, 1957,* p. 4.
* 23 per 1,000 in England and Wales in 1957 (Reg.-Gen.).
5 Para. 626.
6 Source : Government Actuary's Department and Registrars General (one per cent sample. *The Economist,* 29 December, 1956, p. 1112.

The new Index of Retail Prices, 1956, which measures changes in the cost of living, is based on an exhaustive study of family expenditure.

These records may be regarded as giving an average picture of the expenditure pattern of practically all wage earners' households and of most households of small or medium salary earners.[14]

The figures showing the percentage outlay on the various items of expenditure are in themselves proof of the relatively high level of living of the average family. The essentials of life, food, rent, light and fuel, and clothing, take only 60 per cent of the family budget; about fifty years ago 96 per cent of the family income went to meet these essential needs. Certain commodities and services appear in the new Index for the first time as items of family expenditure of sufficient importance to influence the average figure : replacements for television sets, vacuum cleaners, car and motor cycle tyres, and washing machines may be singled out. Not many years ago none of these goods would have been found in the manual worker's home : to-day, they are far from exceptional.

Housing and Re-Housing Policies

Accompanying the rise in family incomes has been the demand for better housing. A slum-clearance programme begun before the war, accelerated in some places by destructive bombing during the war, has become a major rehousing policy of the public authorities since 1945. Old property has been cleared from the centre of towns, and blocks of flats have been erected; housing estates have been thrust out to the perimeter of great cities, and further afield satellite towns and new towns have been created. Recently sociologists have been giving attention to the results of this policy, and have been questioning the social theory, or lack of it, upon which the immense and necessary enterprise has been planned.[15]

One such study, by Young and Wilmott,[16] has emphasized the interaction of kinship and length of residence as the basis of security —emotional, economic, and moral—in an old-established, densely populated area like Bethnal Green, and has shown how severely this

[14] *Method of Construction and Calculation of the Index of Retail Prices,* 1956. H.M.S.O.

[15] See *Neighbourhood and Community: An Enquiry into Social Relationships on Housing Estates in Liverpool and Sheffield.* University of Liverpool Press, 1954. *Two Studies in Oxford.* by J. M. Mogey. O.U.P., 1956. *Family and Kinship in East London,* Michael Young and Peter Willmott. Routledge and Kegan Paul. 1957. cf. "Growing Pains at Crawley", special articles on a New Town in *The Times,* 13 and 14 August, 1957.

[16] See previous note.

security is undermined when these two factors are ignored in the creation of a new estate some twenty miles away. In the old society a kinship network centres on the maternal grandmother : it is at her home that her daughters and their families meet; she is their guide and confidant in matters personal and domestic; it is she who cares for the younger children at times of sickness, confinement, or other crisis, or while their mother is at work; and in return, she is cared for, in her home, when she is sick or old. The bonds of kinship are strong, extending even to the control of entry into trade union chapels and lodges—the printers', the market porters', and the dockers'. With kinship goes friendship : family friends, school friends, mates at work—all are about one, for all live closely together.

> Bethnal Greeners are not a lonely people : whenever they go for a walk in the street, for a drink in the pub, or for a row on the lake in Victoria Park, they know the faces in the crowd.[17]

With the removal of the second generation, with their children, to the new estate, all this network of kinship and friendship is broken up, and the old security is broken with it. Wives especially said that they bore the loneliness and the quietness only because of the better house and "for the sake of the children". Grandparents are no longer at hand either to give the wonted support or to receive it; family meetings are more difficult; the neighbours are un-neighbourly; the journey to work is long, exhausting, and expensive; the shops are unfamiliar and "unfriendly"; the pubs and the cinemas are few, and the dog-track is far away. Rents are about three times as high as before; fares, shoes, food, clothing are all more expensive; there are probably hire-purchase payments on the new furniture, the television set, and perhaps on the car. In the first sixteen years, 26 per cent of the tenants had gone back to Bethnal Green, though the rate was slowing down.

Nevertheless, the picture has its other side, and a new pattern begins to emerge instead of the old. The husband in the home replaces the matriarch at the centre of the kin : he has to contribute more to the family budget, and give up some of his smoking, drinking, and gambling to do so; he has to work in the house and garden to "keep up" with the neighbourhood; in his home he finds some of the social satisfactions of which by his removal he was deprived :

> Husband and wife are together and a closer partnership here can make isolation bearable. He is now the one who leads the active life of society, not only on the job but, sometimes too, on his round of the relatives after the work is done. He is the messenger who

17 Op. cit., p. 92.

brings back to Cambridge Avenue the news from the larger world of work and the smaller world of kinship. She is more dependent on him, for news and for the financial sacrifice which will sustain their domestic economy. If, now that he does not have to share her with so many others, he plays well his rôles of messenger, earner and companion, the strains of the new life are not without compensation.[18]

The newcomers are surrounded by strangers instead of by kin. Their lives outside the family are no longer centred on people : their lives are centred on the house. The change from a people-centred to a house-centred existence is one of the fundamental changes resulting from migration.[19]

In this "un-neighbourly" life, possessions take on a social importance; status rests "on the trappings of the man, rather than on the man himself" :

> The lonely man, fearing he is looked down on, becomes the acquisitive man; possession the balm to anxiety; anxiety the spur to unfriendliness.[20]

Clearly, adjustment to a disrupted pattern of life like this makes demands on character and personality which people and families meet differently, according to their ability. Moreover, the disruption will repeat itself, for there is no room on the estate for the next generation to settle near *their* parents when they marry and found their own families : they will have to move again; without the three-generation pattern, without long family residence in the same locality, the network of kinship and friendship, upon which so much depends, cannot establish itself.

> We can now see how fraught with consequence is the decision to move young couples out of the city. A district which comprises a stable population of all ages is able to go forward to meeting its own housing needs. Houses (though we may sometimes regret it) usually last for more than a lifetime, and grandchildren take over the houses of grandparents (their own or someone else's) when they die. But once upset the age structure by moving out the children as a group, and the relation of population to housing is so much disturbed that further disruptions are almost inevitable later on. For purposes of housing, if for no other, a three generation community has evident advantages.[21]

[18] Ibid., p. 120. [19] Ibid., p. 127.
[20] Ibid., p. 136.
[21] Ibid., p. 140. Cp. *The Family Life of Old People*, by Peter Townsend. Routledge and Kegan Paul, 1957.

This study was limited to one London borough and one new estate. From two other enquiries, made in a wartime estate in Liverpool and and a pre-war estate in Sheffield, the authors concluded that

> It is only too probable that the people who are moved from congested areas to suburbs will find that they have merely exchanged the physical dirt and disorder of one kind of slum for the loneliness and anxieties of another.[22]

For different reasons, therefore, the authors of both of these studies argue that the housing policies pursued by public authorities need to be reconsidered. The urgency of this reconsideration becomes apparent when we realize the magnitude of the task still confronting the housing authorities. England and Wales are among the most densely populated countries in the world; and, moreover, 40 per cent of the population lives in 4 per cent of the area, the highly industrialized parts of the country where work is to be found.[23] Enquiries show that 80 to 90 per cent of families prefer houses to flats : but to rebuild at low densities in the centre of cities is not an economic possibility. The study quoted from Bethnal Green, and Mogey's study of two areas in Oxford, suggest that if new communities are to be founded, grandparents must be able to move with the young families (by no means necessarily to the same house), and that the children, when they grow up and marry, must be able to settle in the same neighbourhood. The planners have hitherto overlooked the reality, even in Britain to-day, of the extended family, and the mutual reliance of the generations in the life of working people. But there is evidence that not all of them are impressed by the case in favour of leaving established communities undisturbed. The Editor of *The Town Planning Review* has written :

> To break up a long-established community is, as we have said, a regrettable thing, the more so as many modern communities are in an uneasy and untidy state of change. But change is the nature of our world, and nowhere in *Family and Kinship in East London* do Messrs Young and Willmott seem to appreciate that if Bethnal Green remained unchanged while everywhere else was changing, it would in the end be a very bad thing for the people of Bethnal Green.[24]

Clearly more thought is required upon the purpose as well as the direction and method of change.

[22] *Neighbourhood and Community.* 1954. p. 148.
[23] *Cities in Flood,* by Peter Self, 1957, p. 19.
[24] Vol. xxviii, no. 2, July 1957, p. 87.

Wives at Work

The real income of many families to-day is higher than it has been ever before. This is due in part to full employment and high wages, and in part to the work of married women. In 1931 10 per cent of married women were working outside their homes; in 1951 the figure was 20 per cent.[25] During this period the *total* number of women workers has remained remarkably stable, at about 30 per cent of the total labour force : the proportion of women workers to men has risen only from 424 per thousand to 442. The increase in the number of *married* women workers, therefore, reflects the increased proportion of married women in the population, the lower age of marriage, and a changed attitude to remaining at work after marriage.[26]

In 1931 there was widespread unemployment, and the social services did not afford the help to families that is available to-day. It is pertinent to enquire, therefore, why the number of married women seeking paid employment has doubled in these twenty years.

The increase in work available to women in which they find better pay and wider interest must have exercised an influence. Women have tended to move from the traditional women's occupations, domestic work and textiles, for example, into light engineering, the making of electrical equipment, and a host of other new industries. The higher wages paid in the new industries have forced up wages in domestic service, with considerable effect upon the households in which servants used to be employed.

All professions are now open to the educated woman, except the Stock Exchange and the ordained ministry of the Church; and in many, university teaching, the medical profession, the British Broadcasting Corporation, for example, women receive equal pay with men. This extension of the field has probably influenced many educated women to combine their home duties with gainful employment.

Some married women are driven to work by sheer economic necessity : husbands may fail, for one reason or another, to earn sufficient to support the home, or, though earning an adequate income, may fail to fulfil their obligations. But it is probable that to-day most married women take paid employment, not because of dire necessity but to provide a standard in the home which they deem necessary. Future income may be heavily mortgaged in hire purchase commitments undertaken in the furnishing of a new home; rent in a

[25] "Analysis of the 1951 Census", *The Economist,* 19 July 1952, p. 147.

[26] Whereas there are those in England who regret this, the Population Commission of the Irish Republican Government, 1948-54, actually desiderated it as a custom to be introduced into Ireland as an encouragement to earlier marriage. *Report,* paras. 169f.

new council house is sometimes three times what it was in an old, rent-controlled one; or there may be a mortgage due to a building society. Two incomes meet these charges better than one. A recent enquiry in South-East London, yet to be published, establishes that the bulk of the women's earnings are devoted to improving the home, providing better clothes and more toys for the children, and saving for such extra expenses as holidays.

The changed economic and social status of women has certainly influenced some women to continue at work after marriage. They value the independence which an income of their own affords; especially is this true of the trained or professional woman who before marriage may well have been earning an income equal to that of her husband.

Clearly these are generalizations, and in no sense do they exhaust the motives which influence a married woman to take paid employment. The older woman, her children grown up while she is still, by earlier standards, "young", may seek relief from loneliness in the companionship of work. The younger woman, living with relations, may wish to escape from the friction of the home. The home may be but two over-crowded rooms which afford little scope for real home making. These and many other reasons have been advanced by married women who take paid employment.

A question of crucial importance is the effect of this work on the married woman's family, more especially on her children. All would agree that the circumstances would have to be very exceptional to justify the absence from home of a woman with a young child; in fact mothers with children under school age seldom go out to work; in working-class areas the whole weight of public opinion is against it. For the older children, school meals solve the problem of the mid-day meal, and part-time work, which is becoming more common, may enable the mother to be at home when the children return in the afternoon. The enquiry into working and home conditions in South-East London, mentioned above, shows that in that area the majority of mothers who are not back from work when the children arrive make careful arangements for children to be cared for by relatives and neighbours. The children with latchkeys tied round their necks are the exception and not the rule. The extent to which the working mother puts home and children first may be gauged by the reluctance shown by employers to employ married women at all, their "absentee" rate being so much higher than that of the other workers.

It is frequently alleged that a major cause of juvenile delinquency is to be found in the absence from home of the mother of the family; this may be so, though, taken alone, the view is not supported by recent studies of the subject. Mr Mays considers that neighbourhood and environment are the chief factors inclining a child to acts of delinquency, although he himself is in no doubt that

> the family is the most significant group to which young people belong. During early years the family exerts the most powerful formative influence on a child's character, and relationships within the home circle, particularly with the mother or mother-substitute, are vital determinants of future development.[27]

Dr Ferguson, the co-author of three studies in Glasgow, one of them on the young deliquent, writes categorically :

> In this study the fact that the mother of the family is out at work has not been found to be of any great importance in relation to delinquency.[28]

He confirms this conclusion in his study of the young wages earner.[29]

Doubtless there are families in which family life is gravely impaired by the absence of the mother, but there are others where the contrary may be true. There is evidence to suggest that the greater comfort of the home made possible by the mother's earnings serves to draw the family together. Husbands are prepared to spend their time on painting and decorating; better domestic equipment makes it simple for the whole family to share the home duties; the home, in fact, becomes a joint enterprise in which the whole family takes a pride.

The part played by television in uniting the family has been commented upon by many observers; the increasing consumption of bottled beer for use at home rather than of draught beer to be drunk on licensed premises suggests that more men are spending their evenings in their own homes; many publicans have registered a loss of trade, though this may be offset in part by the increase of licensed clubs.[30]

Whatever view is taken of the desirability of married women going out to work, we have to realize that as industry and the professions are organized to-day it would be extremely difficult to dispense with their services; still less shall we be able to do so in the

[27] *Growing up in the City,* J. B. Mays, Liverpool University Press, 1954, p. 83.

[28] *The Young Delinquent in his Social Setting: A Glasgow Study,* by T. Ferguson, 1951, p. 24. Figures, Table 8.

[29] *The Young Wage Earner.* By T. Ferguson and J. Cunnison. 1951. p. 174. Figures, Table 112. See these authors' further study, *In Their Early Twenties.* 1956. Table 26.

[30] In 1930, 13,526 clubs were registered; in 1955, 22,736; the estimated total in Sept. 1957 was 25,000. (*The Times,* 1 Oct. 1957.)

years to come. In industry, married women are largely employed on unskilled or semi-skilled automatic processes; their work is essential to production, and in 1951 half the total number of women employed on this work were married. We are short of teachers, but classes would be larger still if married women had not returned to the profession; they number about one-third of all women teachers.[31] In social work the same proportion holds good, and the nursing profession is having to take back into service the nurses who marry and to adjust their hours to fit in with their home duties where possible.

The Church and the community at large have tended to regard the married woman going to work as an unfortunate and temporary deviation from the norm : women, it is argued, will, or ought to, return to their homes and devote themselves to their families. If our analysis is correct, we should perhaps accept the situation as it is, and apply ourselves to the task of meeting the special needs of the married woman at work and particularly of her family and family life. This positive approach was outlined by the Bishop of Sheffield in a notable speech with which he opened a debate in the House of Lords on "The Wellbeing of the Family", in June 1953.[32]

Location and Demands of Work

For married women to be at work is one part of the social cost of our high level of living based on intense industrialization. The long journey to and from work imposes on many men and women undue fatigue and prevents them from sharing to the full their family life and the religious and social life of their neighbourhood. Of importance to the Church as to all social organizations is the increase of overtime and, in particular, of shift work : the furnaces burn, the machines run, and therefore work continues, weekdays, Saturdays, and Sundays alike. Increased use of automation may well increase the number of men on shift work, for the capital cost is so high that the plant has to be run continuously to make the installation profitable. The economics of the present high standard of living, from which we all benefit, are calculated to a nicety : the social costs have been examined with less care.

The Middle-Class Family

The changes which have been discussed in this paper have, of course, affected the families of the middle class, some 26% of the total number of families. The range of occupations and incomes is

---

31 "Analysis of the 1951 Census", *The Economist,* 19 July 1952, p. 147.
32 Parliamentary Debates, Lords, Vol. 182, April-June 1953, col. 662ff.

wide, and whilst some families are better off than in pre-war days a certain number have suffered a reduction in income. The families of farmers and shopkeepers, for example, are frequently better off than before the war; the real incomes of many professional men have diminished, though the time-lag in adjusting salaries to rising costs of living has in some professions been overtaken in recent months.

The majority of middle-class families have benefited from the State education and health services; on the other hand those families in the higher administrative and professional classes who strive to send their children to the public schools have to meet a crushing financial burden, which, if they have married at an earlier age than formerly, falls upon them before they have reached their highest salary scales.

The almost entire absence of adequate domestic help has been responsible for marked changes in the middle-class home, more particularly in the younger households; domestic duties and the care of children are now frequently shared by both parents; the change in the status of women is accepted, and one sees the pattern of family life based on partnership as a living reality.

Family Integrity

A closer partnership between husband and wife has been observed also in other than middle-class families. Young and Willmott, in the preliminary chapter to their study of the family and kinship in East London, remarked that while some husbands maintain their old attitudes, and are, e.g., secretive about their wages, more are sharing in the responsibility for the home :

> These preliminary impressions suggest that the old style of working-class family is fast disappearing. The husband portrayed by previous social investigation is no longer true to life. In place of the old comes a new kind of companionship between man and woman, reflecting the rise in the status of the young wife and children which is one of the great transformations of our time. There is now a nearer approach to equality between the sexes, and though each has its peculiar rôle, its boundaries are no longer so rigidly defined nor is it performed without consultation. The grand assumption made by Church and State (but thrown into doubt by earlier surveys) can be re-established.[33]

This may or may not be true of other localities; but it is a straw in the wind.

This social change has been reflected, in the century since 1857, in the steadily changing legal conception of the position of the wife

[33] Op. cit., p. 15.

and of the integrity of the family, with the welfare of the child as a paramount consideration.[34] Some of the recommendations of the recent Royal Commission on Marriage and Divorce 1951-1955,[35] would carry this process of integration further, forcibly asserting the interests of the children and of the family as an institution against the too-ready acceptance of divorce as a remedy for marital discontents. Family Law in the last hundred years was the subject of an important recent study edited by R. H. Graveson and F. R. Crane.[36] In this, Professor Graveson writes :

> The change in the legal position of the married woman . . . is one of the most outstanding features in both law and society during the past century, but it is not the only change of importance. If it is the highlight in the pattern of social change, it is so only because of the important position of the wife in the family unit.[37]

It is against the changes which have been sketched—demographic, economic, social—that the vicissitudes of the family in British society, and its standing to-day, have to be judged. They go a long way to account for the apparent avidity with which increased facilities for divorce were seized—which perhaps prompted the remark of the Master of the Rolls that

> perhaps the fault lies somewhat in ourselves in that, as men, we have not yet sufficiently learned the office of the twentieth century husband.[38]

Since 1947 the number of divorces has fallen, giving in 1955 the lowest figures since the war—28,314 petitions, and 26,816 decrees made absolute, including 554 of nullity. By these divorces some 34,000 children were affected.[39] Statutory Instruments,[40] operative since April, 1957, have given judges in the divorce courts increased powers to secure as best they can the interests of these children, and at present the combined weight of opinion in the social and welfare services is against the inflicting of suffering upon children through a selfish parental seeking after divorce. Despite the figures quoted

[34] For the purposes of the Guardianship of Infants Act, it is *the* paramount consideration.

[35] Report, Cmd.9678. H.M.S.O., 1956.

[36] *A Century of Family Law, 1857-1957.* Edited by R. H. Graveson and F. R. Crane, 1957.

[37] Op. cit., p.1.

[38] Ibid., p. ix.

[39] *Registrar-General's Statistical Review, 1955,* Part II, Tables, Civil.

[40] 1957 No. 619 (L.4). 1957 No. 176 (L.2). H.M.S.O.

above, Professor R. M. Titmuss, writing in 1952, can give it as his opinion that

> It is probable that the proportion of broken marriages under the age of 60, marriages broken by death, desertion and divorce, is, in total, smaller to-day than at any time this century despite the rise in the number of divorces.[41]

Within the family, patterns of authority have changed. Especially in middle-class homes, old forms of discipline have sometimes been abandoned before a new working arrangement for the preservation of harmony within the family group has been achieved. In the workers' families the high wages now being paid to school-leavers—and to schoolboys and girls in holidays—have tended to undermine parental authority. Two world wars and the teachings of psychology have also thrown the old authoritarianism into the melting pot. It has nevertheless been remarked that

> It may well be that in many cases the weakening of the bonds of authority has led to a strengthening of the bonds of affection between parent and child.[42]

The state social services have taken from parents not a little of their responsibility for the medical care and education of their children, though there is little foundation for the view that as a result of State action parents are less responsible than they were, and are not deeply concerned for their children's welfare. The number of children committed to the "care" of a local authority—one in every 200 of children under the age of 18 in England and Wales—is no evidence against this opinion : about half of these children have parents who are ill or temporarily incapacitated, and, with the breakdown of the locally-resident extended family, have no one else to care for them;[43] the others, the homeless, the ill-treated or neglected, and the 30 per cent committed by a court under a "fit person" order, are "in care" precisely because society has accepted a concern for their welfare. We have travelled a long way since the days of Shaftesbury and Dickens.

The family is a conservative institution, with deep roots in the past and with wonderful resilience. Slowly and sometimes painfully it is adapting itself to radical changes in the wider society of which

[41] Quoted in Young and Willmott, op cit., p. 8.

[42] Graveson and Crane, op. cit., p. 143.

[43] "About half the children coming into care in the course of a year are received because of temporary difficulties in the home, usually confinement or temporary illness of the mother, and many of the children remain in care for only a few weeks." *Seventh Report on the Work of the Children's Department,* H.M.S.O., Nov. 1955, p. 1.

it forms part; and, far from disintegrating, the modern family is in some ways in a stronger position than it has been at any period in our history of which we have knowledge.

7. FAMILY PLANNING POLICIES

The economic, social, and demographic problems which arise in an economically under-developed country seeking to raise the level of its inhabitants have been indicated briefly in the preceding pages. Reduced mortality and undiminished fertility with the consequent growth of population are endangering the success of plans for agricultural and industrial progress as well as holding back the extension of social services. Faced with this situation, a certain number of countries are allotting government funds to the study of family planning techniques and the dissemination of knowledge through government-sponsored agencies; some countries are allowing voluntary agencies to undertake the same service, sometimes aided by government grants.

Puerto Rico

The population of Puerto Rico is increasing at a pace hardly equalled in the rest of the world. The population for some years has been increasing at the rate of some 3 per cent per annum. The government is gravely concerned at this situation and for about twenty years it has been actively assisting a family planning policy, but with little success.

Crude birth rates per 1,000 of population [1]

1947	1950	1953	1955
42.2	39.0	35.1	35.0

Crude death rates per 1,000 of population

1947	1950	1953	1955
11.8	9.9	8.1	7.2

Birth and death rates of this order give a population increase of 2.78 per cent per year.

The population of Puerto Rico is still largely rural, but within the past half century the urban population has increased from 15 to 40 per cent of the total population; the fertility of the rural areas is higher and this is accounted for in part by the differences in marital status : a larger proportion of rural families is based on marriage than in the towns.

The inhabitants of the island have American citizenship, so there has been considerable emigration to the United States; any fall in

[1] U.N., *The Demographic Year Book*, 1956.

the birth rate in recent years may be attributed to the departure of considerable numbers of young adults.

Puerto Rico has been favoured by United States federal benefits, by American military installations, by American citizenship facilitating emigration, and by American capital and technology. It is also blessed by a stable government and by far-sighted leadership. The government has invested its revenues in a broad program of industrialization aimed at providing more non-agricultural jobs for the population. Its efforts have added roughly 200 new industrial firms and 12,000 employees to the island's economy within the past decade. But the impact of this formidable accomplishment is largely vitiated by the fact that every year there are 16,000 more entrants into the labour force. Thus the gains of industrialization tend to be consumed by the rapidly growing population.[2]

The level of living is the highest in the Caribbean area with the exception of Cuba; the level of literacy has steadily increased and it is estimated that three-quarters of the population can read and write.

As already stated, the government of Puerto Rico for the past twenty years has been striving to bring about a reduction in births through a family planning policy. There are, in 1957, 160 clinics where a family planning service is available (as well as opportunities for female sterilization in the hospitals).

Since 1939 a network of government sponsored birth-control clinics has provided information and free materials to all those who desire and need them. Despite this fact, there has been little appreciable change in the crude birth rate. Apparently then, materials are not enough, and the neo-Malthusian assumption that, given information, people will act rationally and apply it, would not seem to hold in Puerto Rico.[3]

The Social Science Research Center of the University of Puerto Rico has been engaged for some years now in a study of attitudes relevant to fertility and birth control. The book by Dr Stycos already cited is a report on the first phase of the inquiry.

The results of the Stycos inquiry emphasize the immense importance of understanding the cultural, economic, and psychological factors which influence the attitudes of parents to family planning in widely differing cultures. Puerto Rico is predominantly a Roman Catholic community, though the attitude of the Church to

[2] J. Mayone Stycos, *Family and Fertility in Puerto Rico,* Columbia University Press, 1955, p. 6.

[3] Ibid., p. 7.

agencies, financed from public funds. The governments of these countries are aware that their plans for raising the level of living through the improvement of agriculture and the furthering of industrialization may well be defeated if the population continues to grow at its present rate. The death rate is declining; the birth rate, except in Japan, is remaining at its previous high level and may even be increasing. In all these countries there is a high proportion of dependent children and every year workers are added to the labour force for whom work is not available.

Japan

Crude birth rates per 1,000 of population

1947	1950	1953	1955
34.3	28.2	21.5	19.4

Crude death rates per 1,000 of population

1947	1950	1953	1955
14.6	10.9	8.9	7.8

Fertility in Japan during recent years deserves special attention. Wide use of contraception and a large number of induced abortions (legally permitted by the Eugenic Protection Law passed in 1948) are clearly reflected in the trend of the Japanese birth rate. The rate declined continuously from 1950 to 1955, . . . Japanese fertility, however it is measured, is now lower than that of many Western countries.[8]

In 1952 a law was passed extending the provision of the 1948 Act legalizing sterilization in certain circumstances. A number of Japanese speakers at The Fifth International Conference on Planned Parenthood deplored the widespread use of abortion, the chief means by which the fall in the birth rate had been obtained.

Since the revision of the Eugenic Protection Law in 1952, abortions have increased sharply, amounting to 1,140,000 in 1954, and it is estimated that the number of abortions increased so much last year that, if unreported abortions are included, the total number of abortions differed little from the number of births (1,760,000 in the same period). It is, therefore, essential to take measures to spread the practice of family planning based on rational conception control.[9]

---

[8] U.N. *Report on the World Social Situation*, New York, 1957, p. 8.

[9] "Family Planning and the New Life Movement". Paper read at the Conference on Planned Parenthood, Tokyo, 1955, by Toru Nagai, Director of the Foundation Institute for Research in Population Problems, Japan, p. 117.

114

It is generally recognized in Japan that to permit abortions and sterilizations is to destroy the idea of family planning, but Japan's limited resources, and the impossibility of migration on a scale which would affect population growth, prevent the government from taking steps to end the present situation; the remedy, as seen in official circles, is the wide-spread use of contraceptives. Various government councils and committees have been formed for the study of population problems and the means by which contraceptive advice can be spread throughout the country. Much research is being carried out and the specialized training of doctors and midwives capable of giving advice on contraceptive procedures is being pressed forward at both national and local levels. The Ministers of Health and Welfare are responsible for policy and for aiding the local authorities and the voluntary associations with advice and financial help.

China

Factual information from China is regrettably slight and sometimes contradictory.

Until fairly recently the family was the main exception to the communist predilection for planning. The Chinese did not differ in this respect from the Russians. When the startling results of the previous year's census were published in 1954 (claiming a total population of 601.9 million, of whom 582.6 million lived on the mainland; 7.6 in Formosa; and 11.7 million abroad) the Chinese dismissed as "Malthusian nonsense" any outside suggestions that such a pressure of population might be an obstacle on the road to prosperity; they even argued that fertility must be encouraged. Now, however, the line has changed completely. At the last meeting of the People's Consultative Conference Mrs Li Teh-chuan, the minister of health, made an impassioned plea for birth control. If the campaign begun a year ago for disseminating contraceptive measures was not rapidly expanded, she argued, many women would resort to abortion and sterilization, which are now freely permitted.[10]

In a despatch from Hong Kong the correspondent of the Manchester Guardian states,

Mrs Li Chien-Sheng, vice-director of the Peking Public Health Bureau, today issued a warning about the dangers in the Government's new policy of legalizing abortion and sterilization. Hospital investigations, she said, had shown that abortion was harmful to

[10] *The Economist*, 23 March 1957, p. 986.

women. She did not propose making abortion illegal, but to discourage it she thought those who wanted an operation should have to pay for it themselves. She also criticized early marriages.[11]

It is estimated by the Minister of Health, Mrs Li, that the Chinese population is increasing at about 15 million a year; as a result of better care in child-birth and the improvement in the medical services the death rates are declining. Officially the birth rate is given at 37 per 1,000 of the population and the mortality rate at 17 per 1,000, but it is probable that both these rates are underestimated; it is considered that the Chinese population may well be increasing at the percentage rate of 2.5 a year.[12]

China's population is overwhelmingly rural; 500 million people live in villages or in scattered farms; the immense difficulty of training doctors and nurses and of supplying material to launch an effective birth control campaign is evident, but the attempt is being made. The traditional desire for sons to support the parents in old age and to perpetuate the family presents an obvious barrier to the acceptance of family planning; nevertheless it is reported that the barrier is being overcome :

> Birth control [is] now being advocated in every Chinese home, with all the persuasive apparatus of the omnipresent State. . . . Many people think that the Chinese, a realistic and not very religious folk, will take easily to this new practice. In fact, they are already doing so. Ministry of Health vans drive round even the distant co-operatives with supplies on board.[13]

The Times in a leader, "The Good Earth is Not Enough", commented on two exhibitions held in Peking during the spring of 1957. One was to show the urgent necessity of increasing agricultural output, the other to explain the importance of birth control. China needs more food for her growing population and for export in order to pay for much-needed imports. The relation of the two exhibitions is clear.

> There are 630 million people alive in China at this moment. How can they be kept alive? The mystique of Marxism can do nothing to flip this awkward question aside, for it is the very root and foundation of China's future.[14]

11 *The Manchester Guardian,* 9 March 1957.
12 *Population,* Oct.-Dec. 1956.
13 *The Times,* 2 Oct. 1957.
14 *The Times,* 11 March 1957.

The Chinese government is now concentrating propaganda on the need to produce more from the land and to diminish the number of mouths to be fed.

Singapore

Immigration is now strictly controlled in Singapore so that the large yearly increase in population is due to natural growth, the increase in the number of births over the number of deaths.

Crude birth rates per 1,000 of population[15]

1947	1950	1953	1955
45.9	45.7	48.7	47.6

Crude death rates per 1,000 of population

1947	1950	1953	1955
13.3	12.1	10.3	8.7

(In 1934 the crude birth rate was 43.26 and the crude death rate 24.07.)

The 1955 figures give a population increase per annum of nearly 4 per cent. In 1921 the population numbered 420,000; in 1955 it numbered 1,211,000. At a constant rate of increase of 3 per cent per annum, a population increases by 50 per cent in less than 15 years, and doubles itself in less than 25 years.

In 1949 the first Family Planning clinics were opened and the government to-day allots a sum of £11,718 to this voluntary association which now operates twenty-seven clinics. Radio talks are given on the subject of family planning, and booklets giving particulars of the Association's work are distributed in various languages. The vote of the government grant to the Family Planning Association gave rise to a debate in the Legislative Assembly in November 1956. There was a certain amount of opposition from the Minister of Health (who contended that were the money allotted to his department his clinics could be extended), from certain members on moral grounds,[16] and from others that the budget could not carry the extra expense. Members of the Assembly speaking for the continuance of the government grant stressed the need of family planning both for the sake of the families striving to feed and educate more children than their resources allowed, and for the sake of the community. The difficulty of providing work for the increasing numbers was stressed by more than one speaker. Mr Lim Koon Teck, for example, stated :

[15] U.N. *Demographic Year Book*, 1956.

[16] *The Times* correspondent, reporting the debate of a year before, remarked that "the speakers hesitated to make a definite stand, either for or against birth control, in the name of any denomination other than Roman Catholicism". (*The Times*, 23 Nov. 1955.)

To my mind, we have the example of China, India and Japan whose governments have adopted family planning and they do so not because they want it but because of necessity, because of over-population and the impossibility to feed and clothe all the children being born in those territories. These countries will not adopt family planning unless it is vitally necessary and we in Singapore are coming to that stage. We have now over 20,000 people unemployed and their numbers are increasing, and this has been confirmed by the Minister for Commerce and Industry. On top of that, we have those people who are now leaving school and trying to find employment, and their numbers will be increased. . . . If we can save a few hundred women from the worry of an unplanned confinement and going through the sufferings of ill health and having to visit a quack doctor in order to obtain abortion, which may injure their health and possibly cause their death, then we shall have spent this money well.[17]

The opposition amendment was lost, and the grant was not only continued but increased.

India

The importance attached by the present Indian government to family planning has been emphasized earlier. The problem facing the government is a formidable one. There is the difficulty of reaching the peasants, 70 per cent of the population, many of them illiterate and living in villages difficult of access. Much emphasis is now being laid on training doctors, nurses, and social workers, but their numbers are still far below those required to carry out the government's programme. Continuous research is being made to find a contraceptive which would prove efficient and acceptable to the Indian people.

Dr John B. Wyon read a paper at the Third All-India Conference on Family Planning, on "Motivation for Family Planning with Special Reference to Field Studies". He said that

Never in the history of man has any nation yet reduced its birth rate by a conscious and planned application of contraception. Success in the effort now being made in India, Japan and elsewhere will depend to a great extent on an adequate understanding of motivation and factors affecting motivations which determine use of family planning.[18]

[17] *Singapore Legislative Assembly Debates, Official Report,* 21 and 22 November 1956.

[18] Paper published in *The Medical Digest*, February 1957, Bombay, p. 66.

118

In India, surveys, one of them by Dr Wyon, are being conducted to try to discover the motives which influence people in refusing or accepting the techniques of family planning; at present it is estimated that at the most only about ten per cent of women are willing to employ family planning methods, though over half the women consultated state that they wish to plan their families.[19] The need to establish the factors which influence motivation is imperative for the success of the Indian plant; the brief account of family planning in Puerto Rico has made this clear.

Pakistan

Crude birth rates per 1,000 of population[20]

1947	1950	1951	1955
20.7	19.0	21.2	Not available

Crude death rates per 1,000 of population

1947	1950	1951	1955
13.2	12.2	11.9	Not available

These figures are more or less accurate; births and deaths are probably understated.

On November 7th 1953, a Family Planning Association was founded at Lahore. Three clinics have been opened in that city to educate women and to help in the foundation of new clinics. In November 1953, the Minister of Food and Agriculture, Abdul Kan, declared : "The senseless race between increase of food and increase of population must not continue any longer." The Minister has asked the Food and Agriculture Organisation to add to its program designed to increase food production, an educational program to reduce the over population.[21]

The Central Government has allocated a sum of £37,630 for family planning in 1957. Clinics are now established in Karachi and Peshawar; Lahore in 1957 has six clinics.

[19] Ibid., p. 69.
[20] *Population*, April-June 1955, p. 291.
[21] *Demographic Year Book*, 1956.

the peculiar sufferings and service and joys of marriage "beareth all things . . . hopeth all things, endureth all things".

Again, while we might bestow all our goods to feed the poor, and might in this way have a concern for social well-being, without displaying *agape,* the converse is certainly not true. *Agape* is "the very bond of peace and of all virtues" without which, with or without material possessions, people are counted as dead before God.

Further, it is *agape* which, recognizing the limitations of human knowledge—though we "know all mysteries and all knowledge" we only "know in part"—can bind people together in a fellowship and unity to be distinguished from any which a strong administration by itself could create.

So *agape* is the theme which links together these four papers which treat of the bearing of the Christian gospel on questions of family and population in the contemporary world.

1. THE THEOLOGY OF MARRIAGE AND THE FAMILY

During the past thirty years theological thought about marriage has developed considerably.

(1) Full weight has been given to New Testament teaching[1] about the union of man and woman in "one flesh" and the analogy it bears to the union of Christ and his Church. It is now fairly generally recognized that the union of man and wife ought not to be regarded mainly as a means to bringing children into existence, but as a "two-in-oneship" which has value in itself and glorifies God. It has become common to think of children as the "fruit", rather than as the "end" of the marriage union; and monogamy is more often defended by reference to the demands of love and of the gift of self which is made in marriage than by reference to the needs of offspring.

(2) In keeping with this development a new value is ascribed to *coitus,* which, as the specific and consummating act of marriage, is seen to be no mere means to generation, but an act of positive importance for the marriage union and for the perfecting of husband and wife. This intrinsic value is affirmed as against the old opinion that *coitus* always needed the "good" of generation to justify it. Since the unitive virtue of the act depends partly on the manner in which it is performed, value is attributed to love-making also.

(3) Lest the new orientation of thought about marriage should cause procreation to be regarded as merely subsidiary to the personal relationship of husband and wife, there is renewed insistence in some

[1] See "Extended Note" after this Section, p. 127.

quarters on the dignity of parenthood as participation in the creativity of God and on the fact that the procreative purpose is part and parcel of marriage, not an optional *addendum* to it.

(4) Increased understanding of the cycle of fertility in woman has made deliberately non-generative *coitus* a practical possibility even for those who reject contraception. In consequence new moral questions are posed. On the one hand, to what extent may man and wife rightly use *coitus* with sole reference to their own relationship? On the other hand, how are man and wife to determine the extent of their procreative responsibility? Is there a discoverable "duty" to have children, or should procreation be regarded as a matter of vocation rather than of duty? In addition there is still the vexed question whether contraception is admissible or, if it is admissible, in what circumstances it may rightly be used. On these matters which are relevant to population problems, debate continues.

(5) The importance of the family as the basis of a wider society continues to be underlined. The family-community is a model situation in which the meaning of human relationship is learnt. In particular, it is one of the few groupings in the modern world in which human persons have status and are respected simply because they are human persons, and not because they are useful. This is what makes the family the principal school of charity. Wherever, on the contrary, children are either valued for the potential contribution to the family's wealth or, in different circumstances, regarded as economic liabilities, family life is bound to be corrupted.

(6) Eucharistic doctrine has been used to illuminate the meaning of Christian marriage, and this is to be welcomed. We can usefully develop, as far as it will go, a parallel of which we are reminded by the last general rubric attached to the form of Solemnization of Matrimony in the English Prayer Book of 1662 : "It is convenient that the new-married persons should receive the holy Communion at the time of their Marriage or at the first opportunity after their Marriage." For marriage, like the Service of Holy Communion, is set in a social context—there is the need to be in love and charity with our family as with our neighbours— and it has a social outcome. Each is an offering of a human fellowship for a divine empowering. Further, just as in the Service of the Holy Communion, the natural elements of bread and wine are those means by which the grace of God is received, so we may think of the most intimate relationships of marriage as being elements in space and time whereby God's grace is given to enable a man and wife to continue in such a fellowship together as enables them to "do all such good works as [God has] prepared for [them] to walk in". We need not argue that every theme

123

mentioned, could be justified in refusing to do anything to reduce the number of births. It is true that in the event predictions may be falsified—for instance, if disease were unexpectedly to escape from control; but a government can only act on the best information obtainable. It has to be recognized that birth rates have already been influenced by State action. It will be generally allowed that justification for such action could hardly be stronger than it is in the Indian situation.

(2) But what are the limits of justifiable intervention? We have become accustomed to financial inducements being offered to parents to encourage procreation. Where it is discouragement that is aimed at, it would seem to be unjust positively to penalize parents who think it right to have more children than seems good to the government. As for propaganda, there can be no reasonable objection to a government's publicizing the need for fewer births and using its resources to persuade people to act accordingly. Moral difficulties emerge only when a government actively encourages methods of birth-prevention of which the moral lawfulness is disputed. The Church cannot acquiesce, for instance, in policies of abortion or sterilization for limiting births. What about contraception? The morality of this means will be discussed further below.

(3) A question that needs further consideration is whether a situation of the Indian kind imposes a definite obligation on parents to limit their family in accordance with State recommendations. As has been remarked, man and wife now have it in their power to choose generative or non-generative intercourse. Consequently, quite apart from situations like the Indian, it has to be considered on what principle the extent of procreative possibility is to be determined. This is a comparatively new question which has not so far received any very clear answer. It may be that it should be answered in terms of "vocation" rather than of "duty". As a rule the vocation to seek to have a family large enough to be a school of human relationships is implicit in the vocation to marriage; but it has usually been allowed that there may be exceptional vocations to childless marriage although husband and wife are, as far as they know, capable of procreating. In the past such a vocation was assumed to involve abstinence from intercourse. Whether there can be vocations to have intercourse only on occasions when conception is impossible or very improbable is a new question to which the answer is not immediately apparent.

If procreation is rightly regarded as a vocation, then it seems that it is not within the competence of a third party to determine that a couple have not that vocation, however undesirable the birth of a child may appear to be in the particular circumstances. In other

126

words, if in a situation like the Indian a government were to declare against families of more than a certain number, the question for parents would not be one of obedience or disobedience, but rather one of discerning vocation in the light of all the circumstances, including the governmental declaration. The predicted consequences of more births, to society as well as to the children themselves and to the families concerned, may not be disregarded; but parents are entitled to reflect that predictions may be falsified and that in any case unfavourable circumstances do not destroy the value of existence.

(4) Alike in situations that seem to demand a reduction of the birth-rate and in situations which seem to demand an increase the chief concern of the Church will be to foster the sense of responsibility and vocation in its married members. Whether it is proper for the Church to help to promote morally legitimate measures which States may take on the basis of predictions is a difficult and delicate question which can only be answered by those who know all the circumstances. Where the future of a nation seems to be in danger it may seem intolerable that it should "sit on the fence". But as a rule it is undesirable that it should tie itself to any general policy, whether of "many children" or of "few children"; for the impression must not be given that the family exists for the sake of society; and this matter of procreation must be kept personal—whatever the circumstances.

EXTENDED NOTE: MARRIAGE IN BIBLICAL TEACHING

It cannot be doubted that the Bible for the most part[2] would emphasize the high significance of marriage. This emphasis arises in at least three ways :

[2] The most obvious exceptions occur in the Old Testament where polygamy is not only recognized, but generally practised. We may recall the large harems of David and Solomon. We have, further, divers examples of a matriarchal type of marriage, when the husband resides in the wife's clan and the children are counted as her family. Such a concept of marriage lies behind the story of Jacob and his marriage to the daughter of Laban (Gen. 31) and behind the story of Shechem and Dinah (Gen. 34); and it is not unrelated to the *mot'a* or *sadiga* marriage such as Samson contrived to contract (Judges 14), a marriage in which the wife remained with her people, being visited from time to time by her husband.

On the other hand, the levirate marriage (Deut. 25. 5) is sometimes traced to polyandry; and a depressed concept of womanhood lies behind the association of a wife with a man's chattels (Ex. 20. 17) and behind the provision that a son could inherit his father's concubines. (Cf. the resentment of Ishbosheth when Abner took Rizpah, one of Saul's concubines.)

That some of these examples from the Old Testament find ready parallels in certain countries today should make us all the more cautious in our appeal to the Bible, whose authority must necessarily reckon with some doctrine of "progressive revelation". The authority of the Bible as a whole is not something which belongs mechanically to any and all of its parts.

(a) *By talking of God in terms of words and phrases and incidents that have to do with marriage*; for example, the marriage covenant between the Israelites is associated with Yahweh's covenant with his people (Mal. 2, 10-16); there are the familiar similes of the woman in travail (Isa. 13. 8; Rom. 8. 22; Gal. 4. 19) and of birth (Isa. 37. 3; 66. 9; Hos. 13. 13); and use is often made of the pictures of bride and bridegroom (Isa. 61. 10; Jer. 2. 32; Matt. 25. 1; John 3. 29; Rev. 21. 2; 22. 17). Further, God is "known" as a husband "knows" his wife.

(b) *By the actions of our Lord himself*, for example at the marriage in Cana of Galilee.

(c) *By our Lord's teaching*, which emphasizes above all the significance of the one-flesh unity which marriage brings (Matt. 19. 6).

But these positive themes which would emphasize the high calling of marriage, in which the most physical and fleshly of relations can be hallowed and informed by God, were, until recently, often neglected because of a different emphasis which is to be found in St Paul.

For St Paul, marriage is undoubtedly a second best, with celibacy and virginity as ideal courses (see 1 Cor. 7—especially vv. 1, 5, and 9). But it has to be emphasized that, equally for St Paul, marriage is not in any way sinful. The reference we have just given does not of course by itself in isolation represent St Paul's total view, which in fact stems from presuppositions with which it is integrally related. For St Paul, when he wrote this epistle, considered that the end of the world was at hand and a time of great tribulation was imminent. In these circumstances he commended celibacy and virginity on prudential grounds. At such a critical period people without little children to care for would be fortunate indeed. At the same time Paul's views on marriage are not at all ascetic in character. He never considers that marriage is an evil thing which the Christian should utterly renounce. It is true that he chose celibacy for himself, and as we have said, advised it for others, though he had no wish to restrict people's freedom or to "throw a halter on them" (1 Cor. 7. 35). Above all, his high view of marriage is clear from his exhortation in Eph. 5. 25; "Husbands love your wives, as Christ also loved the Church and gave himself for it." We could hardly imagine a greater significance being given to married life than this. Further, we can recall that in Ephesians 5, St Paul echoes the gospel teaching and takes the one-flesh mystery of husband and wife as an apt model for the relation between Christ and his Church.

128

2. CONTRACEPTION

To consider the family in contemporary society, whether, for example, in Great Britain, or India or the West Indies or Japan, is to raise for various reasons the question of family planning and consequently the question of using contraceptives to that end. In Great Britain contraception is widely advocated and used not only where there are grave objections to the birth of children, but also for spacing births without interrupting intercourse and for facilitating earlier marriage of the two-stage pattern which has already been mentioned. In India and Japan it seems to many to be the only practical solution of economic and demographic problems, unless abortion (already legalized in Japan) or sterilization are to be countenanced. There is therefore urgent need to establish, if possible, an Anglican attitude to this practice.

There are annexed to this Section three separate treatments of the moral problem, in which contraception is considered as a relatively isolated matter and the question of intrinsic moral quality is raised.

(1) In the first (Example 1) *coitus*, like marriage itself, is said to have a "given" pattern to which metaphysical significance attaches, and to be a sign of union which effects what it signifies; and it is argued that if certain essentials of the "given" pattern are not preserved there can be no assurance that the metaphysical blessing will be received. In short, the metaphysical apparatus which belongs to the *ex opere operato* view of the Christian sacraments is here extended to *coitus*. The conclusion is that contraception makes an act of intercourse a misleading counterfeit of the *coitus* to which the promise of union in one flesh is annexed, and that therefore it cannot rightly be regarded as a positive good, capable of enriching the marriage relationship. The paper then goes on (1B) to inquire whether intercourse modified by contraception can be justified in certain situations which morally exclude the "given" act, and suggests that it can.

Some will think that this treatment of the question founders on the difficulty of demonstrating that something in the metaphysical realm is bound up with an empirical event of which the essential features can be unalterably specified. In this instance (it may be asked) can we specify exactly those empirical features which are needed to safeguard union? Can we be absolutely sure that any different features necessarily exclude that union? Morover no one would maintain that each and every detail of *coitus* is "given" and unalterable. There is thus the added difficulty of distinguishing "inventions" which destroy the metaphysical significance from legitimate developments of sexual behaviour which preserve it. Again, if we combine 1A and 1B, we have to make room for the possibility that approximations to the "given" act may be permissible on occasion. Some will see here an ultimate appeal to insight; and if such an appeal has to be made, the hope of establishing something incorrigible and guaranteed beyond question remains unfulfilled.

The philosophical difficulty is that of conceiving a metaphysical language which is translatable into unmistakable empirical terms. While every Christian must agree that God's revelation in Christ is "given", not every Christian will thereby conclude that in the same sense the particular empirical features of every Christian situation are likewise "given" or that a comprehensive deductive metaphysical pattern is also "given".

(2) The second treatment (Example 2) takes the customary categories of moral theology and seeks to show that they have been wrongly used in this matter as a result of imperfect appreciation of the function of *coitus* in marriage. It is argued that, in view of certain empirical considerations which are discussed, it is misleading to speak of procreation as "the primary end" of *coitus*; that *coitus* inevitably serves different ends on different occasions; and that contraception can represent a responsible use of human freedom in the interests of a joint development of personality and, through that, of the family as a whole. Thus a justification for contraception is found, not in any special circumstances, but in the nature of the marriage relationship itself.

A weakness of this treatment, some will think, is that it does not provide a firm basis for making a moral distinction between *coitus* modified by contraception alone and other sexual actions for which a certain relational value may be claimed, but which are generally condemned by Christian moralists.

(3) The third treatment (Example 3) exemplifies a quite different approach. Eschewing any kind of *a priori* starting-point, except the broadest background of Christian doctrine, it begins by postulating a case in which man and wife have conscientiously decided that in their particular circumstances the use of contraceptives can be made part of the offering of their marriage to the glory of God. Here is a claim to valid insight. The paper then proceeds to discuss, by way of point and counter-point, certain objections to their decision that the couple might be called upon to face; and it concludes that none of these is sufficient to invalidate the claim to insight.

This approach to the matter is that of the spiritual adviser rather that that of the ordinary moralist. Those who adopt it do not claim to enunciate incontrovertible Christian principles of universal validity which could stand as axioms for the development of a deductive ethic. The appeal to insight is, in their opinion, fundamental and their concern is to teach those who have decisions to make to bring their particular situations, in all their empirical complexity, alongside other situations in which the Christian response is recognizable through their understanding of the Christian faith.

Some may see a difficulty here. If the discussion of objections in this paper bears only upon the particular case postulated at the outset, and if the refusal to formulate general principles is absolute, no guidance at all can be offered for the future. All we can say, on the basis of actual insights known to us, is that contraception has sometimes been justified in the past: we cannot predict that it will ever be justified in the future, still less adumbrate the sort of situation in which it might be justified. If on the other hand it is only a certain kind of general principles that is repudiated, viz. a kind which purports to be "incontrovertible" and "of universal validity", then it seems that the position here adopted is not after all so very different from the position of the ordinary moral theologian, who would say that, at the most, only a few primary principles can be of this kind. However that may be, if this second interpretation is correct, it can then be asked what guidance for the future emerges from this paper; and the answer seems to be that the refutation of objections to contraception, if held to be adequate, establishes human liberty by the negative method of showing that there is no certain evidence that contraception must always be wrong. On the general question whether contraception should be regarded as a normal element in the relations of husband and wife, or only as a permissible response to particular emergencies, this method can of course give no guidance.

In spite of the manifest divergences between these three treatments of the question, there is a meeting-point of practical importance in the judgement that a conscientious decision to use contraceptives would in certain circumstances be justified. Even the kind of argument found in Example 1A does not necessarily conflict with such a conclusion; for although some who endorse that argument would say that contraception so alters the nature of intercourse that no conceivable circumstances could make it permissible, others would argue as in 1B that there are circumstances of such urgency as to make contraception relatively the lesser evil and morally eligible.

EXAMPLE 1

It is necessary to distinguish two opinions in favour of contraception:

A. that contraception is a positive good—a discovery which enables human beings to realize more fully the potentialities of

131

kind of submission meant here is not to be confused with an un-reasoning and fatalistic "Let nature take its course". The rational nature of man shows itself in seeking to understand the biological processes better and in making use of the knowledge gained, not to supersede the processes by human inventions, but to fulfil the implicit pattern more completely. So, for instance, study of the processes reveals that there is a place in marriage for "relational" *coitus*; but it does not support the notion that it is proper to man to enjoy such *coitus* at will : the pattern disclosed is one that imposes definite limitations. (It should be noted, by the way, that this view of the matter does not involve any *universal* proposition about man's dominion over his body. *Coitus,* like marriage to which it pertains, is a special case.)

(2) If we see *coitus* simply as a spatio-temporal event, which can be fully described in physiological and psychological terms, then it may be possible (though some may question this) to regard *coitus* during sterility artificially induced as ontologically and morally equivalent to *coitus* during the sterility which is found in the biological process. But if we believe that *coitus* has metaphysical implications, then the equivalence disappears. It is only to the act which is "given", and not to any human counterfeit, that the metaphysical union in one flesh is attached. Here again we see the analogy with marriage. In order that union in one flesh may be *initiated,* man and woman must submit themselves to the divine ordinance concerning the gift of self : if some other form of consent is substituted, their union may possibly be valid in a purely legal sense, but there can be no assurance that it is metaphysically valid. Similarly, in order that the same union in one flesh may be *consummated,* man and woman must submit themselves to the specific act as "given"; if some modification is substituted, there can be no assurance that anything is achieved in the metaphysical realm.

It therefore seems that those who advocate contraception are either denying, or at least ignoring, these metaphysical implications of *coitus,* and treating the act simply as a spatio-temporal event. They seem to be content with the outward aspect of the act—penetration, orgasm, and the physical and psychological consequences of orgasm. That is not equivalent, as opponents of contraception have sometimes unfairly suggested, to saying that the *pleasure* of the act may be sought while the *end* of the act is frustrated; for even on the spatio-temporal level the act has "relational" value. But it is certainly to ignore the analogy between *coitus* and sacraments. In a sacrament the promise of a supernatural gift depends on due per-formance of the rite according to the divine ordinance; in *coitus* the metaphysical union in one flesh depends on submission to the act as "given". In brief, there is no assurance that *coitus* during contraception can constitute consummation in more than a merely legal sense.

As a rule those who approve of *coitus* with contraceptives condemn *coitus interruptus*. But once the notion of "givenness" is jettisoned, it becomes difficult to find adequate grounds for this condemnation. It is indeed maintained that *coitus interruptus* is bad for health, while *coitus* during contraception is not; but although ill consequences may suggest that the act they follow is contrary to human nature, they are not by themselves sufficient to settle the question. Perhaps the main ground of distinction that is alleged is that *coitus interruptus* lacks "relational" value. But so does *coitus* during contraception, if we include under "relational" the consummation of metaphysical union. If on the other hand only the spatio-temporal is to be considered, more careful research would be needed before a worth-while conclusion could be come to. "Relational" value seems to attach itself to the oddest sexual activities. It is well known that many people cannot find any satisfaction at all in the normal act of *coitus,* but find it in variations that most would condemn. On what grounds are we to say that these are not pioneers in the development of the sexual life?

It is in this connection that the spread of contraception gives rise to a fear that may or may not be justified, but which at least suggests caution. It is, to say the least, suspicious that the age in which contraception has won its way is not one which has been conspicuously successful in managing its sexual life. Is it possible that, by claiming the right to manipulate his physical processes in this matter, man may, without knowing or intending it, be stepping over the boundary between the world of Christian marriage and what one might call the world of Aphrodite—the world of sterile eroticism against which the Church reacted so strongly (perhaps too strongly) in its early days? For one of the characteristics of the latter world was (and is) the exercise of unlimited self-determination in sexual activity. Once submission to the "given" pattern is abandoned, all kinds of variations on the sexual theme which heighten satisfaction can appear to be enrichments of the sexual life. Admittedly this is a very difficult subject to handle; for in sexual matters the usual Christian counsel of "indifference" to pleasure simply does not apply. The sexual act as "given" seems to demand, for its due performance, deliberate heightening of, and abandonment to, sensation. But that is all the more reason why the definite limitations imposed by the "given" pattern are necessary.

Is any scientific research possible in this field? It could only deal with the spatio-temporal effects of various types of sexual activity;

135

but that would be something. It would certainly be a help to have some factual material to work on. For instance, are the effects of *coitus* during normal periods of sterility and *coitus* during induced sterility the same or different? It has been suggested here that the two acts are ontologically different; they are apt to be psychologically different : are the consequences also different? Is *coitus* during contraception a *sedatio concupiscentiae*? or does it perhaps stimulate appetite? One receives an impression that the answers which have so far been given to this sort of question have owed too much to prejudice and too little to evidence.

The upshot of all this, it may be suggested, is that it would be very unwise at this juncture for the Church to endorse in any way the opinion that contraception is a positive good needing no special circumstances to justify it.

B. *The opinion that contraception, though normally to be avoided, can be justified by circumstances.*

In 1930 the Lambeth Conference gave majority support to this opinion; but the background of the committee's discussion and of the resolution which was then passed was very different from the circumstances of to-day.

(1) The theological revaluation of *coitus* as a symbol of and means to the union of man and wife in one flesh was then only in its early stages. To-day few would commend prolonged abstinence from intercourse as "the primary and obvious" method of preventing conception; for if *coitus* is the characteristic act of marriage, which differentiates it from other relationships, and the seal of marriage union, then prolonged abstinence is contrary to the nature of marriage and requires either special vocation or strong circumstantial justification.

(2) In 1930 the scientific basis of what has come to be called "the rhythm method" of controlling conception was only just being established; and so the Conference spoke as if choice was confined to abstinence and contraception alone, and as if intentionally non-generative intercourse stood or fell with contraception. To-day it is recognized that nature itself provides for purely "relational" intercourse; it is generally allowed that such intercourse is permissible during natural infertility; and the question at issue is whether such infertility may be reproduced artificially and, if it may, in what circumstances.

(3) The background of the 1930 discussion was concern about "the decline of the birth-rate throughout the civilized world". To-day, on the contrary, minds are chiefly exercised by the overpopulation of certain territories.

A contemporary argument for the occasional justification of contraception starts from a belief that it is desirable that such limitation or spacing of families as vocation or circumstances require should be achieved without enforced abstinence over long periods. It is held that often the rhythm method affords the means to this end, but that in circumstances where it is not eligible, and the choice lies beween abstinence and contraception alone, contraception may be chosen.

Is this judgement reconcilable with the view of *coitus* given above (in 1A)? Some would say not. They would argue that no circumstances can have the effect of changing a counterfeit into the genuine "given" act of *coitus*. On the other hand, others would say that, although circumstances cannot alter the ontological status of *coitus* with contraceptives, they can and do alter its moral status; that the modified act, though ontologically different from *coitus* during natural infertility, may on occasion be morally equivalent, being the best symbol of love and union that is eligible in the circumstances.

It is remarkable that hardly any attempt seems to have been made to indicate the kind of situation in which this latter judgement would hold good. Perhaps the reason is that, if procreation is to be treated in terms of vocation rather than of duty, no brief and simple guidance can be given. For the same reason, and also because more co-operative work on the question is badly needed, the casuistry of the matter cannot be discussed here.

The implications of this type of judgement on contraception for people living in Indian or similar conditions calls for special consideration. The existence of such conditions does not immediately justify contraception in any particular case, since rhythm *may* still be negligible. It may be that there are many whose education or intelligence does not enable them to use rhythm, but who can yet be taught to use contraception. Again, it may be argued that the Indian house is on fire, and that the only fire-brigade action that has the slightest chance of being effective is a State campaign in favour of contraception. But these considerations do not suffice to show that contraception is permissible for all.

EXAMPLE 2

Notes
on the Morality of Contraception
considered with reference to
the "Ends" and "Object" of Coitus

I.   In moral theology the traditional determinants of the morality of an act are its object, its circumstances, and the agent's intention;

6

and of these, the object is regarded as primary. It has been described as "that natural tendency or result which, when adequately qualified or defined, specifies the action as being one of a particular class".[3] In practice it is difficult to consider the object of an act without making reference to its end (*finis operis*); and this is particularly so in the matter now under discussion—the morality of *coitus* with the use of contraception. Consequently moralists have usually been inclined to treat this problem in terms of the *finis operis* of *coitus*, rather than in terms of its object; and we shall follow their practice here.

II.   *Coitus*, considered in itself, comes within the category of indifferent acts, such as walking and eating, and is therefore morally neutral. Regard, therefore, must be paid to circumstances, and to the agents' intentions, when attempting to decide whether any concrete act of *coitus* is good or bad. In general, we may say that the good act of *coitus* must be (1) free, that is, it must be an act to which both parties consent, knowing to what they consent, and there must be no constraint due to force or fear; (2) conformable to reason and to the divine will, as they are seen to relate to sexual and coital behaviour; (3) adequately related to the end or ends of the act. This means, in effect, that *coitus* must occur within the context of a certain kind of responsible sexual relationship, which may be defined theologically as the common life of one-flesh, and institutionally as "marriage" (recognizing that more than one form of institutional relationship between the sexes may conform to reason, and that different institutional forms may co-exist—e.g., the ecclesiastical and the civil).

Consideration of circumstances leads to the conclusion that the morally neutral act of *coitus* becomes bad when it occurs in conditions which contravene the above requirements, such as fornication and adultery. But is it true, on the other hand, that every act of marital *coitus* is good? And in particular, is marital *coitus* with the use of contraception morally good?

III.   Before considering the question, What is the end (*finis operis*) of *coitus*? it is well to bear in mind the kind of human act with which we are dealing. No treatment of *coitus* is adequate or realistic which fails to recognize the profoundly mysterious nature of this particular mode of human intercourse. Even the Bible regards it as a distinctive means by which one person attains a certain "knowledge" of another which cannot be mediated otherwise, but the full content and significance of this unique relational experience can neither be apprehended nor expressed by the individual, for its character and

[3] R. C. Mortimer, *The Elements of Moral Theology*, 1947, p. 66.

meaning are as infinitely variable as is the structure of sexual relationship itself.

Appreciation of the mystery of *coitus* and a deeper understanding of the relationship between man and woman make it difficult for the modern theologian to speak with the same confidence as his predecessors about the proper ends of *coitus*, or to regard it merely as one among many comparable human acts. Traditionally, the principal end of *coitus* has been defined as generation—though other subsidiary ends, such as the relief of incontinence and mutual endearment, were also recognized; but such a classification hardly does justice either to the complexity of the act or the realities of experience. If the true ends of *coitus*, as determined by God's purpose, are to be apprehended by means of the exercise of an informed reason, then it would seem that some redefinition is necessary.

IV. *Coitus* may be said to have a two-fold end (or, if it be preferred, two separate ends).

(1) Biologically, its purpose is *generative*—that is, the fertilization of the ovum by a spermatozoon.

(2) On the personal plane, its purpose is *relational*. Husband and wife become one-flesh in principle at the physical consummation of their union, and their *coitus* plays an important part in the progressive realization of all that one-flesh implies. It serves to direct creatively the powerful (and potentially disruptive) sexual impulses, so that they are expended in acts which develop and enrich the relationship; it is a means for the expression of love; and it is also an important aspect of the "mutual society, help, and comfort" of married life. Finally, it is in a very real sense "sacramental" of the whole meaning of wedlock.

One very important aspect of this relational purpose deserves special mention, and suggests a legitimate extension of the meaning of "procreation". It would now be generally agreed that procreation implies co-operation with God in his creative work—that it is really creation on behalf of God. It would also be agreed that such co-operation in the divine work of creation involves the education of the child to maturity, and not merely its begetting and birth. Consequently the procreative task of parenthood is not completed until the last child is fully adult.

To this task, the parents' *coitus* makes a valuable contribution. Once conception has occurred, it plays an important part in the maintenance of harmonious relationship between the couple, and thus promotes the well-being of the child, first before birth, and then during the whole period (some seventeen or more years) of growth towards maturity. Especially in the vital formative years (up to the age of five or six) it can thus help to ensure the stability and security of the child.

V. It will immediately be apparent that this two-fold end is not, and cannot be, attained with every act of *coitus*.

(1) Generation is so controlled by biological and other factors that its achievement is uncertain and, relative to the total incidence of *coitus,* comparatively rare. Conception cannot occur during the infertile period of the menstrual cycle, nor after the menopause, yet *coitus* can take place satisfactorily at those times. Furthermore, male sterility or physiological defect in the female may prevent *coitus* from resulting in conception.

(2) The relational end of *coitus* is always attained, either (*a*) constructively, in the expression of love, the building up of the one-flesh union, and the fulfilment of the "procreative" task of parenthood (in the sense explained above—see IV. 2) or (*b*) destructively, in the expression of lust, and in exploitation of another person, whether in or outside marriage (cf. 1 Cor. 6. 16). *Coitus* is a personal act of such a kind that it is seldom without its effect upon the characters of the participants, either for good or for ill.

VI. The two-fold nature of the end (*finis operis*) of *coitus* is not denied by traditional systems of morality, but it is always assumed that the generative end, though least certain of attainment, is nevertheless primary and determinative. Accordingly, it has been held that every act of *coitus* must at least (to use the customary phrase) be *aptus ad generationem*—"suitable for generation". This requirement is not interpreted to exclude *coitus* during times of infertility; it is sufficient that nothing be done which would prevent conception, were conception possible. It is not necessary that the act be performed always in circumstances which ensure or favour conception; but no artificial contraceptive measure is permissible.

It has yet to be shown, however, on what grounds (other than *a priori* ones) generation is determinative among the ends of *coitus*. Such an assumption was doubtless natural and inevitable at a time when the relational significance and the intrinsic mystery of *coitus* were not recognized; then it was easy to regard the act principally as a generative mechanism to which, in consequence of the Fall, a certain remedial function is now annexed in marriage. But it is difficult any longer to maintain such a view, and it is at least arguable to the extent of probability that any attempt to classify the ends of *coitus* in order of supposed importance or priority is misconceived. On the other hand, every consideration of coital morality must take account of two things. (1) Human *coitus* is an act of unique quality and significance involving to a greater degree than any other the whole person as a psychosomatic unity. (2) Human *coitus* cannot be treated as an isolated and self-subsistent act. Being an act of the whole person, it is in some sense expressive of an attitude to life and to God. Each act of *coitus* between husband and wife must be seen, therefore, as part of a total pattern of relationship.

With this caution against attaching greater importance to the individual act of *coitus* than to the general pattern of coital relationship which is one aspect of the common life of husband and wife, two alternative approaches to the problem of contraception may be proposed.

VII. According to certain moral theologians, the good act of *coitus* must be *aptus ad generationem*; but generation is only one end of *coitus*, and that the least certain of attainment. Moreover, an act which, while *aptus ad generationem*, is an exploitation of one spouse by the other, can hardly be regarded as other than morally bad. The good act of *coitus*, therefore, might better be defined as that which conduces to fulfilment of the act's proper twofold end (or, if it be preferred, the act's proper ends).

Such a re-classification, however, does not take us very far. It avoids any isolation of the generative end, but it does not escape the error of treating the individual act of *coitus* as a self-subsistent entity, rather than as a single element in a complex relational pattern, the morality of which must be assessed as a whole. In the latter connection the following facts need consideration.

(1) The "proper two-fold end" (or the "proper ends") of *coitus* are impossible of fulfilment in every act, because generation and procreation (using these terms in the sense already defined) depend upon favourable biological conditions, and upon the existence of parental responsibility.

(2) Fulfilment of the relational end of *coitus* is possible independently of the attainment or the non-attainment of the other end.

It is arguable, then, that the morally good act of *coitus* is really that which forms part of a pattern of relational acts consistent with the "proper two-fold end" (or the "proper ends") of sexual intercourse in marriage. In the normal marriage, husband and wife will desire certain coital acts to be both relational and generative, and others to be only relational; in selecting against generation, are they to be morally restricted to periods of natural infertility, or may they extend such periods artificially by the use of contraceptive appliances —provided always that this is done in such a way that it does not render the general pattern of coital relationship inconsistent with the

141

"proper two-fold end" of *coitus* within marriage? The answer made to this question will depend upon two further considerations—the extent of human freedom, and the nature of the "given" structure of the coital act; and to these we shall return later.

VIII. Alternatively, it is arguable that moralists have over-simplified the problem of contraception by treating *coitus* as if it were simply one species of physical act—whence (partly) their preference for discussing this problem in terms rather of the act's end than of its "object".

On the contrary, it would seem that there are actually two species of *coitus*, or two kinds of coital act. These have sometimes been described as "relational" and "generative"—but the distinction is hardly accurate, since it suggests that the act is either relational or generative, whereas all *coitus* is necessarily in some sense relational. It is preferable to say that there are two species of *coitus*, or two kinds of coital act : (1) the "generative", performed under conditions which are biologically favourable to conception, and (2) the "non-generative", performed when conception is biologically impossible.

This abstract distinction takes no account of the agents' intention. By observing the biological processes of the human body, however, man can determine what conditions are favourable or unfavourable to conception; consequently he can decide, within the limits set by those conditions, whether any particular act shall (at any rate, in intention) be generative or non-generative. This capacity for selecting between the two kinds of coital act represents in itself an advance also in man's understanding of his nature. A further advance is marked by realization that non-generative *coitus* has a positive value of its own, as a relational act—that it is not merely a "safe" form of sexual indulgence.

Growing appreciation of the relational value of *coitus* has been accompanied by greater understanding of human biological processes, and of the means whereby these processes can be subjected to rational control. Not only has more accurate observation of the bodily functions made selection between generative and non-generative *coitus* easier, but contraception now enables man to decide more or less at will, by the employment of artificial methods, whether or not *coitus* shall be generative; and there is good ground for believing that scientific research will eventually place in his hands even simpler and more reliable means, such as preparations designed to produce temporary sterility. Even now, therefore, the question of selection hardly arises; rather, we have to ask whether it is morally permissible to render a particular act of *coitus* non-generative artificially by creating conditions which make conception impossible.

Many would hold that such a revision of the natural coital pattern, in the interests of the marital relationship, the family, and the community, is a rational development by means of which biological processes can be controlled and directed in order to serve personal and social ends. The distinction between generative and non-generative *coitus* still holds good, but both kinds of *coitus* derive a new and enhanced significance from the fact that each becomes a responsible act chosen with reference to a specific situation. This choice, however, must be justified as a legitimate exercise of human freedom, and as consistent with the intrinsic nature of coital acts.

IX. Discussion of the morality of contraception is often confused by the different senses in which the words "nature" and "natural" can be used. Dr Kirk draws attention to this when he asks what is meant by describing the contraceptive appliance as unnatural:

> Is "unnatural" the same as "artificial"; and if so, is all "artificial" interference with the processes of nature—all control of those processes by the methods of science—to be adjudged immoral? Or is it only this process [i.e., generation] which may not be so controlled or modified? And if so, why is "artificial" (i.e., scientific) control debarred from coming to the aid of natural control (i.e., complete abstinence) in this matter alone?[4]

Clearly it is incorrect to treat "unnatural" and "artificial" as synonymous, for human artifice may serve to assist nature; and it is not simply because contraception involves the use of artificial means that certain moralists regard it as unnatural. It is important, therefore, to clarify the customary terminology.

In the traditional usage of moral theology, "natural" means consonant with the true nature of a person or thing, as that nature has been given by God and is perceived by the exercise of an informed reason. That is natural to man which is consistent with human nature as designed by the Creator—and "nature", in this sense, cannot be controlled or manipulated; man can only either conform to his nature, or violate it. If, therefore, the structure of *coitus* as determined by biological and physiological factors is seen to be given to man as part of his "nature", then any interference with that structure (such as by contraceptive methods) will appear "unnatural"; but selection between generative and non-generative coital acts by the use of the "safe period" will be accepted as "natural".

On the other hand, to theologians or philosophers who think in other than traditional moral-theological terms, "nature" will

<hr/>

[4] *Conscience and its Problems*, 1933, p. 295.

143

it necessarily has metaphysical implications; but these implications are nullified by any interference with the act such as to destroy its "natural" character. In other words, the introduction of a contraceptive appliance has an ontological effect; it changes true *coitus* into a specious imitation from which the appointed relational benefits are withdrawn. Hence contraception is both morally wrong because it is contrary to human "nature", and powerless to secure the benefits at which it aims because it immediately converts the act of *coitus* into a transaction void of metaphysical significance, and therefore void of positive value.

Impressive though these arguments are, it is by no means easy to sustain them on other than *a priori* grounds. It is by no means certain that if human *coitus* has a "given" structure, that structure is disclosed or determined exclusively or even principally by physiological or biological factors. *Coitus* is only "natural", or consonant with man's true nature, when it exhibits all the characteristics of a responsible personal act expressive of a certain integral relationship between the man and woman concerned. But any attempt to define abstractly the empirical features which guarantee that *coitus* is "natural" must be regarded as misconceived and doomed to failure, for by its very "nature" *coitus* between human beings is not an act of such a kind that it can be so defined. It cannot be considered as "given" apart from the relational context within which it is "given". And it is arguable that it is fully consistent with the "nature" of human *coitus* as "given" that man, by the responsible exercise of his freedom, should modify certain of its "mechanical" details in order to increase its relational potentialities.

So, too, with the second argument. *Coitus* certainly has a metaphysical significance, but since this is derived from its personal character, it can never be nullified; this has been expressed in another way by the statement made earlier that *coitus* is always relational, even though its effect may be destructive. Likewise, it is evident that certain benefits are annexed to *coitus*—but it is impossible to define the precise empirical conditions which must be fulfilled in order to secure such benefits. Again, all that can be said is that the relational blessings conveyed by the act depend upon the quality of the personal relationship of the pair in question, who will receive from their intercourse proportionately to what they bring to it.

The difficulty about both arguments (that from the "natural" or "given" structure of *coitus*, and that from the conditions supposedly prerequisite in order to ensure the benefits of the act) is that they are so easily countered on empirical grounds—and this is deliberately stated as a difficulty in the way of accepting the arguments, rather

146

than a proof that they are wrong, since in this matter especially the empirical approach is apt to be regarded as suspect. There is abundant evidence to show that *coitus* can be both "natural" and relationally immoral (as when man and woman exploit each other), and that contraception appears to promote the highest personal ends of sexual union. These facts cannot be ignored or dismissed as insignificant; they suggest that the allegedly "natural" performance of the act cannot *per se* guarantee the benefits attributed to it, and that those benefits can follow in impressive measure from acts which are alleged to be morally "unnatural". It is pertinent, therefore, to ask whether "natural" *coitus* (in the traditional moral-theological sense) is not simply an arbitrary *a priori* concept to which there is no correspondence in reality.

Is there, then, no objective criterion by which the morality of physical sexual acts between man and woman can be assessed? Surely we may say that for human *coitus* to be "natural" it must above all have integrity as a responsible personal act—although (because of its unique and mysterious quality [see §§ III and VI]) it is manifestly impossible to define in advance the precise general conditions which ensure integrity, since many factors are involved which elude or defy definition. A valid conception of the "given" structure of *coitus*, therefore, must take fully into account the fact that personal and relational factors are "given" no less than the physiological and biological factors—and that the former must not be separated artificially from the latter.

XII. Thus, whether we consider the unique and mysterious character of human *coitus* (§§ III and VI), its relational significance (§§ III; IV, 2; V, 2), its proper ends (§§ IV, V, VI, and VII), its species (§ VIII), and its "nature" and "given" structure (§§ IX, X, and XI); or whether we consider the range of man's legitimate freedom consequent upon his paradoxical situation as a being at once involved in, and transcendent over the natural order (§§ X and XI); we reach the conclusion that there are very strong moral-theological grounds for regarding the responsible use of contraception by married persons as morally right.

Appendix

Dr Niebuhr's treatment of contraception in the context of his discussion of human freedom has already been mentioned. It may be useful, as an Appendix to these notes, to summarize the teaching of another eminent modern theologian, Dr Karl Barth, who deals with family limitation in *Die Kirchliche Dogmatik*.[7] His argument is

7 III, pp. 300-11.

147

responsible parenthood in general demands some family limitation. Again, it may happen, as in India, Japan, and the West Indies, that economic circumstances compel births to be severely restricted. In such circumstances, the use of contraceptives enables planning to occur without a man and wife having to exclude altogether some realization of the one-flesh unity which, as we have seen, is a distinctive feature of Christian marriage.

When family limitation is a grave necessity, contraception may provide the only possible means by which there can be some realization of that one-flesh unity without which marriage can become no more than an external bond—or at best a companionship of friends; at worst, a progressive isolation of man and wife.

(1)   Against this view, and while agreeing on the importance of the unitary aspect of marriage, it would be argued that the use of contraceptives mars the act and detracts from the one-flesh unity. Now this may be an empirical assertion. In this case we can agree that something of the spontaneous unity is lost by the use of contraceptives, however much certain contraceptives may in this respect be less unsatisfactory than others. At the same time, three observations must be made :

(i) That all "safe period" calculations likewise mar and tamper with the act. Indeed, the only occasion when an act could not be said to be "tampered with" or to be "marred" would be when it was utterly spontaneous. But then, of course, it might have other characteristics not at all morally praiseworthy.

(ii) Further, is there ever *any* intercourse which is *not* as *a matter of empirical fact* "defective" and "marred" in some way? Is there ever any complete and perfect self-giving? Again is sexual intercourse to be considered in any case as an act *complete in itself*? Supposing that children are likely to originate from the act and that such children are then condemned to malnutrition, famine, and so on, the situation is not merely the simple one of choosing the one symbol which is better than another. The question now becomes, which life—one with contraceptives, the other without, and all those in the setting of famine and malnutrition—which life is best offered to the glory of God? In short, in such a case the problem is not one of contraceptives as such, but of the procreation of children in a certain economic situation. It might be said that here we have background considerations somewhat comparable with St Paul's presupposition, and it is plainly a situation which we could answer in St Paul's way. The difference is, however, that the contemporary presupposition does not anticipate direct intervention of God. What it emphasizes is that in defending contraception, we ought positively

150

at the same time to be working out a theology of rapid social change and betterment. It is in the working out of such a theology that the moralist must "enter into the genuine anguish of mind" which besets so many of his contemporaries. Meanwhile, the leading question will always be : Is it better to have no intercourse at any time so as to avoid children altogether, or, on occasion, to use contraceptives? Which of these makes the better offering to the glory of God?

(iii) Finally, let it be noted that in no circumstances can sexual intercourse with contraceptives be rightly called an act of "self-love". As an empirical description this plainly falls.

If the argument that contraceptives mar the act and make it defective is, however, an *a priori* assertion, it would follow from the claim that *coitus* without contraceptives completely pictures and reproduces an element in Christian doctrine. Such a supposition surely brings with it the most profound epistemological difficulties; nor in any case need we take such a view of the structure of Christian doctrine in itself. Nor can it be seriously supposed that there are any "biological laws" which somehow picture irrevocably God's will, unless "biological laws" are being used in a sense which makes them incapable of any empirical modification, in which case the assertion might be true without being particularly informative. Otherwise it sponsors a view of the laws of nature that could hardly at this time be substantiated and a view that carries with it a metaphysical picture which is hardly an essential part of the Christian tradition.

(2) The second argument is based on the premiss that the use contraceptives is "unnatural" or "against nature", and that its being so makes it necessarily wrong.[8]

Once again, this assertion could either be metaphysical or empirical. If it is metaphysical it would be a claim that the use of contraceptives conflicts with "natural law" or with a "given" metaphysical pattern. But we should then have to ask the grounds on which such claims are made, and we can anticipate great problems arising both in regard to the concept of natural law and in the epistemology which lies behind the metaphysical claim. If, however, the claim is empirical, it amounts to very little. To say that the use of contraceptives interferes with what "nature" would do if left alone is no answer to the question, unless we identify God with the physical order after the manner of those who see more of God in earthquakes than in the devoted labours of those who toil to rescue their victims. But for the Christian the physical world, as it is given to us, is the raw material out of which by God's grace he is to fashion a world

[8] The following paragraphs are closely based on a discussion of contraception in Dr L. Hodgson's book, *Eugenics* (1933), in the Standpoint series, edited by the late Dr K. E. Kirk.

more in accordance with God's will than it is when he finds it. The only sense in which the "unnatural" is wrong is that according to which the "natural" is the perfection of creation towards which we aspire, and the knowledge whereby we are enabled to control the actual and mould it after the image of the ideal comes to us by the grace of God working through the devotion of scientific investigators. If it enables us to deflect the course of gametes into channels through which they will contribute to the making of a better civilization than would result from their being left alone, it is showing us the way to use actual "nature" for the creation of the ideally "natural". To confuse the two senses of "natural" is nothing but confusion of thought, and the resulting position belongs to pantheism, not to Christian theism. To prove that contraception is wrong because "unnatural", it would be necessary to show that it is inimical to the best development of human life. This is a question we shall have to face in section 5, below.

(3) The third argument is based on an appeal to the sacredness of life. Here it is important to distinguish between Christian and non-Christian views of life, for their are some kinds of reverence for life which are distinctly not Christian, e.g. the reverence for life which underlies the child-marriage of India and also favours the unchecked spread of vermin. The same non-Christian attitude to life can be seen in the view that the birth of children is somehow an inexorable working out of a "natural force" within us : as well as in the view that children like chattels are the expression of a parent's property and material wealth, and so the more, the better. Such attitudes to children can be found to-day in, e.g., the West Indies.

For the Christian, however, life is not God but God's. Our duty is to ask what God wills it to become, and to reverence physical life as the raw material of spiritual life. Now life, as we have seen, exists in countless living creatures, and its existence is maintained by the processes of reproduction in their many forms. The whole system culminates in mankind, where there appear creatures capable of development *as individuals* into citizens of Heaven. According to the Christian view of the world, its purpose is to produce human beings and train them for their eternal life of communion with God.

Now we see the full importance of the difference of status between gametes and zygotes. If it is true that the *individual* human life begins with the formation of the zygote, then it follows that reverence for the sacredness of life requires of us that we should so control the behaviour of gametes as to make of them the best zygotes that we know how to. If we can enlist in this endeavour the discoveries of medical science, and the ingenuities of modern manufacturing methods, this will not necessarily involve any failure in reverence. On the contrary, the refusal to make use of them might well be held to argue irreverence both towards the Spirit of God in his guidance of doctors and machine-makers, and towards the true sacredness of life. Any other view seems to imply that superstitious reverence for life which reveres it not as the instrument of God's creative purpose, but as itself, in all its manifestations, God.

(4) The fourth argument is an appeal to authority. It is stated, and stated truly, that to many saintly people the thought of contraception is so repugnant as to argue a radical incompatibility between those practices and the development of holiness of character. "When in doubt on such matters," it has been said, "I think it is wisest to trust to the instincts of the holiest men and women I know, and they are against them."

This argument deserves serious attention. If the testimony of those most advanced in that life is against any practice, that is a very weighty argument against its morality.

But, in the case before us, this testimony is far from being unanimous enough to provide a simple solution of our problem. One knows other Christians, not less advanced in holiness (so far as one can judge in these matters), who have no such "instincts". How is one to judge between them? Only if there are independent arguments which convince us in favour of the one or the other.

(5) The fifth argument we need to consider would stress the virtues of self-control and would argue that the use of contraceptives is likely to weaken moral fibre. Now, without doubt, an invaluable contribution has been made to moral progress by the necessity to wrestle for the mastery of sexual desire. Further, we can be suspicious of any popular demand for contraceptives in an age when moral calibre is on the decline.

At the same time is must be pointed out that even with the use of contraceptives, marriage quite obviously leaves much room for the exercise and learning of self-control. In every marriage there are occasions when one partner desires intercourse and the other does not. Contraceptives are no use here; self-control is the only alternative to cruelty. We thus return to our original point that contraceptives are not to be seen as substitutes for self-control where self-control is called for, but as instruments to make possible a joint life of the quality which a Christian marriage demands.

(6) Finally, the case of death seems not without its parallels. Death might be said to have a Christian significance; yet we do not hesitate to bring "human tamperings" to bear on it. The empirical approach would see this situation as in principle parallel to the question of birth control. For in the use of contraceptives we begin to be

"scientific" about the most precious and responsible of all activities, namely procreation, as we have for years been "scientific" about death.

Admittedly, the greater our lordship over nature, the stronger our moral calibre needs to be, and the greater we need to realize our dependence on God. It is not without significance that the greatest moral problems of our age arise from scientific developments in relation to birth and death : contraception on the one hand; atomic warfare on the other.

Along with any justification of the use of contraceptives then, there needs to go an emphatic effort to increase a sense of moral responsibility generally. But we conclude that there are no satisfactory arguments against the position set out at the start which claims that a Christian marriage may justifiably include the use of contraceptives.

3. The Christian Attitude to Material Development

A. In this matter it is important to do justice to the full Christian tradition, not least because it incorporates two different if only superficially incompatible themes.

(1) The importance of the material world is implicit in any doctrine of the Incarnation. It was human flesh that our Lord took upon himself and which he glorified. It was the Gnostic and Manichaean heresies which belittled the significance of the material world and even denied its "reality". Moreover the Christian belief is that man has been given a certain dominion over God's creatures. It is proper to him to learn to realize the potentialities of the material world; and as a rule human persons need to possess and administer at least some material things in order to develop fully the capacities of human nature.

(2) Along with this, however, goes an emphasis on the supremacy of the eternal, so that the material world gains all the significance it has in virtue of being taken into the creative and redemptive purposes of God. Apart from God, the world must be viewed as no more than a Cosmos (Κόσμος). "The world" in this sense is something apart from God, supposedly self-sufficient, and in this way misdirected in its character. Cf. John 1. 10; 1 John 2. 15; James 4. 4; 2 Peter 2. 20.

Sometimes material prosperity, sometimes sheer poverty, can blind people to the significance of the eternal. Both can prevent us from seeing "the world" in relation to the purpose of God.

B. With that background we can now take up one or two particular questions.

(1) What of the "holy poor"? Has the Christian never to pursue a better standard of living?

154

Let it be said at once that for some people, and in certain ages, asceticism will be a Christian duty. For this may be the only way in which the supremacy of the eternal can be emphasized. Now it is true that in our own age, when material resources are being so greatly developed, when there is, as never before, the chance of a high standard of living for humanity generally, the importance of the eternal calls for emphasis. It can and has been only too easily asserted that progress is entirely to be measured by a "high and rising standard of living" (Paley report). But the importance, nay supremacy, of the eternal can be emphasized not by denouncing material development but by showing how these increased resources can be made part of a Christian offering.

In this matter it is relevant to remember that many in Europe think of North America as materialistic because of its higher standard of living, and of themselves by contrast—and since they are conscious of economic difficulties—as avoiding a materialistic emphasis; but spiritual insight does not necessarily increase with economic difficulties. Europeans need to remember that they appear to Africa and the East as the Americans do to them.

Do we accept the current division of wealth between countries and continents as part of the divine purpose? Plainly not. Material development will therefore be welcomed and made part of a Christian offering in so far as at every point there is an endeavour to share it on a world scale.[9] The Christian who fixes on material welfare alone will surely be self-condemned—"he who would save his life shall lose it". But the Christian who sees material welfare as something which in his own life might be made part of a Christian offering ("for my sake and the Gospel's") will be fulfilling a Christian duty. Nor must the Christian despise pleasure or see it as in essential conflict with virtue. Pleasure need not be excluded from the Good Life.

(2) This brings us close to the next question : Can we resolve the tension in Christian morality between mortification and self-realization?

Without doubt every Christian is called to mortification. But material development does not exclude mortification : it simply offers different possibilities of exercising the same virtue. No matter how far material development extends, the Christian welcomes it not for its own sake, and not only for the material comfort and pleasure it may bring to him, but as something which brings with it many opportunities for moral decision as well. These we see at all times of rapid social change. In short, welcoming a material development

[9] See above, Report, pp. 9-11, and Appendix 1, pp. 53f.

which we must not as such denounce, let us see it as creative of more occasions of moral decision,[10] and of more occasions when we may recognize our own relative powerlessness. In this way it can then all the more deepen our vision of what abides, and our awareness of that power not our own, which is the heart of the Christian gospel.

(3) In so far as the Christian welcomes material development, he will also welcome the work of all those who search out, develop, and use the gifts of God to meet human needs—and scientists, economists, social scientists, and so on among them. But he will see all the greater need for a constant interchange between those who are concerned with the creation of material welfare, and the clergy and others who are—or should be—guardians of man's spiritual life. For there will be times when a situation seen as a basis for scientific and economic enquiry brings also with it moral demands and the discernment of obligations which, together with man's response to them, are essentially religious activities. This is not to say of course that the more "religious" a man is the more "moral" he will also be. So it is that statistics, which are often given nowadays to show that there are as many believers as unbelievers annually convicted in the courts, do not show anything more than that Christians need to be more faithful stewards of their manifold gifts of grace. They do not show that Christian faith has little moral significance; they show all the greater need for matching material development with increased faith and conviction.

Material development is not to be denounced but seen as a challenge which needs to be made part of a Christian offering. To do this will need co-operative thought and action on the part of many Christians united in an adventure of faith and content to follow where that faith may lead.

(4) In particular, at a time when the most staggering differences of wealth are no longer between persons and persons, but between nations and nations, problems raised by material development are problems which for a Christian solution will need a far greater emphasis on the concept of the Church Universal. Contrariwise, as these problems are solved, the difficulties which are overcome and the sacrifices which are made will in their own way lead us to an increased awareness of the significance of the world-wide Church.

Material development, therefore,

(i) needs to be matched by an increasing spiritual insight such as the Christian faith can give; and we need not suppose that there are any absolute priorities[11] as between economic development and the

10 See previous note.

11 In this we would agree with the Government of India Planning Commission, *Second Five Year Plan*, p. 22. Quoted above, page 54.

development of social welfare services, for both these developments would for the Christian be tested with regard to the "spiritual development" of which each can and ought to be a part.

(ii) has to be welcomed not only for the new material comforts and pleasures it brings but for the new moral decision it provokes;

(iii) suggests an increasing co-operation between those concerned with its production; and

(iv) at the present time brings problems that for their solution will need a much greater awareness of a concern for the Church Universal.

4. RELIGION AS A SOCIAL BOND

It is a commonplace to say that there are countless definitions of religion. But among all those definitions two broad and fundamental themes may be discerned.

(a) The religious man is one who appeals to certain *situations*, to situations which are "what's seen" and more; and the Christian in particular appeals to situations in which he discerns that power of God which is the Gospel.

(b) But besides "religion" relating to certain situations as these, it is also plainly expressed in *institutions, doctrine, and so on.* In other words, with every religion goes some kind of established culture. Christopher Dawson in *Religion and the Rise of Western Culture* notices that for something like three centuries there was once a spiritual tide steadily making for unity. This found, he would say, a climax in the philosophical systems of the thirteenth century, what Gilson has called the great "cathedrals of ideas". Here there seemed to be the possibility of a magnificently planned culture of a religious kind. But what happened? Dawson says : "On the contrary, it inaugurated a period of intellectual criticism and cultural change which is of the utmost importance for the history of Western culture, but proved fatal to the synthesis of religion and culture that seemed to have been achieved in the previous centuries."[12] Later he remarks : "It is as though the spiritual tide which had been steadily making for unity for three centuries had suddenly turned, so that everywhere in every aspect of life the forces that made for division and dissolution were predominant."[13] What was the mistake? The great mistake was to suppose that a unitary culture could be translated into an unambiguous intellectual pattern. The mistake was to suppose that a religious situation could be translated without

[12] Op. cit., p. 238.
[13] Ibid., p. 239.

157

reduction into politico-scientific terms, into a metaphysics which was neither more nor less than a super-science. The medieval mistake was to fail to distinguish between that fellowship and unity which a religion can give to its believers, and the unity which a political system or a strong administration can create between people.

So it is that the Christian religion will always supply to the culture of a people two influences which are to react permanently on each other :

(a) the influence of a fixed tradition, which will look for uniformity, for firm plans and settled administration, and

(b) a drive for prophetic novelty.

Religion, therefore, will on the one hand be creative of a unity which a political system can neither copy nor do justice to; it will also supply prophetic insight which leads to permanent dissatisfaction with things as they are. It will always sponsor institutions and doctrines that can give stability to society; it will also provide the source of inspiration to ensure that the society which is stable is also flexible and adaptable.

Practical Corollaries.

(1) When a society is disintegrating under rapid social change, religion can be relevant in three ways.

(a) It will hesitate to sponsor any particular political administrative pattern, but, if anything, will encourage diversity; no pattern of society will be sponsored for its own sake.

(b) In its worship it will seek to provide a unifying bond which can be found nowhere else; nor will this fellowship, once known in worship, be restricted to the worshipping community in the narrow sense. It will more and more leaven the whole society.

(c) It will also teach that Christian contentment is no synonym for utter placidity and inactivity : it is one which comes from bringing to suffering and change the power of the gospel.

It has been pointed out that on the face of it science to-day often provides a harmony and coherence where religion fails. Further, the bonds by which science links both its workers and beneficiaries seem so much the more evident and real than the intangible and shadowy bonds which religion (it might be said) at best would supply. But we have to recognize that developments in science itself are making us all the more aware that scientific procedures and techniques will never supply us with bonds that satisfy the whole man. If scientific development over the last two decades has shown us anything, it is, as the scientists themselves would be first to recognize, that scientific method and techniques alone are not adequate for any fellowship which embodies the whole man. This is not to deny the need and importance of scientific and technological developments : they can, in principle, be welcomed and encouraged. The Christian must denounce none of them, nor the material development they bring, but must emphasize what *more* is needed.

(2) When the Christian faith meets an ancient non-Christian civilization, there are, besides these earlier considerations, some important points. To what extent must it be, in relation to this ancient civilization, nothing but a disintegrating force?

The extent to which it can be more depends in large measure on our theological views as to the relation between natural and revealed religion. Distinctive and unique though Christianity be, we need not deny all significance to other religions nor need we condemn *in toto* the institutional, doctrinal, cultural pattern to which they have given rise. Further, the possibility of regarding missionary work as with, rather than for, non-Christian people can come from recognizing that God's grace is given in some measure to all—even the "heathen" have some kind of moral insight (Rom. 1 and 2).

(3) Here is raised again a practical point which we have made elsewhere. Without doubt much of the disintegration of society has come from the intensive development of different intellectual disciplines. How can we recapture the unity that academic development seems increasingly to deny? For the first time for centuries we are beginning to seek a unity whose need has only been discerned when the different disciplines of knowledge have proved so singularly successful in developing that knowledge, as to bring with them disintegration as the price which we have paid for success. Further, on all sides there is a growing awareness of the inadequacy of these departmental languages to deal with the total situation in which man finds himself; besides this, there has been now, at least in the West, for almost a century, a growing interest in personality. The conclusion is that the unity of which our age stands in need is likely to be recaptured in that personal bond which is basically religious, and which will (we may hope) be created when men of like disposition, though working in different fields, come to work together with their different disciplines on a common problem. So there arises the suggestion that to meet increasingly complex social problems, whether at home or abroad, we need to work out increasing co-operation between the clergy, economists, and social workers of all kinds. This same practical conclusion is being suggested from all kinds of directions. It is also raised, for example, as a need between doctors and clergy. It is further raised by the need of an entirely fresh approach to women's work in the church.

This kind of background would also suggest the great value of permanent Commissions sitting between successive Lambeth Conferences, since the bearing of the Christian faith on practical behaviour is something which can be worked out only as the result of co-operative study between experts. Certainly it would seem in our own time to be a theological, philosophical, and practical necessity, and we should like to recommend that the Bishops give earnest thought to the practicability of providing opportunities for such discussion in which churchmen would join with others, not all of whom would necessarily profess the Christian faith. Whether within this formal framework or not, only in this way in the present complex situation will religion succeed in supplying a cohesive bond.

(4) Further, when with rapid social change there are emerging new patterns of community, there is an urgent need to ask whether the older, parochial patterns of the Christian Ministry will without modification be suited to the new types of community. If, for example, there are communities which are rather functional unities than geographical units, do they not require that the pattern of ministry be conceived as in part functional? At any rate, if the Christian faith is to preserve its prophetic character, it will not suppose that there is anything fixed or unalterable about the parochial system as it occurs to-day. To suppose that would be to do an injustice to one of the two themes which, as we have urged at the start, belong basically to religion.

9. AN ESSAY IN CRUSOE ECONOMICS

THE ECONOMICS OF OVER-POPULATION

(Contributed)

The essential features of a complex economic question can often be identified by the use of a simple image—the device known as Crusoe economics.

Let us consider two neighbouring islands, each of which is inhabited by a single family. Let us suppose that both families maintain themselves by the use of one single commodity, namely, coconuts, which grow on both islands, and that no other resources are known about.

Now suppose that one of the families, A, possesses a technical advantage not shared by family B. Family A has invented ladders, made of coconut fibre, by the use of which the members of the family are able to collect coconuts far more easily than by shinning up the palm trees.

Finally, let us suppose that Mrs B., the mother of family B, changes her procreative conduct by producing twin babies, and continues thereafter to produce pairs of twins for an indefinite period ahead.

Until Mrs B. has produced her first pair of twins, the economic conditions of islands A and B may be summed up as "developed" and "underdeveloped" respectively. When the twins arrive, however, the population of island B will manifest the feature known as "the pressure of population upon resources", or, in short, over-population. For, until the twins have grown to a size at which they are able to climb the palm trees in search of nuts, the other members of the family must either work harder to maintain the twins or, if they work no harder than before, consume less of their products per head, in order to feed the twins.

Now let us suppose that the members of family A, having leisure, by taking thought, discover the values of Christian ethics. These values lead them to believe that it is their duty to do whatever may be possible to assist family B to escape from the dilemma of over-population.

It is clear that, so long as Mrs B continues to produce twins, there must be a tendency for the standerd of living of her family to decline unless, sooner or later, contraception, infanticide, abortion, sexual

161

abstention, or some other practice can be introduced to reduce the birthrate at least to the level which it had been before Mrs B's procreative habits changed. Nevertheless, whether Mrs B continues to produce twins or not, family A, being now Christian, is determined to assist family B in some way or other.

There are, of course, many ways by which family B can be assisted by family A, but the following are perhaps the most obvious and important.

(i) A member of family A may visit family B and teach the people there how to make ladders. This is technical assistance.

(ii) Family A may invite a member of family B to come over to island A and join the labour force there. One of the twins may be invited or one of the adults. This is migration.

(iii) Family A may lend to family B a few ladders, receiving by way of interest part of the extra produce which will accrue from the use of these capital resources, which are "invested" in island B. This is capital investment.

(iv) Family A may make an interest-free grant of equipment to family B, with or without conditions attached. This is economic assistance.

The essential economic features of all the various methods by which island A may help family B are the following :

(i) Family A must, either temporarily or permanently, go without something which it hands over to family B.

(ii) There must be freedom of movement, either of goods or of people, or of both, between the two islands.

It is important to note that each of these conditions may prevail in any degree and that neither is of an absolute character. With regard to the first, namely, the necessity for family A to make some sacrifice if it is to help family B, the sacrifice may be very large or very small. Likewise, the freedom of movement of people or goods between the two islands may be great or small. It is clear, however, that some degree of sacrifice and some degree of mobility are necessary if the Christian motives of family A are to be achieved.

By starting with this simple abstract illustration, we may introduce, one after another, assumptions to show how each or both of the necessary conditions in which family A may help family B may be limited. The usefulness of the illustration is enhanced if such assumptions correspond, in principle, with conditions in the real world. The following examples may be useful :

(i) Suppose that there are two "developed" islands, A and A.1, instead of one only, and that each of them lives in fear of an attack

162

from the other. Although the people of A and A.1 may be very anxious to help island B, they may be so afraid of each other that they feel it necessary to devote a very large part of their labour forces —say ten per cent—to accumulating coconuts which may be used as ammunition for throwing at the enemy, in case of need. In such circumstances the amount of assistance which may be given to island B will be greatly restricted. Moreover, if A does more than A.1 to help island B, it may feel itself to be relatively weak when it comes to preparing to meet a warlike threat from A.1.

(ii) Let us suppose that the people of family A consist of poor and rich members. In such circumstances the opinion that "charity begins at home", and that it is the duty of family A to look after its own needy members before doing anything to help family B, may be strong.

(iii) Let us suppose that the skins of family A are green and those of family B violet. The members of both families may attach importance to the preservation of their own skin colour and object strongly to any miscegenation between members of the two "races". This may severely restrict the mobility of persons between the two islands.

(iv) Let us suppose that, although the two islands are "neighbours", they are separated by a fast moving ocean current which makes the journey between them very hazardous. This also will restrict mobility.

(v) Although the majority of members of family A may be very anxious to help family B, and the members of family B would welcome such help, it may be very difficult to find members of either family who are actually willing to change their way of life, especially by paying a protracted visit to the other island.

What lessons are to be learnt from the analogy of the islands by Christians in the modern world? Surely the answer is simple. It is the duty of Christians (a) to support policies which involve sacrifices by the developed countries on behalf of the undeveloped ones, and (b) to advocate policies designed to increase the mobility of capital and labour between the developed and the underdeveloped parts of the world.

The existence of "pressure of population on resources" in many parts of the world to-day can be explained, perhaps wholly, as the consequences of political and physical restrictions on the mobility of capital and labour in the past and of the selfishness of the developed countries, a selfishness due mainly to the political divisions between the various parts of the "developed" world and between social classes in each "developed" country.

Appendix 2

THE FAMILY IN THE UNITED STATES

CONTENTS

1. Changed Function of the Home

Until the twentieth century the home was an economic production unit in which the members of the family co-operated to produce the necessities of living—food, clothing, heat, even some implements and toys. As industrialization and distribution have grown, economic production has shifted from the home so that the majority of families now purchase most of these necessities from outside. This is as true of families in rural areas as it is of those in urban areas. It has changed the character of the home and even of the family. Large amounts of physical space are no longer necessary, and dwelling units have become smaller. Children are not now necessary as helpers in production, and until recently the numbers of children per family were dwindling. Grandparents and unmarried relatives, no longer helpful auxiliary workers and now able to purchase their own essential commodities, are not often found living with the family unit. Even the members of the family itself spend less time in the home. Fathers spend a major portion of the waking day at a job earning the money to purchase what they formerly produced. Mothers often work for salaries, but more often use the time released by mechanical household helps and processed food to shop, visit friends, or give their services to Church or community. Children spend increasingly more time in school, beginning at an earlier age, and stopping at a later age, and a considerable portion of their play is outside the home.

In spite of the changed character of the home, there is little or no evidence that it is less basic to American life now than formerly. As its production function has disappeared, it has continued to hold its more basic function of providing a centre of relationship for the man and wife, and a centre of growth, development, and training for the children.

2. Social and Economic Trends affecting the Family

Industrialization and Automation

A rapid rate of industrialization is nothing new in the United States. Beginning with the second world war, however, and accelerating constantly, there has been development of ever larger production units, usually in new areas, employing more workers in spite of the increasing proportion of work done by machines rather than men. The steady growth of the population itself multiplies the results of industrialization. It may be that changes in the economic cycle of the world situation will slow down this development, but it is affecting the whole of American society so drastically that its results are a basic part of any study of the American family.

The development of larger production units dependent upon complex machines has altered employment. Frequently hundreds and even thousands of persons are employed in plants covering acres of land. The space and labour requirements of large industrial units have led to decentralization and the spread of such plants into the South and the Far West. The need for workers and the nature of the work have brought hundreds of thousands of women into the labour market. New techniques of management have multiplied many times the amount of clerical or paper-work involved. The necessity for skilled personnel to design, service, and operate the elaborate machinery has created a demand for technical education as well as more general education. At the same time, the number of routine machine-tending jobs has increased, and service occupations are growing even faster than industrial occupations.

The acceleration of industrialization has brought about great improvements in material living for the majority of the population. Jobs are plentiful, salaries are high, and products, from food to television sets, to automobiles, are easily available. The presence of two or more incomes within many family units improves even more the standard of living. It is an economy of abundance. There is, furthermore, a widespread psychology of abundance. The prevailing goals for "success in life" place high priority on material possessions.

Arising largely from industrialization, but also from philosophies of government and education, there has been an almost complete emancipation of women—economically, socially, and politically. The education of women through the secondary school level is now approximately at the same rate as that for men. The era when women voted "as their husbands told them" is past. There are few cultural groups remaining where the social status of women is inferior. Although their salary rates are not equal to those of men for the same jobs, women are employed in almost every occupation. Indeed, the present rate of industrialization would not have been possible had the emancipation, and thus the employment, of women not occurred.

Urbanization and Suburbanization

Acceleration of industrialization has heightened the trend toward the urbanization of the growing population and increased its

168

mobility. The United States Census Bureau reports that the rate of growth for metropolitan areas is now four times as great as that for non-metropolitan areas, and this becomes more important in view of the rapid growth of the total population. Further, the average family moves eight times during its existence, and each year one family in every five moves across county lines.

Concomitant with urbanization has been a trend toward suburbanization. It is an obvious result of the increased pressure of population in the cities, but it is also encouraged by higher incomes, improved transportation, and the decentralization of industry. Commutation from suburbs to the central city by train, bus, or automobile is now possible for distances up to one hundred miles. Suburban areas are developing as stratified communities housing homogeneous income groups so that they become symbols of the social status of their residents.

The metropolitan area of to-day and to-morrow is a confusing and demanding complex of central city and clusters of suburbs, with residential, industrial, and commercial units in each, interwoven by train and bus systems and great superhighways, all interdependent for their very existence. The typical pattern of the metropolitan area is that of a central city housing hotels, business headquarters (and increasingly some luxury apartment units); this central area is ringed by blighted areas with deteriorated housing and industrial sites (dotted by new, large, public housing projects for low income groups); these, in turn, are surrounded by older residential areas, deteriorating and often transitional between middle and low income families; beyond, extending for dozens of miles, following transportation arteries, are the new suburbs.

The size and complexity and mass living of metropolitan areas have fostered standardization. Familiar now is the suburban housing development in which houses are all so similar that even the owners have difficulty in recognizing their own units. Urban apartment developments need complex systems of numbers for identification. Powerful nation-wide advertising has further standardized the appetites and households of most Americans. Already mentioned is the establishment of a value system which almost universally rates achievement by the possession of these standardized material assets. Such conformity not only tends to stifle individuality—and often the individual—but also builds up great power structures in which the leaders are able to dictate the patterns of living for masses of the people. Commercial, financial, and industrial organizations have become power centres affecting the whole society.

Combined with easy transportation is the phenomenal growth in easy communication. The mass media of the press, radio, and television have hastened the trends towards urbanization and conformity. It is not only those who live in cities who are urbanized—hardly a farm or village in the country is so remote as to have avoided the effects of what has become an urban culture with its standardization of material living and social values and goals.

Although urbanization has completely changed the ratio of city people to country people, there are still over 54 million persons in the United States living in rural communities (under 2,500 population). The fact that the development of the culture is away from rural areas has affected the life of this large minority. Standardization has changed living patterns. Depletion of population and easy transportation have lessened community consciousness and services. Local schools have been replaced by regional schools. Resident clergymen have been replaced by clergymen covering several towns, often at great distances from each other. Thus urbanization has affected the total population, whether they live in cities or not.

Internationalization

The changing status of the United States in international affairs has also had far-reaching effects. Not only has increasing international interdependence hastened industrialization, but it has also changed the whole prospect for the future of the individual. The necessity of military service, the danger of attack with atomic weapons, the emphasis on defence production, the threat of economic inflation or depression, and world conflicts of political ideologies have created insecurity in society and in individual citizens. Mass communication gives to everyone knowledge of day-to-day events throughout the world. Willingly or unwillingly, actively or passively, most citizens of the United States know that they are citizens of the world and are involved in what happens in far countries.

3. Emerging Family Patterns

The Mobile Family

The industrial shift which has removed economic production from the home has also removed the ties which bound a family's home to a particular house, a special piece of ground, a familiar and close-bound community. Since livelihood is dependent upon jobs, the home of the family must be where jobs are. It is no longer rooted in the soil or in the comfortable established social patterns of a town where many of the inhabitants are distant cousins and the rest at least share anecdotes of the past. Families must be highly mobile, as is the economy. Their possessions must be limited to what can be moved from apartment to apartment with some ease. Their ties with other families must be tenuous enough to be broken without disrupting their own lives. Because they have cut their familial and cultural roots, they are dependent upon more superficial and less personal associations in whatever community happens to be theirs at the moment. They are also more dependent upon the members of their immediate family unit.

It is one of the paradoxes of our time that urban culture has brought so many people to live so closely together that they are alone and isolated in the midst of multitudes. Wherever city people go, there are crowds—to work, to school, to shop, to the movies, to the beaches or the lakes, or even to their homes—yet in the crowds there is seldom a person whom they know by name or who knows them by name. Identity and the individual personality are threatened by mass living and the lack of familial roots. Even the tenuous ties acquired in the factory or school or apartment house can be quickly lost by yet another move to a "better" apartment, or a new city, or even a new state.

Security and Conformity

The modern American family, in spite of its mobility, has more material security than its predecessors. The standardization which threatens its individuality at the same time provides a pattern of living into which it can fall comfortably in each new community. Its improved standard of living, while subject to the hazards of economic fluctuations, has a bulwark of publicly sponsored insurance against crippling, unemployment and death, as well as both public and industry-sponsored provisions for retirement income. The mass employment of women has led to the prevalence of "two-salary families" where the husband's income is supplemented by a smaller income from the full or part-time work of the wife. The higher level of education is gradually offering the security of steadier employment. The reliance of the American family upon security has become so widespread that there is resultant loss of individual initiative and the will to pioneer.

Conformity to the dominant cultural patterns of American life is almost universal. The United States has been called a melting pot because of the many cultures and ethnic groups represented in its population. This image, often criticized because it implies the loss of identity on the part of diverse cultural groups, becomes more and more apt as differences disappear in conformity. This conformity in itself is felt to be a kind of security against failure.

171

encouraged through more participation in planning and activities.

There is some tendency upon the part of American families to be self-centred and concerned with their own happiness and welfare to the exclusion of the welfare of their communities and the world. The nightly absorption of many families in television entertainment is offered as proof of this. Television has greatly affected the daily habits of families, but has had both positive and negative values. It has drawn families together for longer periods each day, but has also diminished the interplay of the members upon each other. It absorbs time which may have been given to reading or other occupations, but it is increasingly offering programmes which are instructive in human relations and general fields of knowledge. There is no question that widespread television has reinforced the trend toward standardization, but it has also broadened the horizons of millions of Americans. Eventually it may help in counteracting the present tendency of the American family to be self-centred.

A-typical Groups of Families

To set forth the facts about the American family invites the obvious deduction that almost no family fits the pattern in every detail. Yet particularly in the United States to-day, because of standardization and conformity, there is a clearly recognizable majority of families which can be described as fitting the norm. There are two groups which are a-typical—those with less and those with more than the advantages possessed by the preponderant middle classes.

In spite of the economy of abundance, there are large numbers of Americans with very low incomes. In 1955, 22 million multiple or single person family units had incomes under $4,000 (currently estimated as the minimum adequate income); of these, 8 million earned under $2,000. A high proportion of these were families subsisting on farming. Others fall into groups with occupations now outmoded. Many come from the minorities varying from the norm in racial or religious background. Some have low education or limited mentality. Some are physically handicapped or of advanced age. Some are new-comers from Puerto Rico, Mexico, or elsewhere, possessing language and educational handicaps.

Overlapping with a-typical groups with low income are those with low social status. Possessing many of the same handicaps—race, creed, physical or mental difference—families of low social status frequently face discrimination in housing, education, and personal relationships which deeply affect their family life.

Families with abnormally high incomes or social prestige form a very small proportion of the population of the United States but

174

exert great pressure on the culture and its adaptations. Because of their positions of leadership in industry or commerce, as well as their relatively unlimited resources, they are free to be exceptions to the prevailing patterns of family living which they help to set.

4. CURRENT PROBLEMS IN AMERICAN FAMILY LIFE

Communities in Transition

Changes in industry have brought serious problems to many American communities and the families within them. Hardest hit are the towns and cities which, having owed their existence to factories for generations, are now losing those industries to other areas of the country where land and labour are cheaper and more abundant. Examples of these depleted communities can be found throughout New England, in Detroit, and elsewhere. Younger families usually shift with industry, but many others either choose or are forced by circumstances to remain and cope with unemployment and its results.

Also suffering from changes in industry are communities existing on supplanted products such as anthracite coal and some textiles. Families and communities basing their livelihood on dwindling production and consumption of these products face lowered income and the necessity of finding other sources of income.

Economically sounder but just as disrupted are those communities which suddenly find themselves housing vast new industrial units and unprepared for the needs of the swelling population. The dearth of facilities in newly industrialized areas has given rise to such phenomena as caravan camps, barracks living, and mobile stores, schools, and even churches. All families in such communities suffer, the older residents as well as the new strange families.

Agricultural communities are experiencing a new kind of influx of workers, that of imported or seasonal labour. Gangs of workers, sometimes in families but often the men alone, are brought in from Puerto Rico, Mexico, or elsewhere to harvest a crop or work on a construction project, and are then sent elsewhere. Such a labour force is seldom integrated into the community or has any semblance of normal family life.

Agricultural communities themselves, apart from migrant workers, might well be classified as in transition. They suffer generally from depleted community services and the lack of funds or personnel to improve services. Much of the young adult population of such areas is drawn off into the mobile industrially employed group. Families find it constantly harder to subsist on farm income alone, and the

175

whole economy of purely agricultural areas is subject to great fluctuations of the national market.

A primary fact about family life in communities in transition is that its lessened stability creates greater need for social resources. When accustomed patterns of living are withdrawn, the community is called upon to reinforce the existence of the family through the services of its governmental and voluntary social agencies, its schools, its Churches, and its whole structure.

Mass Urbanization

The community and its social resources assume constantly more importance in all aspects of increased industrialization. This is as true of all urbanized areas as it is of areas in transition. The loss of personal associations and roots which comes with mass living must be offset by common opportunities to secure help in times of trouble, fellowship in times of leisure, protection from harm or loss. By and large, American communities have accepted their responsibility for the welfare of families, but there are still great gaps in essential resources for health, welfare, and education. The lag in social adaptation on the part of all institutions, including the Churches, has aggravated these unmet needs. With certain exceptions, such as in suburban areas where Churches have become vital centres of community life, Churches and schools have been particularly slow in changing to meet changing needs.

Another problem is the growth of conformity in the American culture. It has become so widespread that initiative and independence in thought, speech, and action are often feared. There is even some abridgement of civil rights, such as free speech and free press, in the interests of conformity, although it is not widespread or general. Recent decisions of the United States Supreme Court have done much to protect civil rights. Though conformity is not a new manifestation and is characteristic of every culture, its enforcement through mass living and easy communication gives it a new dimension.

Allied to conformity and dependent upon the same social and economic factors is the problem of the growth of power structures in the United States. The centralization of industry and finance gives to those who control them, both in management and labour groups, influence over the lives and fortunes of most American families. Since this control extends into politics and government, it exerts public as well as industrial influence and touches many aspects of family life.

Suburbanization and the Growth of Metropolitan Areas

Housing shortages are a problem in almost all parts of the United

States, but they are most acute in the inner city and in those areas where decentralization of industry has moved families about by the thousands, creating constant demand for new houses, new schools, new roads. Suburbanization adds to these demands and also adds to the difficulty of meeting them because of the scattered nature of the areas to be served. Again the community must assume responsibility for expanded services and for planning. Metropolitan areas use water, electricity, sanitation facilities, streets, food, personnel, fuel, everything in quantities unimagined until recently. Planning is necessary to provide for them, and it must be planning on a vast scale, crossing the boundaries of counties and even of states. The rigidity of town, county, and state lines constitutes a problem in the kind of administration necessary for metropolitan areas.

A source of anxiety is the change in the nature of the central city and its suburbs. Increasingly families able to afford it or even hoping to afford it in the future are moving to suburbs. This increases the proportion of the underprivileged families in the central city. The relatively few high income families moving to luxury apartments in "downtown areas" do not as yet affect the general trend. Because of dwindling income from real estate, taxes, schools, and other services are beginning to decay in the central city although population still increases and huge state or federal housing projects for low income groups multiply. The suburbs, although dependent upon the central city for their existence, are unwilling to share in its administration or support. This is again a problem of creating a sense of community responsibility which transcends the immediate neighbourhood.

The Current Value System

Basic to family living and the ways in which the members of the family behave is the value system which motivates their thoughts and actions. The dominant series of desirable goals or values emphasizes economic and social status. There are very clear symbols of achievement in the form of material possessions—automobiles, furniture, a "ranch-type house", fashionable clothing, a television set—all standardized symbols of success in life, usually to be acquired through loans or instalment buying. This dominant system creates the problem of families striving for material achievement at the expense of the development of their own personalities and of their relationships with God and with man.

The emphasis upon material success as a goal, furthermore, is increasing at a time when the community is called upon to give more and more service to its families. Since the helping professions of the ministry, social work, teaching, and others are less remunerative than industry or commerce, the personnel for service is sadly lacking.

7*

Scholarships for graduate study in these professions are often unused because of the absence of candidates. Since the goal is to earn money fast, and since jobs are plentiful, there are comparatively few persons who will sacrifice to serve. The drive for education is powerful, but it is education for a good job in industry or commerce, or at least in a profession such as medicine, law, or the physical sciences where financial possibilities are good. There is constant pressure to improve salaries in the helping professions and there has been some progress in recent years, although standards are still far from adequate.

World Unrest

Two manifestations of world tensions affect the lives of American families. The first is the constant threat of war, which not only brings to some families the fear of atomic disaster but enters the life of each family through the necessity for military service on the part of the male members. The second is distrust of any political ideology not accepted by the dominant power structure, and the resultant limitation of differing thought, speech, and action.

The Effect upon those with Low Social Status

It is apparent that many of the problems generally affecting family life weigh most heavily upon the families with economic, social, racial, religious, or physical differences from the norm. Abridgement of civil rights, housing and school shortages, lack of achievement in material success are all more prevalent in the groups which start out with handicaps. Although geographic areas vary in the severity of the handicaps imposed, none is free entirely from discrimination. In this aspect, industrialization has had and will increasingly have a good effect. Because of its impersonal nature, industrialization, with the growth of employment and education, tends to obliterate differences. The need for more workers in more places in more occupations absorbs the socially, physically, or racially handicapped as well as others. Military service, labour unions, nationally broadcast entertainment, and commercialized sport have also helped integration, as has the immigration of some 400,000 refugees from Europe and Asia. The social lag of Churches and educational institutions has made them slower to absorb the minorities. There are still serious problems for most families with handicaps, but progress has been quite rapid in the past two decades.

Another group suffering from low status at the present time is the aged. No longer members of a large family unit, they are lonely. They find themselves "unemployable" and unprepared for the

178

rewarding use of leisure during retirement. Because of their increasing proportion in the population and their improved physical capabilities, their future is more promising in status.

The Socially Maladjusted

The problems which are most widely discussed in the United States, such as the increase in crime, particularly juvenile delinquency, the upswing in mental illness, the increase in alcoholism, the prevalence of divorce, and the growth of sexual promiscuity, are not in themselves basic problems, serious though they are. They are rather symptomatic behaviour growing out of basic problems. When family life is disturbed by one or more of a number of the social and economic factors already described, a member of the family may exhibit visible evidence of this. When the system of values places such heavy emphasis on material success, individuals who are unable to achieve this success frequently respond with hostility which results in anti-social behaviour. Recent studies of juvenile delinquency, for example, show that more cases arise from the desire to improve status than from the failure of family life. The care of maladjustment, in addition to treatment of the individual, involves removing the basic problems which are the causes.

5. THE STATUS OF THE CHURCH IN RELATION TO THE AMERICAN FAMILY

Renewed Interest in Religion

Since the second world war, American families have shown a steadily growing interest in religion. This is a reversal of the trend during the period between the two world wars when Churches of all kinds, particularly those in urban areas, were experiencing a falling-off of participation to the point where 40% of all city people were unchurched. The new trend toward church affiliation is not of long enough duration to show in figures except in a slight increase in membership rolls, the rapid growth of schools of religious education, and indirectly in the increase of financial giving. Mounting evidence from all Churches, however, shows steady growth, not only in newly developed or expanding areas, but also in fairly static areas. (The notable exception is the very large cities where church strength continues to decrease.) There was dramatic increase in "fundamentalist" sects—"storefront Churches"—all through the period of fall-off in the more organized Churches. Since 1950, there have been just as dramatic examples of growth in the organized Churches.

There is little evidence that the increased participation of American families in Churches has affected great changes in the spiritual

179

life of the family. Rather, it is a means of social identification and relationship. It is also directly related to the new feeling of conscientiousness about family life and to the new rôle of the father. Two clear proofs of this are the popularity of Family Services and the presence in all services of worship of a greater proportion of men. Participation of men has not yet reached the point where men's organizations have anything like the size of women's organizations. Men are more active, however, in those phases of church life where they can participate with other members of their families, and this may continue to be their method of greater involvement.

Adaptation of the Church to Urban Culture

One reason for the lag of the organized Churches between the two world wars was their slow pace in adapting to the rapid shifts in population, whereas "storefront Churches" could move rapidly and adapt quickly to the people surrounding them. For the past decade, the organized Churches have been making nationwide efforts to understand and meet the spiritual and social needs of families in an increasingly urban culture. Regional and national units have been formed to finance urban, suburban, and rural expansion and adaptation. Research and experimentation in such ministries are being conducted in all parts of the United States. There are training programmes for workers in town and country work and in urban work. Recent evidence of the interest of the public in the new rôle of the Churches is found in the number of Foundation grants which have been given to church groups for research and demonstration projects. The common core of most of these projects is to establish the relevance of religious insights and principles to the patterns and problems of urbanized society. The presence of economic abundance has meant that the new efforts of the Churches have been able to find sources of financial implementation.

Every national unit in the Episcopal Church is now working to increase its relevance to urban culture and the changing nature of the family. Each unit has conducted research and experiment upon which to base its present and future work so as to meet more adequately the needs of people for the Church's ministry. It is making wide use of the findings of psychology, sociology, and other social sciences to provide insights into the ways in which it can serve individuals, families, and communities.

The Church in Relation to Current Problems in Family Life

Churches are seldom exceptions to the problems faced by institutions in communities in transition. Churches in depleted rural or urban communities find the needs of their families increasing at the

180

very time when their resources are decreasing. Churches in communities where the population is changing culturally find it difficult to blend into their membership the old people and the new people. Churches in rapidly expanding communities find swelling congregations and schools of religious education outgrowing the available personnel and physical facilities. In all these situations, the Churches are more aware than they were in the past of their responsibilities to the community and their responsibilities to minister to the families around them. This attitude of ministering to the total community and the total family is rapidly replacing the earlier pattern of identification of certain cultural or ethnic groups with certain organized Churches. The question is whether the new attitude and the actions which grow from it can spread rapidly enough to keep pace with the rate of transition in the United States. The further question is whether the Churches can meet the rising need for community identification which stems from the impersonal nature of modern living.

Mass living, with its resultant loss of personal relationships, is one of the most important factors which the Churches face. Even the normal channels of church affiliation and fellowship are more difficult to find and utilize for families in cities. Within the Churches, the heterogeneity of the congregation, as well as its size, makes necessary new approaches to secure the active participation of the total membership. The growth of multiple organizations and units within the congregation has been a response to these needs. There is a dichotomy, however, between the growth of these organizations which are usually based on age or sex groupings and the drive to minister to the whole family in its new consciousness of unity.

One aspect of urban culture requiring drastic adaptation on the part of Churches is the growth of metropolitan areas. As these areas cross county and state boundaries, so also they cross jurisdictional boundaries within the Churches. For example, in the Episcopal Church, they cross archdiaconal and diocesan lines. An effective ministry in metropolitan areas is beginning to demand a strategy which is jointly planned and co-ordinated by all the jurisdictional units involved. The mobility of the population, furthermore, produces the need for more adequate systems of communication between regional units and even local Churches throughout the country.

Organized religion, throughout history, has been subject to the danger of conformity to the culture of which it is a part. A difficult balance must be maintained between sufficient conformity to enable the Churches to minister effectively and sufficient independence to witness to the sins of man and society. In modern urban culture in the United States, the tendency to conformity is so universal that the danger of acquiescence on the part of the Churches is very great. Such conformity creates resistance to change and makes more difficult the necessary constant adaptation to changing need.

Not only the prophetic witness of the Churches, but also their ability to minister to people is hampered by strict conformity to prevailing cultural values. The growth of the new sense of unity and relationship within the American family is dependent upon the degree to which the individual is able to work out his own personality in relation to the other members of the family. Too great a conformity to patterns for the "successful" personality is a handicap to such development. The Churches' rôle in fostering personal development is based more upon its conviction of the sacredness of human personality than upon a code of ethics based upon acceptable patterns.

Undue emphasis on conformity is a problem in itself, but, when the dominant value system emphasizes material achievement, the problem is a more serious one for the Churches. The Judaeo-Christian tradition seeks to promote a code of spiritual and moral behaviour which is at variance with such a value system. The constant indictments of contemporary society as secular and materialistic reflect this anxiety. Even the Churches themselves are sometimes accused of measuring their own success in terms of material achievement, and church families are often accused of using their Church for economic and social advantage. If the American family's renewed interest in religion is to be of more than passing worth in improving the value system, the Churches must discover effective ways of incalculating Christian faith, its goals and standards, in the members of the family. They must also find more effective ways of recruiting persons for vocations in the Church in order to extend and widen their ministry to the family.

In a society in which social and economic status are so important, the Churches have assumed a special responsibility to those groups of families and individuals where status is lessened by racial, cultural, physical, or mental difference. Although the mission programme of the Churches has always served such groups, and social services to them are traditional, widening of these concepts is now occurring. The mission of the Church is being seen as a total ministry to all persons everywhere, and the Church itself seen as an integrated Church. Were the Church not impelled to this broad concept by its own theology, it would be forced into it by the mobility and urbanization of the culture.

The Churches have a further, corporate responsibility to groups of families with low social or economic status, and that is to oppose the abridgement of their civil or personal rights. American Churches, among them the Episcopal Church, have regularly taken official action in support of desegregation and an end to discrimination on the basis of race, creed, or nationality. The national policy of the Churches, both separately and through major interdenominational bodies, has uniformly supported equality and integration as a goal. The application of this policy, however, has lagged in local congregations and occasionally even in regional programmes. Although the Churches in the Southern area of the United States are currently receiving the most criticism for their segregationist practices, most Churches throughout the United States are still far from having achieved complete integration in their work and worship.

Other families for which the Churches have a special responsibility are those affected by juvenile delinquency, divorce, alcoholism, or other forms of social maladjustment such as homosexuality or narcotic addiction. The social service, psychological, and medical agencies of the Church and those of the community have a continuing function in the treatment of such families, but it is increasingly becoming a part of the pastoral ministry of the clergy to understand and help persons and families caught in these situations.

The Episcopal Church, by reason of her understanding of herself and of the nature of the spiritual life, has been less inclined to take positions on some of the moral issues affecting American families than have other American Churches. Such practices as the use of beverage alcohol, tobacco, or birth control and others are still matters of individual choice for Episcopalians, whereas the Roman Catholic Church and the more fundamentalist Churches seek, in many issues of this sort, to bind the conscience of their members by authoritative rulings. There seems to be little tendency on the part of the Episcopal Church to formulate rigid positions on these issues, with the exception of divorce, but there is considerable current interest in the theological exploration of them and the setting forth for church members of the social and moral principles involved. There are indications that the absence of widespread consideration of moral issues by some of the Churches with traditions like those of the Episcopal Church leaves their adherents without guidance on these issues and increases the public attention given to the more rigid positions taken by the Churches which are more authoritative.

The Churches' Rôle in Social Reform and Social Change
During the period between the two world wars, some American Churches were very active in movements of social reform. It has been held, however, that this activity was limited to what might be called "resolutionary Christianity" and to certain groups of church members with special conviction. Whether this is true or whether

life—it may perhaps be argued that the laity is within its rights when it asks from its shepherds some more definite guidance in particular ethical questions. The situation is complicated by the fact that the American Episcopalian is surrounded by friends and colleagues and sometimes by members of his own family who, belonging to Churches of authoritarian character, have no apparent problems of conscience, for they have been told exactly what to think and do in virtually every situation. The typical Episcopalian finds himself unable to give an answer to those who "know the answer", and he may harbour a secret resentment against his own Church. This is partly because it has left him defenceless in the face of the assurance of these others, and partly because it seems to have given him nothing but vague principles, noble ideals, glittering generalities, when what he needed—in a highly relative, ambiguous situation—was a direct word of advice about his next step, now, to-day. To their credit, few Episcopalians want commands from a totalitarian ecclesiastical authority; but they do want counsel, quite definite counsel, in such matters as the use of alcohol, the practice of birth control, gambling, and others. Is this a just request from the laity—and from many of the clergy? And if so, can Anglicanism find a way to direct—but without despotism—to offer specific guidance, while not catering to the morbid desire of man to surrender chaotic-ally his responsible selfhood; to develop from the general principles of moral theology a relevant casuistry, though without investing its casuistry with infallibility?

Appendix 3

THE FAMILY AND MODERN SOCIETY
CANADA, 1957

CONTENTS

INTRODUCTION

A comprehensive study of the present-day family in Canada has not been made, or if it has been, the results have not been published. But a considerable amount of research in this area is being planned or is in process. For instance, the Canadian Home and School and Parent-Teacher Federation has as its major project in 1957-8, "A Study of the Problem of the Canadian Family in its Sociological Setting". A research team has been engaged "to conduct a national survey into the Canadian family on a sociological, economic, and psychological plane".

A major Canadian research project which should provide a wealth of insights concerning the family in the Canadian scene has begun its work at the University of Toronto. It is known as the Round Table on "Man and Industry". Its full title is the Round Table on "The impact on Human Well-Being of a Rapidly Evolving Industrialization". The Round Table is described as a type of "action research" in which representatives of a cross-section of the community—finance and industry, organized labour, government, the social sciences, the human service professions (including the ministry)—are meeting for three sessions of five days each at intervals of twelve months, to visit and to make a field study of selected industrial impact areas, and to gather at the University to discuss the results of these field visits together with other research items, so as to study the human situation as it is affected by industrialization. In 1956 the impact areas studied were Iroquois Falls, the St Lawrence Seaway, Downtown Toronto, Scarborough, Blind River and Elliot Lake, and Malton. Any one familiar with the Canadian scene will realize at once that these centres are typical of the many significant social and cultural changes in Canada to-day. This research process has been described in some detail so as to give an indication of the significance of this study and of its relevance to the Church's concern for the whole of life. It is unfortunate for our present purpose that this research has only begun. However, the results of certain preliminary studies are available and reference will be made to these in the material that follows.

A third major study which has been useful is the work done by Canadians in preparation for the International Conference of Social Work which met in Munich, Germany, in 1956. Its theme was "Social Work in Industrial Society". "Position" papers on various

189

aspects of Canadian life were written by a number of specialists, most of whom were social workers, but these papers have not yet been made available in a published form.

This present paper is, therefore, of necessity a very incomplete compilation of some statistics and facts, an attempt to trace trends and to describe some conditions associated with family life in Canada.

1. POPULATION TRENDS

THE FAMILY IN SOCIETY

A study of the family involves inevitably some consideration of various facets of social life of which the family is an integral part. The family has been one of the great formative influences in community, but at the same time has been affected by the intricate web of institutions and forces which constitute community. The family is not isolated; there is a constant interaction with its surroundings. It is possible, therefore, to consider the family from many different angles. For instance, a Montreal Committee on Family Life and Parent Education, in which our Diocesan Council for Social Service has given significant leadership, suggests the following as a definition of the family and its function in society:

The family is a cell of love, created by the life-long friendship between a man and a woman, with complete sharing of body and mind, and with, normally, the procreation of children. The family is not sufficient unto itself; it is dependent upon and contributes to society, and while making possible the richest personality development of its individual members, it also prepares them to serve their fellow men and to live together with them in the wider family of humanity.

It should be noted that the family provides a healthy and necessary balance between the emphasis on the worth of the individual person, and the equally important emphasis on man as a social being with social responsibilities. Society as a whole must ever strive to maintain this balance. Society does not exist for the sake of the individual, nor the individual for society. For, while individual personality cannot flourish where the individual is valued only as a unit in society, on the other hand the individual person cannot reach his highest development without a growth in concern and sense of responsibility for his fellows, fostered in the inter-personal relationships of the family and of society.

190

THE CENSUS FAMILY

Undoubtedly the "Census Family" is a necessary starting point for any study of Canadian family life. Population figures indicate certain conditions and trends which in turn yield much useful information concerning the family.

With a vast land area and with rich resources Canada has only six thousandths of the world's population. The recent census revealed that Canada had a population on 1 June 1956 of 16,080,791. This was an increase in five years of 2,071,362, almost as much as the total increase in the previous ten years. Practically all of this increase occurred in four provinces—Ontario, Quebec, Alberta, and British Columbia—with the first two provinces accounting for almost 1.4 million of it, or two thirds of the national growth during those five years. According to the 1951 census, 61% of the Canadian people were living in Ontario and Quebec; that proportion had risen to 63% in 1956. More than three quarters of the nation's people live in these four provinces. The preliminary report of the Gordon Commission estimates that by 1980 Canada will have a population of 26.6 million, but estimates concerning the distribution of this increase have not been released.

British Columbia led the provinces in the rate of growth from 1951 to 1956 with an increase of 20%; Alberta had an increase of 19.5%, Ontario 17.6%, Newfoundland 14.8%, Quebec 14.1%, Manitoba 9.5%, Nova Scotia 8.1%, New Brunswick 7.5%, Saskatchewan 5.9%, (Saskatchewan had a decline of 7.2% between 1941 and 1951), Prince Edward Island 0.9%, Yukon Territory 34%, and the North West Territories 20.7%.[1]

In 1956, 450,500 babies were born in Canada, an increase of 7,500 over 1955. The 1956 census reflected the continued high birth rate trend which was one of the startling trends revealed in the 1951 census. What has become known as "the bulge in the birth rate" was still evident in the last census in that the total number of children under 10 represented 23.5% of the total population compared with 22.3% in 1951.

A breakdown of the birth rate with respect to provinces is of interest. Based on the 1951 Census the birth rate per 1,000 married women in the age group 15 to 49 by provinces is as follows :

TABLE 1 [2]

Newfoundland	220	Alberta	160
New Brunswick	200	Saskatchewan	155
Quebec	193	Manitoba	147
P.E.I.	186	Ontario	138
Nova Scotia	162	British Columbia	130

[1] Dominion Bureau of Statistics, *Bulletin*, 23 January 1957.
[2] *Canada Year Book, 1956*, p. 204.

Turning once again to the general increase in the population between 1951 and 1956, the biggest increase was in the age group 5 to 9 years, while the 19 to 24 age group declined in proportion to the total, reflecting the low birth rates of the depression years. The 25 to 64 group increased numerically to 7,320,232 but decreased proportionately to 45.7% of the total from 46.5%, and similarly the population 65 years and over, though it increased 26.6% to 1,243,938, declined proportionately from 7.8% to 7.7% of the total. Women predominated in the age groups 30 to 34, 35 to 39, and 70 years and over. In all other groups men were greater in numbers.[3]

It is against this general population background that the family and household which are the concern of this study are to be examined. For census purposes the following definitions are used.

A household is a group of persons living in the same dwelling, irrespective of whether they are related to one another by ties of kinship. A dwelling is defined as a structurally separate set of living premises with private entrance from outside the building or from a common hallway or stairway inside.

A family is a group of two or more persons, living in a dwelling, related to one another either as husband and wife, with or without children, or as parent and child. Other relatives living in the same dwelling, including married children, were not counted as members of the family. However, where a married son (or daughter) and children were living with their parents in the same dwelling or household they were counted as a second family in the dwelling.

| TABLE 2 | | | TABLE 3 | | |
| Persons per Household in Canada [4] | | | Average size of Household and average size of Family in Canada [5] | | |

Census Year	Persons per Household		Year	Average size of household	Average size of family
1881	5.33		1951	4.0	3.7
1891	5.26		1952	4.0	3.7
1901	5.03		1953	4.0	3.8
1911	4.85		1954	3.9	3.7
1921	4.63		1955	3.9	3.8
1931	4.55				
1941	4.25				
1951	4.07				

Table 2 traces the decrease in the number of persons per household for each census year from 1881 to 1951, a drop from 5.33 to 4.07. The estimated average size of households and of families from 1951 to 1955 varied slightly as Table 3 indicates.

[3] *Globe and Mail* (13 June 1957), Report of D.B.S. Release.
[4] *Census of Canada*, Vol. III, Table 1.
[5] *Estimates of Household and Families in Canada*, 1955.

The total number of Canadian families in 1955 was estimated to be 3,685,000, an increase of 1,159,700 over the 1941 figure of 2,525,300. Estimates concerning the size of families are contained in Table 4, below.

TABLE 4

Estimated Number of Families by number of Children, Canada [6]

Families		1951	1952	1953	1954	1955
Total families		3,282,445	3,413,000	3,477,000	3,595,000	3,685,000
per cent		100.0	100.0	100.0	100.0	100.0
Families by						
Number of children						
No children						
	No.	1,059,430	1,114,000	1,139,000	1,176,000	1,155,000
	%	32.3	32.6	32.8	32.7	31.3
1 child						
	No.	770,936	755,000	773,000	380,000	809,000
	%	23.5	22.1	22.2	21.7	22.0
2 children						
	No.	649,862	681,000	670,000	720,000	748,000
	%	19.8	20.0	19.3	20.0	20.3
3 children						
	No.	357,643	396,000	403,000	403,000	441,000
	%	10.9	11.6	11.6	11.2	12.0
4 children						
	No.	189,716	203,000	213,000	217,000	241,000
	%	5.8	5.9	6.1	6.0	6.5
5 children						
	No.	103,633	108,000	107,000	130,000	118,000
	%	3.2	3.2	3.1	3.6	3.2
6 children						
	No.	61,107	67,000	68,000	69,000	72,000
	%	1.9	2.0	2.0	1.9	2.0
7 or more children						
	No.	90,118	89,000	104,000	100,000	101,000
	%	2.7	2.6	3.0	2.8	2.7

Table 5 reveals among other facts that in 1955 41.8% of all Canadian families had children all of whom were under 14 years of age, another way of indicating "the bulge" in the birth rate.

TABLE 5

Families with children, by age of children [7]

Families		1951	1952	1953	1954	1955
All under 14						
	No.	1,343,167	1,394,000	1,409,000	1,465,000	1,542,000
	%	40.9	40.8	40.5	40.8	41.8
Under and over 14						
	No.	437,122	449,000	477,000	488,000	515,000
	%	13.3	13.2	13.7	13.6	14.0
All over 14						
	No.	442,726	456,000	452,000	466,000	473,000
	%	13.5	13.4	13.0	13.0	12.8

[6] *Estimates of Households and Families in Canada*, 1955.
[7] *Estimates of Households and Families in Canada*, 1955.

Marriages and Divorces

The total number of marriages in Canada had increased from 51,073 in 1921 to 128,385 in 1954 according to the Canada Year Book,[8] and a recent release from the Dominion Bureau of Statistics states that there were 132,000 marriages in 1956. In 1954, 9% of the marriages were between persons who had not been married before, while more than 3% of the marriages were of divorced persons. The average age at marriage of bachelors is just under 27, and that of spinsters just under 24 years.[9]

In 1954, 12.6% of Canada's bridegrooms were Anglicans;[10] they married brides of many denominations :

Church of England	8,180	Presbyterian	804
Baptist	575	Roman Catholic	1,966
Eastern Orthodox	93	United Church	3,618
Jewish	16	Other	556
Lutheran	399	Not stated	3
		Total	16,210

In the same year 12.7% of the brides were Anglicans and married as follows :

Church of England	8,180	Presbyterian	996
Baptist	612	Roman Catholic	1,759
Eastern Orthodox	111	United Church	3,506
Jewish	34	Other	636
Lutheran	491	Not stated	5
		Total	16,330

Thus about 50% of the marriages contracted by Anglicans were with fellow Anglicans. This percentage is much lower than the national average. About 71% of all marriages are between persons of the same religious denomination. Among the Jews the percentage was 93%, the Roman Catholics 89%, the United Church 61%, in 1954.

Table 6 is important for this study because of a number of trends revealed.

TABLE 6

Marital Status of the Population by Sex for all Age Groups
1951 Census [11]

		Single	Married	Widowed	Divorced	Total
	Male	3,747,409	3,141,754	186,595	13,115	7,088,873
All						
	Female	3,325,096	3,119,824	456,753	18,883	6,920,556
Ages						
	Total	7,072,505	6,261,578	643,348	31,998	14,009,429

8 *Canada Year Book, 1956,* p. 226.
9 Ibid., p. 227.
10 Ibid., p. 229.
11 *Canada Year Book,* p. 164.

194

In the decade between 1941 and 1951, the number of single persons increased by 13.5%, but the increase in the married population was more than twice as much, 32.2%, the increase in the not inappropriate to consider juvenile delinquency, because, as it will be noted that there is an excess of married males over females, largely due to the number of male immigrants whose wives will join them later; that there is a great preponderance of widows compared with widowers; and also there is the large and increasing number of divorced persons.

At this point reference should be made to the trend in the divorce rate. In 1900 there were 11 divorces in Canada. At census years, the number of divorces granted were as follows : [12]

1901 –	19	1921 –	558	1941 – 2,461
1911 –	57	1931 –	700	1951 – 5,263

The years immediately following the two great wars witnessed a sharp increase, due generally to unsettled conditions and long periods of separation. In 1947, a peak of 8,199 divorces were granted. The year 1954 witnessed the granting of over 5,800 divorces. Of this number 370 were in Quebec and 8 in Newfoundland, the only two provinces in which applicants for divorce must secure a private Act of Parliament.

Juvenile Delinquency

With the rising incidence in divorce and family breakdowns it is not inappropriate to consider juvenile delinquency, because as it will be seen from the following tables, over 20% of Canada's delinquents come from homes that are broken by divorce, separation, or death. Table 7 lists the numbers of juveniles adjudged delinquent in proportion to the total number before the courts.

TABLE 7

Juveniles before the Courts, Dismissed and Delinquent, 1949-53 [13]

Item	1949		1950		1951		1952		1953	
	No.	%	*No.*	%	*No.*	%	*No.*	%	*No.*	%
Before the courts	7,038	100.0	7,304	100.0	7,521	100.0	7,213	100.0	7,829	100.0
Dismissed	166	2.4	197	2.7	195	2.6	178	2.5	216	2.8
Adjourned	674	9.6	689	9.4	682	9.1	967	13.4	1.236	15.8
Delinquent	6,198	88.0	6,418	87.9	6,644	88.3	6,068	84.1	6,377	81.4

Table 8 describes the marital status of the parents of these delinquents.

12 Ibid., p. 230.
13 *Canada Year Book, 1956*, p. 336.

195

TABLE 8

Juvenile Delinquents: Marital Status of Parents, 1953 [14]

		Total	Boys	Girls
Living together	Natural parents Step-fathers or Step-mothers	4,729	4,299	430
Broken homes	Divorced	104	84	20
	Separated	664	549	115
	Widowed	533	448	85
	One unknown	12	8	4
	Both unknown	14	14	–
Both deceased		33	27	6
Marital status not stated		288	263	25
Total		6,377	5,692	685

The mothers of 10.1% of the juvenile delinquents were employed outside the home, and the mothers of another 3.4% were dead. 7.4% of the fathers of these juveniles were dead. Three out of four of the juveniles who appeared in court were from urban areas. 87.9% of these young people were living in their own homes, 5.3% were in foster homes, and 1.4% were living in institutions.[15]

Certain other trends are startling in their implications.

The Aging Population

A pronounced general aging of the Canadian population has been evident for the last twenty years, and there is every sign that this trend will accelerate. Heavy immigration during the early years of this century, followed by the practically non-existent immigration and lower birth rate of the depression years and the second great war, have had much to do with this. But the prolongation of human life is also a significant factor. Substantial reductions in the mortality rates in early and middle years of life have helped to increase the number of persons in the older age groups and to raise the average age of the whole population. For instance, death rates for males up to age 45 have been cut in half during the past quarter of a century, and for women the reduction has been as much as three to four times. The average age at death of males in 1921 was 39.0 years and for females 41.1 years; in 1954 these figures had advanced to 57.3 and 60.0 respectively. In 1951 the life expectancy at birth for males was 66.3 and for females 70.8.[16]

The rising standard of living, better sanitation, an improvement in working conditions including the elimination of many occupational hazards, and the tremendous advances in medical skill and public health service have all had their influence. Table 9 indicates the extent of the resultant changes.

[14] *Juvenile Delinquents,* 1953, D.B.S., p. 38.
[15] *Canada Year Book, 1956,* p. 335.
[16] Ibid., p. 212.

TABLE 9

The Number per 1,000 of Total Population [17]

	Between 40 and 59 years	60 years and over
1921	183	75
1931	201	84
1941	209	102
1951	203.2	113.7

The total number of persons in Canada over the age of 60 years in 1956 was 1,768,855.

The High Birth Rate

Canada's high birth rate, to which reference has been made previously, is not due to an increase in the size of families; in fact the general trend in the average size of the family is downward; but it is the result of a number of factors including the increase in the number of marriages, the earlier age of marriage, and the earlier birth of children after marriage. Dr Elizabeth Govan, of the Toronto School of Social Work, speaking recently of the trend towards earlier marriages, suggested that this is possibly due to "higher wages, the greater acceptance of married women working, less emphasis upon 'enough money to get married on', more emphasis upon capital expenditure out of income, etc."

Whatever the cause, the results demand drastic action if the greatly increased number of young people are to be provided for. The Universities have been very vocal in their concern, and rightly so. With present accommodation over-crowded, it is anticipated that the number of undergraduates enrolled in Canadian Universities will increase in the next ten years from the present 64,000 to 122,000 and the anticipated post-graduate enrolment will be approximately 6,000 as compared with the present 3,000.[18] At a recent National Conference of Canadian Universities, this prospect was described as "an emergency of grave national consequence".

The same kind of crisis is being experienced by an increasing number of Canadian communities and municipalities which have to provide schools for the nation's children.

Education has always been one of the primary concerns of the Church; therefore, our responsibilities in helping the community in its planning and organization to meet this situation are very great, to say nothing of the Church's own facilities and resources, in buildings and personnel, which will need to be extensively expanded if this present opportunity is to be seized and used constructively.

[17] Ibid., p. 162.

[18] *Canadian University and College Enrolment prospected to 1956.* Prepared by Director, Education Division, D.B.S.

Other provisions for children and youth in the community must keep pace as well. Recreation and welfare programmes are two of many such.

Immigration

When compared with previous decades, immigration was not a significant factor in the over-all increase in the Canadian population during the 1941-51 decade. Migration was responsible for a net increase of only 2% because the immigration of 550,000 was counterbalanced by the emigration of 380,000 persons during that period. Recently, however, the picture has changed completely, due to an accelerated movement of immigrants into Canada, and it would seem that immigration will once again be a major determining factor in the size of the population. In 1956, 164,857 persons came to Canada as immigrants. It is predicted that that figure will be increased to over 200,000 in 1957.

But while numbers of people are important for Canada, even more significant is the impact which the newcomers have upon the delopment of particular regions and their total contribution to Canadian life. The following is a useful summary of who the immigrants are, where they settle, and the types of work they come prepared to do.

Of the 155,080 persons from overseas, 51,319 were British by origin, 29,805 were Italian, 29,405 were German and Austrian and 3,016 were French, making up 69 per cent of the total immigration. In addition, 9,777 were formerly residents of the United States. Totals for these groups during the eleven year period ended December 31, 1956 were 419,024 British, 168,401 German and Austrian, 164,962 Italian, 27,258 French, 100,529 from the United States.

Of the number of people who have entered our country to take up permanent residence in 1956, more than 55.0 per cent were destined to the province of Ontario, 19.0 per cent to Quebec, 21.6 per cent to the Prairie provinces and British Columbia, 1.9 per cent to the Atlantic provinces.

A little over 54 per cent were males and 68.4 per cent were less than thirty years of age.

Workers among the total number of immigrants were 91,039. Of these, 1,685 were professional engineers, 1,248 were graduate nurses, 415 were physicians and surgeons. There also were 8,704 domestic servants and 9,128 skilled construction workers. Of the 9,343 professional workers admitted to our country, more than 59 per cent were British and close to 55 per cent of the workers in the managerial class came from the United States.[19]

[19] *Immigration 1956,* Department of Citizenship and Immigration, p.4.

A recent issue of *Citizen*,[20] a publication of the Department of Citizenship and Immigration, describes post-war immigrants in terms of consumers, workers, business men, and investors. In 1951, post-war immigrants had established 62,160 households; 43,000 of these had gas or electric ranges, 32,000 had power-washing machines, 52,000 had radios, 18,000 had electric vacuum cleaners. One out of every three householders owned an automobile. It is estimated that the number of households with the above listed equipment has more than doubled since 1951. In 1955 Canada's post-war immigrants spent approximately 450 million dollars on food alone. These are significant items in the Canadian economy.

Fifty-four per cent of Canada's immigrants since the war have come to the labour force. Approximately 20% of these are skilled workers. The Preliminary Report of the Gordon Commission on Canada's economic prospects emphasized that Canada is facing shortages in almost every skilled occupation, and there is every indication that these shortages will worsen in the immediate future because the number of persons joining the labour force is increasing more slowly than the population, due largely to the low birth rate of the thirties. Hence, the importance of those skilled persons who came to Canada from other lands.

As regards business and investments, in the ten-year period ending in 1955 immigrants brought over 550 million dollars in cash, to which must be added other assets transferred after arrival. Undoubtedly, a considerable proportion of this went into Canadian investments. The *Canada Year Book* of 1955 stated that immigrants had established businesses ranging from an industry employing more than 4,000 workers to small firms hiring two or three to thirty or forty. The Gordon Commission Report said : "It is the opinion of the Commission that immigrants have made a decided contribution to the scale of economic development in Canada."

Reference should be made, too, to the cultural enrichment which newcomers have added to Canadian life. Leaders in architecture, the theatre, art, music, and crafts have brought their artistry from abroad, and Canada is the richer for their coming.

The Church has played its part in impressing upon the Canadian Government and people the need for a continuous and generous flow of immigrants and has shared in the all-important task of welcoming the newcomer and helping in the process of integration. Every Anglican who comes by ship to Canada is referred to the rector of the parish to which he goes by means of the Church's Port Chaplaincy and referral service, and several dioceses have now set up Information Centres where newcomers are advised as regards

[20] June 1957.

parish churches, accommodation and employment, not to mention special provisions made by parishes and individuals for Hungarian refugees in recent months. These and other programmes illustrate the unique contribution of the Church in this aspect of Canada's development which is of first-rate importance.

But it can never be over-emphasized that in this area of concern so much depends upon the individual, who is in daily contact with the newcomer and who, by his attitudes and reactions, can make or mar, delay or facilitate the progress of the immigrant towards full participation in Canadian life. Original Canadians need much help in understanding the newcomer and his values and in accepting him as a fellow-Canadian.

2. INDUSTRIALIZATION AND THE FAMILY

Industrialization

Two definitions of "Industrialization" given during The International Conference of Social Work at Munich provide a helpful starting point for a consideration of this topic. The Australian delegation used the word to refer to "the production method whereby goods and services are produced in accordance with a system into which the individual must fit; as distinct from the peasant and domestic economies in which the individual had a larger freedom in adapting the productive system to his own interest and capacity".

Professor Richard M. Titmuss of the London School of Economics was more descriptive in his definition. He said: "If the first industrial revolution was characterized by the change-over from domestic to factory production, by the invention of the steam engine, and the use of coal and iron, the second industrial revolution bears the mark of the division of labour, mass production, the conveyor belt, and automation."

In Canada this process is developing at a phenomenal pace and is rapidly changing the whole character of our national economy. The gross national product of Canada is approaching $30 billion a year. Manufacturing industries in 1871 had 188,000 employees, paid $41 million in wages, and the gross value of their products was $222 million; in 1955 employees numbered 1,290,00, the wages paid amounted to $4,111 million, and the gross value of products was $19,469 million.[1] "We are the world's largest producers of newsprint,

[1] Royal Bank of Canada *Monthly Letter,* June 1957, p. 4.

200

platinum, asbestos and nickel. We are second in aluminium, zinc, and wood pulp. We are third in producing gold and fifth in copper."[2] The Gordon Commission's Preliminary Report reveals that Canada's industrial growth has been of a dual character. There has been the development of natural resources, oil and gas in the West, uranium in Northern Ontario, iron ore in Quebec-Labrador, and major power projects in many areas. And as previously indicated, there has also been a considerable growth in those industries producing cement, chemicals, electrical apparatus, steel, etc., directed to domestic markets.

All this has resulted in a substantial transfer of workers from primary to secondary industries. About 40% of all workers in 1900 were engaged in agriculture; in 1956 this percentage had dropped to 16. Less than 17% of Canadian workers in 1901 were in manufacturing industries, but about 25% were so employed in 1956. Since the second great war more workers have been employed in manufacturing than in agriculture.[3]

Urbanization

One of the major trends associated with the industrialization of Canada is the dramatic increase in urban living with all its concomitant influences upon Canadian life, and particularly upon family life. The distribution of the population as between rural and urban has been completely reversed in the last 50 years, as Table 1 indicates :

TABLE 1

Canada's Rural Population [4]

Year	Percentage of Total Population
1900	62.3%
1911	54.5%
1921	50.4%
1931	46.2%
1941	45.6%
1951	43.8%
1956	33.5%

Mr Humphrey Carver, Chairman of the Research Committee of Central Mortgage and Housing, has predicted that by 1980 we shall be an 80% town-dwelling nation. Not only are cities more numerous, but there is a decided trend to bigger cities, which is self-evident in Canada to-day. In 1951, about one third of the total population lived in metropolitan areas of 100,000 and over, and about 45% of the

[2] Ibid.

[3] *Working and Living Conditions in Canada,* Economics & Research Branch, Department of Labour, 1956.

[4] "Rural" is defined for census purposes as any area having less than 1,000 population.

population lived in urban centres of 40,000 or more. This trend towards bigness in urban concentrations has been accentuated in British Columbia, the post-war "boom province", Alberta with its oil and gas development, and in Quebec and Ontario with their concentration of industry. For instance, in British Columbia, Quebec, and Ontario, in 1951 more than half of the population lived in urban areas of over 40,000, but even on the Prairies and in the Maritimes nearly one third of the population will be found in urban areas of that size.

The Gordon Commission's preliminary report estimates that by 1980 56% of our population will be living in large cities.[5]

It would be impossible to assess with any accuracy the exact causal relationship between industrialization and the conditions under which Canadian families live on one hand, and on the other, the relationship between these conditions and urbanization. It is self-evident that these two major trends, industrialization and urbanization, are tied closely together and have made a combined impact upon the family, though to describe exhaustively their influence and all the various ramifications of it would be a difficult task. There is no question but that Canada's booming economy associated with industrialization has been a major factor in encouraging the increased flow of immigrant families, the continuing high birth rate and other population phenomena referred to earlier. The remaining sections of this study will attempt to highlight several other aspects of family life in Canada associated with our industrial economy, which are the concern of the Church.

The Standard of Living

A very noticeable upgrading in the standard of living is a characteristic of present-day Canadian life. Between 1941 and 1951, the average wages approximately doubled, while during the same period there were somewhat smaller increases in the cost-of-living and consumers' price indices for all items except food.

A recent study[6] of average weekly earnings in nine leading industries and in manufacturing concerns indicated that "real earning" (a figure obtained by dividing money earnings by the consumer price index), taking 1949 as a base and equal to 100%, had advanced to 126.3% and 128.8% respectively, whereas the consumer price index had advanced to only 116.1%. Industries have introduced or enlarged welfare and pension plans; there has been an increase and a broader extension to more employees of paid vacations and statutory holidays; the work week has been gradually

5 *Monthly Review*, The Bank of Nova Scotia, July 1955.
6 *Working and Living Conditions in Canada, 1956,* Dept, of Labour, p. 33.

reduced; and unemployment insurance benefits have been extended to more workers and benefits have been increased.

There has been a decided increase in the variety of available goods. All modes of transportation have improved. It has been estimated from the 1951 census that there are two cars for every five households in Canada. Radios are in almost every household, and television sets are being purchased in large numbers. There is an increase in owner-occupation of houses, a decrease in the number of persons per room, and a pronounced increase in the number of domestic labour-saving devices used, especially vacuum cleaners, washing machines, etc. Better health facilities and improved educational facilities are also evident.

Some indication of the range of the incomes which have made these material advantages possible is given in Table 2.

TABLE 2

Percentage Distribution of Families by Income Groups, Canada, 1954 [7]

Income Group	All Families	Families whose major source of income is Wages and Salaries
Under $500	1.9	0.5
$500-999	3.7	1.6
1,000-1,499	5.4	3.5
1,500-1,999	5.6	4.7
2,000-2,499	8.2	7.4
2,500-2,999	10.1	10.4
3,000-3,499	11.3	12.7
3,500-3,999	11.1	12.8
4,000-4,499	9.9	10.8
4,500-4,999	7.2	8.5
5,000-6,999	16.0	17.8
7,000-9,999	6.2	6.6
$10,000 and over	3.3	2.6
Total	100.0	100.0

Coupled with improved living standards have come an increased emphasis upon the importance of material things, money, and security in one's job, and status based upon the extent of one's possessions.

The Industrial Worker

With the rapid advance of automation, an "economy of abundance", greater prosperity, and an appreciable rise in the standard of living are predicted. It is also said that much of the drudgery associated with the industrial process of the past will be eliminated. Machines will do the monotonous, conveyor belt type of work, and will do it more efficiently. A shorter working week is anticipated, so

[7] *Distribution of Non-Farm Incomes in Canada by Size, 1954*—Reference Paper No. 66 (D.B.S.). Total family income includes income from all sources accruing to all members of the family unit.

1955, there were some 630,000 persons looking for work. Conditions such as these lead to a feeling of insecurity and bring much hardship and distress to families when the bread-winner is unable to find work. We are fortunate in Canada in that we have a Federal programme of Unemployment Insurance, but many workers are not covered, and frequently the benefits are not enough or are exhausted before the worker is employed again. Miss Touzel of the Ontario Welfare Council has estimated that about 30% of the Canadian workers are not adequately covered by unemployment insurance.

Mobility

Industrialization seems to be associated inevitably with a high degree of geographical and social mobility. Many of the consequent influences on family life are unfavourable. There is the physical and social transfer from the country to the city, with the accompanying changes in ways of life and scale of values.

The industrial way usually involves a considerable journey to work because the place of work is separated from the place of residence. There has been a tremendous development of "dormitory" towns where the worker sleeps, but does not live. Father Levesque of Laval University in an address at Munich last year underlined the dangers inherent in this separation, and declared that it jeopardized the stability of the family. It also affects working habits because of the lost time, the frustrations and frayed nerves, and the traffic jams associated with the commuting problem. Malton is a case in point. A study there reveals that only about 400 employees live in Malton and about 35 times that number commute. The preliminary report states : "There seems no doubt that production in the plant suffers, especially during the first and last half hours of the work-day, just after and just before the traffic ordeal. A similarly disruptive effect on home life is also apparent."[13] But there is a beginning of new planned communities in Canada. One such is Don Mills, near the outskirts of Toronto. It consists of four neighbourhoods, and it is anticipated that the industries within the planned area will provide for about half of the employment needs of the community.

There is much movement too from job to job, from company to company, between neighbourhoods, communities, and, indeed, across international boundaries. The flow of immigrants to Canada, many of whom come to work in Canadian industries, is closely tied in with Canada's increasing industrialization. One of the new uranium mining centres, Elliot Lake, provides an example of the extremes of mobility. Employers report rates of labour turnover of from 15% to 50% per month. This is partly due to the large number of single

[13] *University of Toronto Quarterly*, January 1957, p. 248.

men who do not have the stabilizing effect of a family to support and move, and also to the fact that married men who have been unable to move their families into the area are apt to move out quickly.

There is mobility too between generations, with the younger generation moving from the fathers' occupation to a new and different work. And undoubtedly automation will increasingly be a major factor in the displacement of workers from accustomed jobs, necessitating retraining and re-location for new jobs.

Women in the Labour Force

One of the most pronounced trends and one that has occasioned a good deal of concern is the rapidly increasing number of women in the labour force. Since 1901 when only one worker in ten was a woman, the number of women outside the home has increased five-fold, and the percentage of women in the working force has almost doubled. There were approximately 1,399,000 women with jobs in the labour force during August, 1956.[14] These workers represented 24% of women 14 years of age and over, and about 23% of those having jobs in the total labour force. 38% of the women in the labour force were under 25 years of age, 39% between 25 and 44, and 23% 45 years of age and over.

Some indication of the extent of this drastic change in Canada's labour force is given in Tables 3, 4, 5, and 6.

TABLE 3

Proportionate Increase of Women in the Labour Force by Marital Status, 1941-1951 [15]

Marital Status	Percentage Increase
Single women	9%
Married women	308%
Widows	13%

TABLE 4

Proportionate Increase of Women in the Labour Force by Age Group 1941-1951 [16]

Age Group	Percentage Increase
14–19 years	30%
20–24 ,,	20%
25–34 ,,	21%
35–44 ,,	88%
45–54 ,,	85%
55–64 ,,	65%
65 and over	31%

---

[14] *Working and Living Conditions in Canada, 1956,* Dept. of Labour, p.7.
[15] Women's Bureau, Department of Labour.
[16] Ditto.

TABLE 5

Canada, 1951 (estimates in thousands) [17]

	Female Population 14 years of age and over		Female Labour Force		Women not in the Labour Force	
	No.	%	No.	%	No.	%
Total	4,938	100.0	1,164	100.0	3,774	100.0
Single	1,348	27.3	723	62.1	625	16.6
Married	3,115	63.1	349	30.0	2,766	73.3
Widowed	456	9.2	79	6.8	377	10.0
Divorced	19	0.4	13	1.1	6	0.1

TABLE 6

Canada, 1954 (estimates in thousands) [18]

	Female Population 14 years of age and over		Women with jobs		Women not working for pay	
	No.	%	No.	%	No.	%
Total	5,257	100.0	1,189	100.0	4,068	100.0
Single	1,341	25.5	644	54.2	697	17.1
Married	3,398	64.6	428	36.0	2,970	73.0
Widowed, Divorced or Separated	518	9.9	117	9.8	401	9.9

In 1956, these percentages had changed again; 51% of the women in the labour force were single, 39% were married, and 10% were widowed, divorced, or permanently separated. In the post-war period almost all of the expansion in women workers has been of married women. Of the total number of women gainfully employed, less than 10% worked usually less than 35 hours per week,[19] so that part-time work is not very extensive. It is generally thought that these increases in the number of young women and married women at work will be permanent and continuing.

One of the most controversial aspects of this situation is that of the married women who are working. Part of the tremendous increase is due to the fact that many girls who worked before continue to work after their marriage, some because they wish to, others to help support the family or improve the family income. Some declare that motherhood in the home is being threatened by this trend; others emphasize that it makes possible economic freedom for women,

[17] Census of Canada 1951 Vol. II, Table 1 and Appendix A Table 1; Volume IV, Table II. The Female Labour Force includes women and girls 14 years of age and over who had jobs or who were actively looking for work. Women who are separated from their husbands are included under "married".

[18] The Labour Force, June 1954, Population Estimates by Marital Status, Age and Sex for Canada and Provinces, 1954. Women not in the labour force and women in the labour force without jobs and actively seeking work are listed under "Women not working for pay".

[19] Working and Living Conditions in Canada, 1956, Dept. of Labour, p. 7.

and it opens up many new interests and opportunities for activity. The small apartments with their labour-saving devices do not offer much scope for real home-making, but there is a very real danger of this twofold function becoming so heavy a burden that it endangers the well-being of the family.

The core of the problem is the needs of the children. The total family unit contributes to the healthy development of the child, but the mother in the home has always been regarded as the unifying centre of the family circle. Hence, the concern about the impact which industrialization is having upon the maternal care of children. Not enough is known about the effect that the mother's absence from the home has upon the children, but if the old family pattern, where the mother looked after the children and cared for the household while the father provided for the family finances, is a thing of the past in an industrialized society, then it is certainly the responsibility of industry and the community to ensure that mothers will be able to discharge this twofold function without harmful effects on the family.

The Church in Canada has embarked upon an extensive programme of marriage counselling, with a special emphasis upon preparation for Christian marriage. Diocesan Marriage Counselling Institutes have been held to assist the clergy in their ministry to families and those who are about to be married. In urban centres, deaneries, and parishes, discussion groups and conferences for young people have been convened to help them consider Christian marriage and family life in its modern setting. It is essential that, in all these efforts, young people should be made to face squarely the implications for the family which arise from married women in the labour force. And certainly the Church should ensure that all the necessary services are provided by the community and the parish for the strengthening of family life in this time of transition. For instance, it is strongly recommended that, at least, mothers having children under 3 years of age should stay at home and conditions should be such as to make that possible.

Housing

Each home and family needs an adequate dwelling, and especially do those who are caught up in the industrial process need a healthy, decent, and attractive background for their homes and daily lives. But speaking generally, a developing industrialization does not provide the sort of houses and living accommodation, or neighbourhoods, needed, or that the industrial society can well afford, unless social policy makes provision for them. For instance, up to the present, it has appeared to be practically impossible for the rapidly developing frontier industrial town to cope with the housing needs of those workers who come to swell its population.

Even when much housing is being constructed in major cities, there is little or no attempt to create well-balanced urban neighbourhoods; instead, small pockets of housing are built, each a small segregation of families of similar size and economic status. Humphrey Carver, who discussed this phenomenon in a recent address, describes it in the following terms : "Here is a strip of row-housing. Over there is a cluster of ranch-houses, there a clutch of small homes. Over here a large project of public housing. This separation is the very antithesis of the diversified, cosmopolitan urban society, from which has grown the culture of great cities. We have become so segregated that a child can hardly meet its own grandmother. Children and grandmothers do not drive cars, on which the whole system is based."[20]

In many industrial areas there is a critical land shortage for any kind of housing, but two of the most pressing problems in Canada are the obsolescence of housing, especially in older metropolitan centres, and the scarcity of low-cost dwelling units that provide decent, safe, living arrangements for families in the lower income brackets.

At the end of the second great war Canada was faced with a serious housing shortage because, during the depression and the war, houses were not being built in any appreciable numbers, and it was not until 1954 that the number of houses built kept pace with needs created by the formation of new families. The 1951 census revealed that in spite of an increase of 29.6% between 1941 and 1951 in the number of occupied dwellings, one fifth of Canada's homes were overcrowded and one third of the nation's population was living under crowded conditions. In that ten-year period the number of owned dwellings increased by 49.1%, whereas rented buildings increased by only 4.2%.[21] This tiny increase in rented accommodation is of particular significance in view of the mobility associated with industrialization, and the large percentage of families whose incomes do not allow for the purchase of the types of homes at present being built.

The year 1955 was remarkable for new house building activity in Canada; 138,000 dwelling units were started during the year and 127,900 units completed. In 1956, 135,700 units were completed, but the number of buildings started dropped 8% from the previous year, to 127,300, due largely to the shortage of mortgage credit.[22] But in spite of all this building, it is still true, as Dr Albert Rose, a

[20] "Vision of the Great City", *Community Planning Review*, Vol. 5, No. 2, 1955.

[21] *Canada Year Book*, 1956, p. 167.

[22] *Canadian Housing Statistics*, 4th Quarter 1956, p. 5.

housing authority at the Toronto School of Social Work, declared recently, that "the greatest proportion of new dwellings is well beyond the savings and income capacity of a substantial proportion of the Canadian population".

One of the most disturbing aspects of Canada's housing situation is the public apathy concerning those areas in large cities which, as slums, have lost their function as satisfactory neighbourhoods. Miss Florence Phillpott, Executive Director of the Toronto Welfare Council, speaking at an Annual Meeting said : "No one can afford to be complacent about the number of families who are housed in basements and other substandard accommodation where there is not proper ventilation, refrigeration, toilet facilities, opportunity for privacy." She continued : "We have ample proof, and it is no news to this community, that there is a direct relationship between over-crowded conditions, lack of privacy, lack of opportunity for enter-tainment, and the breakdown of family life."[23]

In its Brief to the Gordon Commission, the Central Mortgage and Housing Corporation stated that "the major cities of Canada now contain about 100,000 dwellings in a serious state of disrepair, many of them concentrated in blighted areas". Speaking in June of this year, Mr C. E. Campeau, Montreal's Director of Planning, is quoted as follows : "Slums and sub-standard districts make up 20 per cent of most Canadian cities and towns. Slums in most Canadian cities", he said, "house one-third of the population, account for 45 per cent of major crime, 55 per cent of juvenile delinquency, 35 per cent of fires, 45 per cent of total city service costs. But they bring in only six per cent of the city tax revenues."[24]

But the possibilities for improvement have been well illustrated in the Regent Park Housing Project, Canada's first major re-development programme, in the heart of Metropolitan Toronto. Commenting on the social improvements achieved in that area, Dr Rose in his paper for the Munich Conference states that crime and delinquency have all but disappeared, the fire hazard has been eliminated, the health of adults and children has improved, children are doing better in school, are better clothed, more regular in attendance, families are spending more on home furnishings and less on alcoholic beverages, drunkenness is virtually unknown, recreational opportunities for all ages are well utilized. "In short, a relatively normal healthful environment has been substituted for one of the acknowledged slum areas in an older section of the city with consequent social effects of profound significance."

[23] *Annual Report, 1954*, Council for Social Service, p. 30.
[24] *Globe and Mail*, 17 June 1957.

employment. A special counselling service for older workers, established first in 1947 in Ontario, has worked wonders in helping older persons to obtain work and in upgrading job opportunities for these workers.

Compulsory retirement at a fixed age is another area of difficulty. When an employee continues to work at full pressure until the retirement age is reached, and then is compelled to stop suddenly, it is extremely difficult for that person to re-adjust to his changed situation. Then too, it is a situation of sheer wastefulness in human capacity and resources when so many people who are capable of producing and of making a considerable contribution to the economy are forced to be supported in idleness by those who are now working. "The psychological factor is also important. Older people resent being shut out from that which occupied so much of their attention previously. It is frustrating for them to feel that they no longer are of any use. Indeed, the lack of employment for the aged has been regarded as one of the contributing factors in the great increase in senility."[26]

Unfortunately there is some evidence of these "employment trends" associated with industrial society creeping into the life of the Church. There are the questions of pension plans with respect to the ordination of older men and the transfer of older men from one diocese to the other, retirement policies, the adequate use of life-time skills in the later years; these and other aspects of Church life must be constantly assessed with a view to recognizing individual differences and providing appropriate activity for those members of the family, who though older, look forward to years of continuing service.

In the general employment scene, attitudes and policies of employers, employees, trade unions, and the public generally must be changed so as to provide opportunity for those who can give effective service in their normal occupations or in alternative work, to continue work, without regard to age, if they so wish. There should be the possibility of transferring workers from more exacting jobs to those that require less strength and more experience, or to another part of the industry where the rhythm of work is not so exhausting. And decisions concerning eventual retirement should be based more upon the worker's capacity for work and less upon arbitrary retirement age limits.

The Church can and should help to influence public opinion in this respect; but above all, in the fellowship of the Church, there is a God-given opportunity to preach and practice the fact that in the economy of God there is no useless person. Every individual, regard-

26 *The Bulletin*, No. 153, Council for Social Service, p. 7.

less of age, is of infinite worth and has a unique place and contribution to make. From that fellowship there is no retirement, for the privileges and responsibilities of membership are valid throughout the whole of life.

Leisure Time

The increased amount of leisure time that industrialization makes possible should not be overlooked in this survey. The 5-day, 40-hour, week is prevalent at the present time, and the 6-hour day and the 34-hour week are frequently mentioned as possibilities. Paid vacations of at least one week and usually two weeks are almost universal, and a considerable proportion of employees enjoy from 6 to 8 weeks paid statutory holidays. This free time may be used for good or ill. It may be enjoyed by the family as a whole, or it may become one of the disintegrating forces for the family and its interests; it may be creative or destructive of human personality and the family. Certainly there are many evidences of "the deadening and stereotyping effect of commercialized leisure", but there are also great multitudes of "do-it-yourself" amateurs and those who by public service, through the arts, and in many other ways, use leisure time constructively.

Sir Geoffrey Vickers speaks of "the developing leisure cultures" of our age and of their importance, for they provide opportunities through which "we can help to safeguard the independence and variety of the human person against the encroaching stereotype of industrial man".[27] It may well be that in the future, man's unique contribution to the life of the world will be made less through his daily work and increasingly by means of his leisure time activities. If a sizeable portion of the population are to find difficulty in satisfying their innate creative urge in and through their daily work (and the advance of automation makes this probable), it will be necessary to discover how large blocks of leisure time may be so used as to give full scope to man's desire for creative activity.

The Christian Church should provide leadership in this respect. It is worth considering that much of the lay work and witness of the Christian Church was done in the past by a leisured minority. In the future, a majority will be freed to thus witness and serve if the Church is alert to the possibilities. Think of the potential students in the faith, educators, evangelists, workers! Is it too far-fetched to suggest that increased leisure may be used as well for meditation and contemplation so necessary for the development of the inner life. Is the Church prepared for her opportunity?[28]

[27] *University of Toronto Quarterly*, January 1957, p. 217.
[28] L. F. Hatfield, *Automation and the Responsibility of the Church*, p. 9.

It may well be the unique function of the Church, too, to ensure that increasingly leisure time will be enjoyed by the family as a unit and that family activities and programmes under the aegis of the Church, or in the community generally, combined with family corporate worship, will unite and strengthen the family.

Conclusion
There are other aspects of family life upon which industrialization has exerted some influence, but the foregoing are the major impact areas. It would seem that one of the major tasks of our nation at the present time is to discover how the opportunities presented by increasing industrialization may be utilized in such a way as to minimize and counteract those conditions that threaten the unity, the stability, and the well-being of the family, and to assist the family to attain to a fulness of life and to perform its proper and unique functions, namely, that of bringing children through the earlier crises of adjustment to life around them, and the transmitting of the culture of the past and present, of which our religious heritage is the most important part.

3. BIBLIOGRAPHY

Annual Report, The Council for Social Service, The Anglican Church of Canada, 1954, 1955, 1956

Bulletin, The, The Council for Social Service, The Anglican Church in Canada ("Old Age, the Persons and their Problems", 1952)

Canadian Housing Statistics, 4th Quarter 1956, Central Mortgage and Housing Corporation, Ottawa,1957

Canadian Welfare, The Canadian Welfare Council, Ottawa, March 1954

Canada Year Book, 1956, Dominion Bureau of Statistics, Queen's Printer, Ottawa, 1956

Carver, Humphrey, "Vision of the Great City", *Community Planning Review,* Vol. V, No. 2, 1955

Census of Canada, 1956, Dominion Bureau of Statistics (Bulletin : 1-7, *Rural and Urban Distribution*; 1-9, *Old Age,* Ottawa, 1957)

D.B.S. Daily Bulletin, Vol. 26, No. 16, 1957, Dominion Bureau of Statistics, Ottawa

Hatfield, L. F., *Automation and the Responsibility of the Church,* 1956

Immigration, 1956, Department of Citizenship and Immigration, Ottawa, 1957

International Conference of Social Work, Munich, August 1956 (Preliminary Reports of various National Committees)

Joint Planning Commission, Report of Spring Meeting 1957, Canadian Association for Adult Education, Toronto

Juvenile Delinquents, 1953, Dominion Bureau of Statistics, Ottawa, 1957

Monthly Review, The Bank of Nova Scotia, Toronto ("The Trend to Bigger Cities", July 1955; "Problems of Growth : The Policy Suggestions of the Gordon Commission", February 1957)

Royal Bank of Canada Monthly Letter, The, Montreal ("Canada's Ninetieth Birthday", June 1957)

Sheffield, E. F., *Canadian University and College Enrolment Projected to 1965,* Dominion Bureau of Statistics, Ottawa, 1955

University of Toronto Quarterly, January 1957

Women's Bureau, The, Department of Labour, Queen's Printer, 1955

Working and Living Conditions in Canada, Economics and Research Branch, Department of Labour, Ottawa, December 1956

Appendix 4

FAMILY PLANNING IN INDIA

CONTENTS

per year. This gap between births and deaths has been aptly termed the "demographic gap". The gap determines population growth. All indications are that death rates will fall still further. Japan's death rate is now only about 10 per thousand. It is difficult to see what might cause India's birth rate to fall in the next 10 years or so, and the death rate will probably fall considerably.

Barring quite unforeseen factors, population growth will continue. Reliable calculations reveal that if India's birth rate is unchanged in the next 30 years and the Five Year Plans do all that is expected of them, the standard of living will rise by 14%. However, if the birth rate can be halved by 1987 the standard of living will be 75% greater than it is now. There is therefore little margin between a small rise and an actual fall in living standards in India in the next 30 years, in spite of tremendous efforts to increase income if the birth rate remains unchanged. A fall in the birth rate would transform the situation.

Human beings can either ignore the facts of population growth, or they can face them. If they are determined to do something about this gigantic problem they will find difficult decisions ahead of them. Their traditional attitudes to reproduction and sex may need revision. All potential parents now have new responsibilities. In a profound sense, whether they like it or not, they have become their brothers' (and sisters') keepers on a national and world scale.

The root of the population problem lies in the difference between birth and death rates. The only possible solutions are :

(1) A rise in the death rate.

(2) Mass emigration.

(3) A reduction in the birth rate. This could only be achieved by :

    (*a*) Postponement of marriage of women until the age of 30 or 35.

    (*b*) Abstinence from sexual intercourse either by life-long celibacy or by complete celibacy within marriage once the limited number of children have been born (on the average three per couple in India according to calculation; see *Census of India Report*, IA, 1951) .

    (*c*) Widespread induced abortions.

    (d) Widespread sterilization.

    (*e*) A modified form of marriage where several men marry one woman (polyandry). The remaining women would have to remain single.

    (*f*) Contraception.

No one wants the death rate to rise. Mass emigration is only a local and temporary solution and is not practical. Few people would consent to postponement of marriage of women to 35, though this has been done to a considerable degree in Ireland since the Irish Famine of 1846-7. Life-long celibacy is a vocation to which few are called. Total abstinence from sexual intercourse is not feasible for most married couples, though some may find this their method of choice. There is also considerable evidence that frequently this is not a desirable plan from the point of view of the happiness of the family. Widespread abortion is an age-old method, and is being employed on a huge scale in Japan, where there are now more abortions than live births every year. The practice of abortion is illegal in most countries and is rightly condemned by the Church under normal circumstances. Widespread sterilization is objectionable, and people would be unlikely to come forward for the operation in sufficient numbers to affect the birth rate. Polyandry is practised in some parts of the world, but it is neither desirable nor feasible for most. We are left with contraception.

Almost universal use of contraception accounts for the fall in birth rates in countries of North and West Europe and North America, Australia, and New Zealand. In these countries birth rates are one third to one fourth of what they were 150 years ago.

A point worth deep consideration is that, where contraception is not available for any reason, large numbers of women resort to induced abortion as the only method of controlling the number of children born to them. All over the world this results in large numbers of sick and dying women. In India and many other countries a considerable number of the deaths of women of child-bearing age is due to induced abortions crudely performed. Another not infrequent result of a woman's fear that she may conceive is that she refuses to receive her husband at all. In desperation he goes to find an outlet elsewhere resulting in deep unhappiness and often illegitimate children. Reliable contraception is an answer to both these problems.

The Indian Government, with little opposition from State Governments, has adopted a policy of attempting to reduce the birth rate by the application of contraception, which is a part of Family Planning. The Government is fully aware of the effect that the growth of the population has on its plans to raise the standard of life of the common people of India. It is therefore essential that the Church, as a responsible body within the fabric of India's society, should make a clear statement of its attitude to Family Planning for the guidance of its members.

2. CHRISTIAN MARRIAGE

Christian marriage is briefly and aptly described in the Prayer Book as "an honourable estate, instituted of God himself, signifying unto us the mystical union that is betwixt Christ and his Church".

The C.I.P.B.C. *Draft Prayer Book*, 1956, gives us three reasons why marriage was ordained :

(1) It was ordained for the increase of mankind according to the will of God, and that children might be brought up in the fear and nurture of the Lord, and to the praise of his holy Name.

(2) It was ordained in order that the natural instincts and affections, implanted by God, should be hallowed and directed aright; that those called of God to this holy estate should continue therein in pureness of living.

(3) It was ordained for the mutual society, help, and comfort, that the one ought to have of the other, both in prosperity and adversity.

It may be noted that more than one interpretation of the three reasons given above has been put forward. The Bishop of Chota Nagpur considers that the fourteenth Biennial Conference of the Christian Medical Association of India has confused the understanding and meaning of the grounds on which Christian marriage is instituted when it maintains "that these are bound together, and the one cannot be said to have priority over the others". The Bishop states that "the traditional teaching of theologians is well summarized in Canon 1013 of the modern Roman *Codex Juris Canonici*, which runs as follows, 'The primary end of matrimony is the procreation of children and bringing up of children; the secondary end mutual help and a remedy against concupiscence'." He further points out that Resolution 13 of the Lambeth Conference of 1930 is in agreement with *Codex Juris Canonici* in stating that the primary purpose for which marriage exists is the procreation of children.

Similarly, the Bishop of Chota Nagpur has questioned the statement of the C.M.A.I. on the third reason for Christian marriage. He considers that a study of the Encyclical *Casti Connubii* of Pope Pius XI is necessary before one can pronounce on the three grounds for Christian marriage, and he refers to the *bona matrimonii* enumerated by St Augustine.

On the other hand, Dr Sherwin Bailey of the Church of England Moral Welfare Council questions the traditional conception of Christian marriage on both theological and historical grounds.

Dr Bailey says,

The conception of marriage implied in both the *bona* and the causes is entirely consistent with the sexual thought of ancient and mediaeval times—and indeed, of the centuries succeeding the Reformation—*but it is doubtful whether they defined marriage in terms which can now be accepted without qualification* [italics ours]. The Anglican tradition itself calls in question the primacy of the procreative end, for, as I have shown in my book *The Mystery of Love and Marriage,* the consensus among the Anglican divines of the Reformation, and the Jacobean and Caroline periods (the age which produced our Prayer Books) was in favour of regarding the mutual society, help, and comfort as the principal purpose of marriage. This would suggest that the order of the causes in the Prayer Book is to be looked upon as one of the enumeration only, and not one of order of importance.

This Committee considered at length the views of both these scholars. It wishes to draw attention to the *Draft Prayer Book* of 1956 of the Church in India in which it is stated that the first cause for marriage is "the increase of mankind according to the will of God". We would like to emphasize the words "according to the will of God", not found in the 1662 Prayer Book. They have a direct bearing on the complex and pressing problem of family limitation. The Committee also draws attention to the second cause for marriage as stated in the *Draft Prayer Book,* 1956 : "It was ordained in order that the natural instincts and affections, implanted by God, should be hallowed and directed aright; that those who are called of God to this holy estate, should continue therein in pureness of living".

The Committee is fully conscious that views on Family Planning differ. One view is that the use of contraceptives is always wrong. Another view is that the use of contraceptives is normal in every fertile marriage. We consider it significant that the Lambeth Conference of 1930 passed the following resolution (Resolution 15, carried by 193 votes to 67) :

Where there is a clearly felt moral obligation to limit or avoid parenthood, the method must be decided on Christian principles. The primary and obvious method is complete abstinence from intercourse, (as far as may be necessary), in a life of discipline and self control, lived in the power of the Holy Spirit. Nevertheless, in those cases where there is such a clearly felt moral obligation to limit or avoid parenthood, and where there is a morally sound reason for avoiding complete abstinence, the Conference agrees that other methods may be used, provided that this is done in the light of the same Christian principles. The Conference records its strong condemnation of the use of any methods of conception control from motives of selfishness, luxury or mere convenience.

This resolution clearly recognizes that there are occasions when the use of methods, other than that of complete abstinence, for the avoidance of parenthood, is legitimate. Dr Sherwin Bailey has something to say about this which is highly relevant when we come to consider the third cause for marriage as stated in the Prayer Book. He writes :

> In human beings, *coitus* is more than a device for reproduction—it is a complex experience, the purposes of which may be described as conceptional and relational. . . . The Prayer Book states that the "first cause" for which matrimony was ordained is "the procreation of children to be brought up in the fear and nurture of the Lord and to the praise of his holy Name". There is sound reason for suggesting that the process of procreation which is begun at conception is not terminated at birth, for parenthood involves many years of creative work with the growing child before that degree of personal maturity is attained at which he becomes fully the human being God intended him to be. Interpreted in this wider sense, the procreative purpose of *coitus* is not limited therefore to the promotion of conception. Those relational acts of *coitus* between husband and wife which cement and deepen their love, relieve their physical and psychological sexual tensions, and contribute to their personal fulfilment and integration, have an effect which naturally overflows the bounds of the one flesh, so that such *coitus* is directly beneficial to the whole family. It cannot too strongly be stressed that the well-being of the family depends to a greater extent than has perhaps been recognised hitherto, on the well-being of the one flesh—and to that well-being regular *coitus* makes a profound contribution.

The natural instincts or appetites of men are in themselves good. It is the abuse of them that is sinful. Self-control through the power of the Holy Spirit is required in the exercise of all the natural instincts; but to advocate self-control in the exercise of an instinct is not necessarily the same as to advocate complete abstinence.

In the exercise of the sex-instinct, complete abstinence is, we consider, not normal for the great majority of married couples. In married life it is right and natural for husband and wife to have sexual intercourse according to an agreed pattern. Where there is the clearly felt moral obligation to limit or avoid parenthood, that relational intercourse, which cements and deepens their mutual love and contributes to their well-being and that of the family, must take place with the use of some method of contraception. Complete abstinence from intercourse might well cause strains and repressions that would be harmful.

In recognizing that there are times when the relational purpose of *coitus* has a value apart from the conceptional purpose, it follows that a limited use of contraceptives is permissible. The committee is however, in complete agreement that there is no justification for the use of contraceptives,

(1) for purely selfish motives, or in the attempt to avoid the proper and necessary self control; or

(2) to avoid parenthood altogether.[1]

In conclusion we maintain that in any consideration of Family Planning the Church must recognize that besides the purpose of procreation, the relational act of *coitus* has an importance in its own right. We would request that authoritative guidance be given by the 1958 Lambeth Conference on whether the relational act of *coitus* is morally justifiable where there are sound moral reasons for limiting parenthood.

3. PRACTICAL RECOMMENDATIONS

A major problem in the mid-twentieth century is that of the Demographic Gap, the difference between birth rate and death rate, that is to say of populations increasing out of all proportion to world economy, thus leading inevitably to mass privation.

Already this situation has been recognized by various individuals and social groups which have taken into their own hands such remedies as widespread abortion, the indiscriminate use of contraceptives, and the search for sexual satisfaction outside the home.

Having defined the problem it is the duty of Christian leaders to point out such solutions as are permissible within the structure of Christian marriage and the dictates of Christian principles.

The Christian Home Conference at Bangalore in February 1953 stated :

While recognizing the joys and blessings experienced within a large family group, it is also recognized that, in the interests of the health, happiness, and welfare of the mother and the child, spacing and planning are necessary. From the Christian point of view children must be wanted and loved, and have a right to be

[1] See *The Threshold of Marriage*, Church of England Moral Welfare Council, 1954.

properly provided for. It is part of our Christian stewardship to plan and adequately to provide for the home, for the health and happiness of the mother and child. The nation is a family on a large scale, and is confronted with the problems of a greatly increasing population and of raising the economic standard of its people from a mere subsistence level to a level of adequacy. The Conference, therefore believes that family planning is essential.

This Committee suggests that the problem should be tackled under the following four heads :

(1) The training of future parents, i.e. child-training.

(2) The training of teachers and leaders.

(3) The teaching of married couples and parents.

(4) Specific advice on family planning to married couples.

(1) *The training of future parents.* In Christian homes, welfare clinics, Sunday Schools, Confirmation classes and youth organizations, children should be taught discipline, health, and regular habits and given simple sex education.

For 12-14 year-olds the filmstrip "How Life is Handed on" from the Sex Education series is invaluable.

(2) *A course on Sex education and hygiene* should be included in the training courses of teachers, clergy and their wives, doctors, nurses, midwives, and leaders of youth groups.

(3) *The teaching of married couples and young parents* should be encouraged through Christian Home meetings and publications, Church meetings, and baptismal functions, and should include teaching and discussions on :

(a) The meaning of marriage, including its spiritual, physical, and emotional aspects.

(b) The bringing up of children to become responsible members of society.

(c) The necessity of unselfishness, self-control, and the right use of contraceptives.

For this group all three filmstrips of the Sex Education series are useful : "How Life is Handed on" 1 and 2, and "Sex and Society", also the three Indian filmstrips on "Christian Marriage" (N.C.C. Film Library, Allahabad). Vernacular literature is required.

(4) *Specific advice about Family Planning.* It is advisable for young married couples to discuss and understand the responsibilities of parenthood and the various courses of action which are open to them.

Parents should give serious consideration to (*a*) the mother's health, (*b*) the children's health and education, (*c*) the economic situation of the home, and (*d*) national world welfare.

If, having sought God's will in the matter, the parents feel that future births should be limited (with the purpose of producing healthy children from a healthy mother at suitable intervals in a healthy economic environment) the following methods of limitation are advocated :

(1) Abstinence from intercourse by self-control wherever this is compatible with spiritual and emotional health of both partners.

(2) If it is felt that lack of relational *coitus* will result in spiritual or emotional deprivation sufficient to harm their Christian family life they may use a suitable method of contraception. If they desire guidance, they should consult a Christian minister, doctor, or other responsible Christian.

(*Signed*) ✠ F. R. WILLIS, Bishop of Delhi

✠ PHILIP PARMAR, Bishop of Bhagalpur

MARGARET F. JOHNSON, F.R.C.S. (Ed.)

JOHN B. WYON, M.R.C.P. (Lond.), M.P.H.

E. MARGARET SCOTT, M.B., D.P.H.

(NOTE. The Bishop of Amritsar attended the meetings but could not sign the Report because he left on furlough immediately after the last meeting; he was, however, in agreement with the Report as submitted.)